ECONOMICS

FOR IB DIPLOMA COURSE PREPARATION

Constantine Ziogas
Marily Apostolakou

T0320775

OXFORD
UNIVERSITY PRESS

Great Clarendon Street, Oxford, OX2 6DP, United Kingdom

Oxford University Press is a department of the University of Oxford.
It furthers the University's objective of excellence in research, scholarship,
and education by publishing worldwide. Oxford is a registered trademark of
Oxford University Press in the UK and in certain other countries

British Library Cataloguing in Publication Data
Data available

978-1-38-200490-9

10 9 8 7 6 5 4

Paper used in the production of this book is a natural, recyclable product
made from wood grown in sustainable forests. The manufacturing process
conforms to the environmental regulations of the country of origin.

Printed and bound by CPI Group (UK) Ltd, Croydon, CR0 4YY

Acknowledgements

We are grateful to the authors and publishers for use of extracts from their
titles and in particular for the following:

Data from **Institute of Alcohol Studies**, The Economic Impacts of
Alcohol, factsheet http://www.ias.org.uk/uploads/pdf/Factsheets/FS%20
economic%20impacts%20042016%20webres.pdf, where it was reproduced
from various **Government Digital Service** sources, compiled from https://
www.gov.uk/, under the terms of the Open Government Licence, OGL v3.

International Monetary Fund: *Growth or Inclusion.* IMF F&D 55:2, June
2018, https://www.imf.org/external/pubs/ft/fandd/2018/06/economics-of-
promoting-inclusive-growth/ostry.htm (International Monetary Fund, 2018).
Reproduced with permission from International Monetary Fund via Copyright
Clearance Center.

G. H. Brundtland: *Our Common Future: The Brundtland Report,* p16 (Oxford
University Press, 1987). Reproduced with permission from Oxford University
Press via PLSclear.

The publisher and authors would like to thank the following for permission
to use photographs and other copyright material:

Cover: Werner Lehmann/Shutterstock.

All other photos © Shutterstock, except: **p74:** Skip Nall/Getty Images; **p128:**
Keng Po Leung/123RF; **p169:** The Sustainable Development Goals (SDGs)
logo, including the colour wheel and 17 icons, are used with permission
of the United Nations https://www.un.org/sustainabledevelopment/ (The
content of this publication has not been approved by the United Nations and
does not reflect the views of the United Nations or its officials or Member
States.)

Artwork by Q2A Media Services Pvt. Ltd.

Every effort has been made to contact copyright holders of material
reproduced in this book. Any omissions will be rectified in subsequent
printings if notice is given to the publisher.

Links to third party websites are provided by Oxford in good faith and for
information only. Oxford disclaims any responsibility for the materials
contained in any third party website referenced in this work.

*To my budding scientists, Daphne, Myrto and Elias and of course to
my Kris – CZ*

Contents

 Online support material can be found at
www.oxfordsecondary.com/ib-course-prep

INTRODUCTION TO THE DIPLOMA PROGRAMME

The Diploma Programme (DP) is a two-year pre-university course for students in the 16–19 age group. In addition to offering a broad-based education and in-depth understanding of selected subjects, the course has a strong emphasis on developing intercultural competence, open-mindedness, communication skills and the ability to respect diverse points of view.

You may be reading this book during the first few months of the Diploma Programme or working through the book as a preparation for the course. You could be reading it to help you decide whether the Economics course is for you. Whatever your reasons, the book acts as a bridge from your earlier studies to DP Economics, to support your learning as you take on the challenge of the last stage of your school education.

DP course structure

The DP covers six academic areas, including languages and literature, humanities and social sciences, mathematics, natural sciences and creative arts. Within each area, you can choose one or two disciplines that are of particular interest to you and that you intend to study further at the university level. Typically, three subjects are studied at higher level (HL, 240 teaching hours per subject) and the other three at standard level (SL, 150 hours).

In addition to the selected subjects, all DP students must complete three core elements of the course: theory of knowledge, extended essay, and creativity, action, service:

Theory of knowledge (approximately 100 teaching hours) is focused on critical thinking and introduces you to the nature, structure and limitations of knowledge. An important goal of theory of knowledge is to establish links between different areas of shared and personal knowledge and make you more aware of how your own perspective might differ from those of others.

The **extended essay** is a structured and formally presented piece of writing of up to 4,000 words based on independent research in one of the approved DP disciplines. It is also possible to write an interdisciplinary extended essay that covers two DP subjects. One purpose of the extended essay activity is to develop the high-level research and writing skills expected at university.

Creativity, action, service involves a broad range of activities (typically 3–4 hours per week) that help you discover your own identity, adopt the ethical principles of the IB and become a responsible member of your community. These goals are achieved through participation in arts and creative thinking (creativity), physical exercises (activity) and voluntary work (service).

Approaches to Learning (ATL)

The ATL categories are a group of strategies, attitudes and skills that help to build successful and engaged learners. They include thinking, communication, social, self-management and research skills.

ATL Skill	Meaning
Thinking	Emphasis is placed on skills such as metacognition, reflection and critical thinking.
Self-management	Self-management covers a wide variety of skills in two categories: • affective skills: resilience, self-motivation and mindfulness • organizational skills: managing your time and your tasks and goal-setting.
Communication	Communication includes the ability to listen, read and understand as well as to write, formulate arguments and communicate in a variety of forms.
Research	Research skills include practising responsible and ethical research and information literacy during independent, self-managed, inquiry learning.
Social	Social skills involve practising self-management of emotions and behaviours while working collaboratively with others towards a common goal, focusing on the ability to understand the perspective of others.

Key features of the IB Economics syllabus

The economics course aims to enable both SL and HL students to:

- develop a critical understanding of a range of economic theories, models, ideas and tools in the areas of microeconomics, macroeconomics and the global economy
- apply economic theories, models, ideas and tools and analyse economic data to understand and engage with real-world economic issues and problems facing individuals and societies
- develop a conceptual understanding of individuals and societies' economic choices, interactions, challenges and consequences of economic decision making.

SL and HL students of economics are presented with a common syllabus, with an HL extension in some topics. Both SL and HL students develop quantitative skills, but HL students will need to further develop these as appropriate, in analysing and evaluating economic relationships in order to provide informed policy advice.

The grid on the following page gives all the IB Diploma Programme Economics course topics. Bold indicates that all or part of a sub-topic is covered in this book.

Unit	Title	Sub-topic	Chapter in this book
1	Introduction to Economics	**1.1 What is economics?**	1.1
		1.2 How do economists approach the world?	
2	Microeconomics	**2.1 Demand**	
		2.2 Supply	2.1
		2.3 Competitive market equilibrium	2.2
		2.4 Critique of the maximizing behaviour of consumers and producers	2.3
		2.5 Elasticity of demand	
		2.6 Elasticity of supply	2.4
		2.7 Role of government in microeconomics	2.5
		2.8 Market failure—externalities and common pool or common access resources	2.6 2.7
		2.9 Market failure—public goods	2.8
		2.10 Market failure—asymmetric information (HL only)	
		2.11 Market failure—market power (HL only)	2.9
		2.12 The market's inability to achieve equity (HL only)	
3	Macroeconomics	**3.1 Measuring economic activity and illustrating its variations**	3.1
		3.2 Variations in economic activity—aggregate demand and aggregate supply	3.2 3.3
		3.3 Macroeconomic objectives	3.4
		3.4 Economics of inequality and poverty	3.5
		3.5 Demand management (demand side policies)—monetary policy	3.6
		3.6 Demand management—fiscal policy	
		3.7 Supply-side policies	
4	The Global Economy	**4.1 Benefits of international trade**	4.1
		4.2 Types of trade protection	
		4.3 Arguments for and against trade control/protection	4.2
		4.4 Economic integration	4.3
		4.5 Exchange rates	4.4
		4.6 Balance of payments	4.5
		4.7 Sustainable development	
		4.8 Measuring development	
		4.9 Barriers to economic growth and/or economic development	4.6
		4.10 Economic growth and/or economic development strategies	4.7

Why this book?

This book provides a comprehensive introduction to the IBDP Economics course. The goal has been to explain key concepts and theories as clearly as possible, to ignite your interest in the subject and to ensure that you are well-prepared to embark upon this course. We will show you why economics is relevant on an individual, local, national, and also global level. Particular emphasis is placed on key elements of the IBDP such as approaches to learning (ATL), theory of knowledge (TOK) and community and service (CAS) to ensure that you are ready to take economics to the next level. This book covers the majority of topics you will encounter at the DP level, assuming that this is your first 'hands-on' contact with economics. It can be used as a preparation guide before you start DP Economics, but it will also prove a useful guide as you move through the DP Economics course.

The features of this book

In the coming pages, you will find a range of features to help you understand and engage with the skills that the Diploma Programme seeks to develop. These features are designed to improve your understanding and support the learning of new concepts.

TOK: During the economics course a number of issues will arise that highlight the relationships between TOK and economics. TOK questions presented in this book will help you understand and explore these relationships.

CAS: The economics course highlights many economic issues that have local, national and global manifestations. The CAS boxes in this book provide ideas that can help you plan, participate and implement CAS activities.

ATL: ATL skills boxes are designed to give you a chance to practise the skills of a learner. These boxes are accompanied by different tasks designed to improve your understanding of the concepts being presented.

Search the web: These boxes guide you to additional information that will facilitate your understanding, as well as the application of concepts and theories explained.

Internal link: These boxes point to other places in this book where a particular topic is discussed.

Key terms: At the end of each section you will be asked to provide definitions of the most significant terms encountered to ensure that these can be effectively used. A full glossary can be found on the book website: oxfordsecondary.com/ib-course-prep.

1 Introduction to Economics

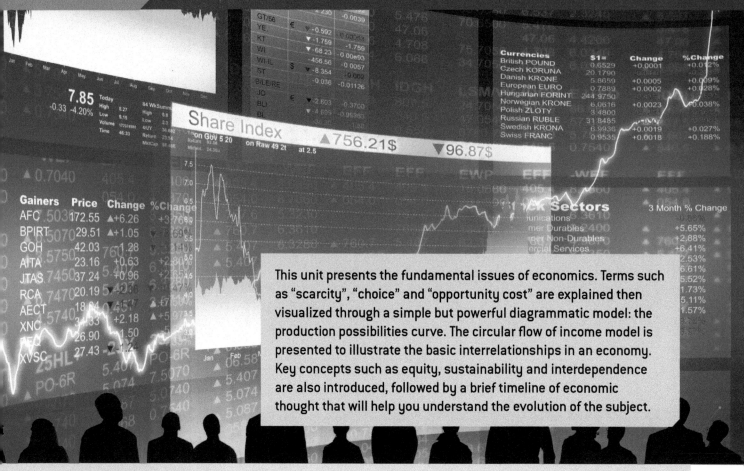

This unit presents the fundamental issues of economics. Terms such as "scarcity", "choice" and "opportunity cost" are explained then visualized through a simple but powerful diagrammatic model: the production possibilities curve. The circular flow of income model is presented to illustrate the basic interrelationships in an economy. Key concepts such as equity, sustainability and interdependence are also introduced, followed by a brief timeline of economic thought that will help you understand the evolution of the subject.

In this unit you will learn about ...

→ scarcity, choice and opportunity cost

→ the production possibilities model

→ the circular flow of income model

→ economic methodology

→ key ideas in economic thinking.

1.1 YOU CAN'T ALWAYS GET WHAT YOU WANT

The issue

This may be your first formal contact with economics, and yet news about the unemployment rate, higher or lower taxes, inflation, recession or growth, income inequality and climate change is constantly on television, in the newspapers and on social media. Economics affects our everyday lives. We constantly face problems or have to make decisions for which a knowledge of economics can be useful. Should I get a new pair of trainers or a new pair of jeans? Shall I buy the newest smartphone or keep my old one a little longer? This section asks: what is economics about?

Scarcity and choice

Economics is the study of scarcity and choice.

Scarcity refers to the excess of human wants over what can actually be produced to fulfill these wants. Human wants are unlimited, as individuals typically prefer to have more and better goods and more services. However, it is not possible to produce all of the goods and services to satisfy these wants. This is because resources are limited. The term "**resources**" refers to whatever is used to produce goods and services; resources are also known as the factors of production, as follows.

- **Land:** inputs into production provided by nature (such as land, metals and mineral deposits, forests, underground water, fish stocks and the atmosphere).

- Labour: the human input, both physical and mental, used in production.

- **Capital:** Produced means of production (such as machines, tools, equipment and factories).

- **Entrepreneurship:** the willingness and ability that some individuals have to take risks and to manage the other three factors of production.

Scarcity has an important consequence, it necessitates choice. Societies must choose which goods or services to produce and how much of each they want, given the available resources. If there were no scarcity, no choices would have to be made. Every choice involves sacrifice. For example, choosing to produce corn using the available land implies that some other agricultural product, such as wheat, has been sacrificed. This alternative that has been foregone is the opportunity cost of that choice. The **opportunity cost** of choosing any activity is the value of the next best alternative sacrificed. If resources were unlimited, no sacrifices would be necessary, and the opportunity cost of producing any good or service would be zero.

The problem of scarcity has a second important consequence. Since resources are scarce, it is important to produce the combination of goods and services that society values the most and also to avoid wasting any scarce resources. This relates to the idea of **efficiency**, which is making the best possible use of scarce resources, minimizing their waste. Therefore, economics is the social science that studies how societies make choices that lead to the best possible use of scarce resources in an attempt to satisfy unlimited human wants. The above definition classifies economics as a social science. **Social sciences** study human behaviour and social relationships and include psychology, anthropology, political science and others.

Besides scarcity, choice and efficiency, there are a few other key concepts that are central to economics and that will be discussed throughout this book. These are as follows.

- Equity: this refers to the idea of fairness. In economics, inequity is associated with rising inequality.

 TOK

What distinguishes a social science from a natural science?

- Economic well-being: this relates to the living standards enjoyed by the members of an economy.

- Sustainability: this refers to the ability of the present generation to meet its needs without compromising the ability of future generations to meet their own needs. It relates to the idea that current generations should be good stewards of the environment.

- Change: the economic world is not static; it continuously changes. In economics the focus of investigations is on change. It is not the level of an economic variable but the change in that variable that economists are typically interested in.

- Interdependence: economic agents such as consumers, producers, governments and nations interact with each other. Any action of any economic agent will therefore impact other agents, indicating that all economic agents are interdependent. The intended and unintended consequences of these interdependencies must therefore be considered.

- Intervention: this refers to government involvement in the workings of markets, despite markets being considered as the best mechanism to organize economic activity. Markets often fail, creating room for government intervention. Note that not only is the extent of government intervention a contentious subject of debate, but also there is no guarantee that the outcome of any intervention will improve market outcomes.

Economics is divided into two main branches: microeconomics and macroeconomics, where "micro" means small and "macro" means big. More specifically, **microeconomics** is concerned with the individual parts of the economy; it deals with individual units within the economy such as firms, consumers or markets. **Macroeconomics** zooms out and is concerned with the economy as a whole; it deals with aggregates such as the overall level of unemployment, output, growth and prices in the economy.

The fundamental questions of economics

Let's return to the basic economic problem of scarcity. Scarcity forces every economy to answer three fundamental questions.

1. What to produce? Choices must be made in all economies about which goods will be produced and in what quantities.

2. How to produce? All economies must make choices on how to use their resources in order to produce goods and services. Should a good be produced using more labour and less capital (machines) or perhaps rely more on capital and less on labour?

3. For whom to produce? All economies must make choices about how the goods and services produced are to be distributed among the population. Should everyone enjoy education and health services? Should everyone enjoy the same amount of all goods?

The form of organization of each economy can lead to different ways of answering the three fundamental questions. At one extreme lies the command economy, where the state owns all

capital and land and so answers the three fundamental questions. At the other extreme lies the free-market economy, where households and firms answer the three fundamental questions through their interaction in markets. Households decide what goods to consume. Firms decide what goods to produce and what resources to use. The resulting production and consumption depend on all these individual demand and supply decisions in markets. In a mixed economy, the answers to the three fundamental questions are given partly by the state and partly through the market. In practice, all economies are mixed, yet the roles and importance of the state and of markets can differ substantially.

The production possibilities model

The **production possibilities curve (PPC)** provides a very simplified but useful picture of an economy at a point in time. It refers to a country with a fixed amount of resources and some level of technology producing only two goods or services. This is unrealistic but still, as you will see, powerful enough to illustrate a number of key concepts. The PPC shows the maximum combinations of these two goods or services that this economy can produce by fully using all of its resources with the available technology—so the points on the curve show no wasted resources and production is efficient. Typically, the PPC is concave (that is, bowed in) towards the origin.

Let's visualize a PPC. Assume that an economy devotes all of its resources to the production of two goods: X and Y (X and Y can be any goods or services, such as wheat and cotton, or health care and national defence.

As shown in Figure 1.1.1, at point A the economy is using all its resources to produce good Y, so no amount of good X can be produced. At the other extreme, point B illustrates that the economy is using all its resources to produce good X, so good Y cannot be produced. At point C, resources are allocated in the production of both good X and good Y: the economy can produce 300 units of good X and 200 units of good Y. At point D, 400 units of X can be produced but only 160 units of good Y. Finally, at point E, 500 units of good X can be produced but even fewer units of good Y, only 100, can be produced.

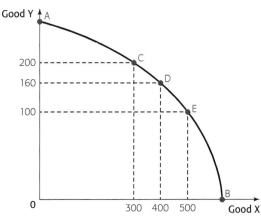

▲ **Figure 1.1.1** Production possibilities curve (PPC)

The PPC also illustrates choice and opportunity cost. As Figure 1.1.1 shows, if the economy chooses to produce more of good X it will have to sacrifice the production of some of good Y. This is shown by moving along the PPC from point C to point D. This sacrifice of good Y is the opportunity cost (OC) of the additional amount of good X that is produced. Specifically, we realize that the OC of producing an additional 100 units of good X (400 units instead of 300 units) are the 40 units of good Y (160 instead of 200) that must be sacrificed. The fact that scarcity requires that producing more of one good necessitates producing less of the other is what explains the negative slope of the PPC.

The PPC also illustrates the phenomenon of the increasing OC. Consider moving from point D to point E. The OC of producing an additional 100 units of good X (500 units instead of 400 units) are the 60 units of good Y (100 instead of 160) that are sacrificed. However, producing these additional 100 units of good X is now more costly as 60 units instead of 40 units of good Y have been sacrificed. This means that as the economy produces more of one good, it is forced to sacrifice increasing amounts of the other good. The reason for this is that resources tend to be specialized. As the economy concentrates more of its production on one good, it must start using resources that are less suitable for its production; that is, resources that would have been more appropriate to produce the other good. The PPC is concave rather than being a negatively sloped straight line because opportunity cost increases as more and more of X is produced.

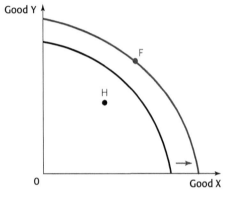

▲ **Figure 1.1.2** Inside and outside the PPC

What if the economy is operating inside the PPC producing a combination such as point H in Figure 1.1.2? In this case the available resources are not being fully utilized, for example, there is unemployment. Point H is therefore an inefficient production combination. It follows that if unemployment increases, then the new point will lie somewhere closer to the origin, as fewer units of at least one of the two goods will be produced. In contrast, if unemployment decreases, the economy will move to another combination closer to the curve itself.

Could an economy be operating at a point outside the PPC, such as point F? No, because the available resources and current level of technology do not allow the economy to enjoy such output combinations. Point F is an unattainable production combination. If more or better resources become available and/or technology improves, combinations of output that were initially unattainable (such as F) can be produced. This can be shown through an outward shift of the PPC.

The circular flow of income model

The circular flow of income model is a simple diagram that allows us to visualize and understand the economy.

Let's start with a simple explanation. Consider an economy with two "inhabitants": households and firms. Households own the four factors of production—land, labour, capital and entrepreneurship—which they offer to firms. In exchange for the factors of production, firms offer payments to households in the form of rent (for land), wages (for labour), interest (for capital) and profits (for entrepreneurship). The sum of these payments makes up income. Firms use the factors of production to produce goods and services that they sell to households; households make expenditures on the goods and services produced by firms.

In this basic view of the economy there are transactions that take place by two kinds of flow: "real" flows such as labour, raw materials, goods or services in one direction, and flows of money that pay for these things in the opposite direction.

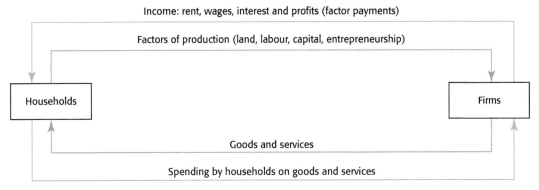

▲ **Figure 1.1.3** Flows in an economy

In Figure 1.1.3, the real flows are shown in orange and the money flows in blue.

The money flows shown in Figure 1.1.3 are equal. The income that flows from firms to households (as payments made for the use of the factors of production) is equal to the spending by households that flows back to firms (as payment for the goods and services produced). This is the circular flow of income.

Now let's go a step further. For our basic **circular flow model** to resemble the real-world economy more closely, we must add leakages and injections.

Adding a banking sector

Households do not necessarily spend all their income on goods and services, because part of it may be saved. Savings represent income that is not spent on goods and services and, in turn, is a leakage from the circular flow. At the same time, it is not only households that spend on goods and services. Firms also spend when they buy capital goods. This is known as investment. Investment is an injection into the circular flow. Savings and investments are enabled by the banking sector. Banks attract savings and then lend the funds that firms need for their investments. In this way, income leaks out due to savings but is injected back through investment.

Adding a government sector

In every economy there is also a government sector. How does this affect the circular flow? Households must pay taxes. This implies that a part of income is paid in taxes and is therefore not spent on the goods and services produced by firms. The government uses the tax revenue collected to finance government spending, such as the building of roads and schools, and so this spending is an injection back into the circular flow.

Adding a foreign sector

Most countries trade with other countries and are therefore "open economies". This means that domestic goods and services are exported while foreign ones are imported. Imports are a leakage as they represent household spending on foreign goods and services. Exports reflect foreign spending on domestic goods and services, so they are an injection back into the circular flow.

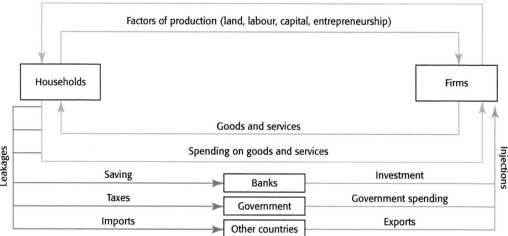

▲ **Figure 1.1.4** Flows in an economy including leakages and injections

The circular flow of income

Carefully draw your own diagram showing the circular flow of income. Explain what would be the effect on national income if:

a. households decided to save more

b. the government decided to initiate spending cuts and raise taxation.

c. the government of a trading partner decides to relax import duties.

 TOK

Is the *ceteris paribus* assumption realistic? Do other disciplines make a similar assumption?

Figure 1.1.4 shows the expanded version of the circular flow, which includes leakages and injections.

Leakages from the circular flow of income consist of savings, taxes and imports. They are matched by injections into the circular flow of income, which are investment, government spending and exports. Yet leakages and injections may not equal each other. What happens then? Think of the circular flow as a swimming pool containing a certain amount of water. Now, imagine there is a crack in the pool and water leaks out while someone is adding water using the garden hose. If the water injected into the pool exceeds the amount of water leaking out, then the pool will tend to overflow. In contrast, if the water leaking through the crack exceeds the amount of water injected, then the pool will tend to drain. In terms of income, if injections into the circular flow are larger than leakages, the income flow becomes larger whereas if injections are smaller than leakages, the income flow becomes smaller.

Economic methodology

The methodology employed by economists is similar to that employed by natural scientists. Economists attempt to construct models that are then used to explain and predict. These models show simplified relationships between various economic variables. Most models can be described, but they can also be represented with diagrams. They are constructed by making general hypotheses about the causes of economic phenomena, for example, that consumer demand will rise when consumer incomes rise. These hypotheses are often based on observations. The aim is to draw conclusions from the constructed models. To arrive at conclusions it has to be assumed that nothing else that can influence the relationship under consideration has changed in the meantime. This is known as the **ceteris paribus** assumption. The Latin **ceteris paribus** translates as "other things being equal".

Models can be judged according to how successful they are in explaining and predicting. If the resulting prediction is wrong, the model must be either adapted or abandoned. This process is referred to as refutation.

Economists play a major role in helping governments to devise economic policy. In order to understand this role, it is necessary to distinguish between **positive** and **normative economic statements.** A positive statement is a statement of fact. It can be proven right or wrong. "Unemployment is rising" or "inflation will be higher than 6 per cent by next year" are examples of positive statements. A normative statement is a value judgment: a statement about what ought to be, about whether something is good or bad, desirable or undesirable. "It is right to tax the rich more than the poor" or "the government ought to reduce inflation", are examples of normative statements. They cannot be proved or disproved by a simple appeal to the facts.

 TOK

What criteria should be adopted for evaluating normative statements in economics?

Economic thought

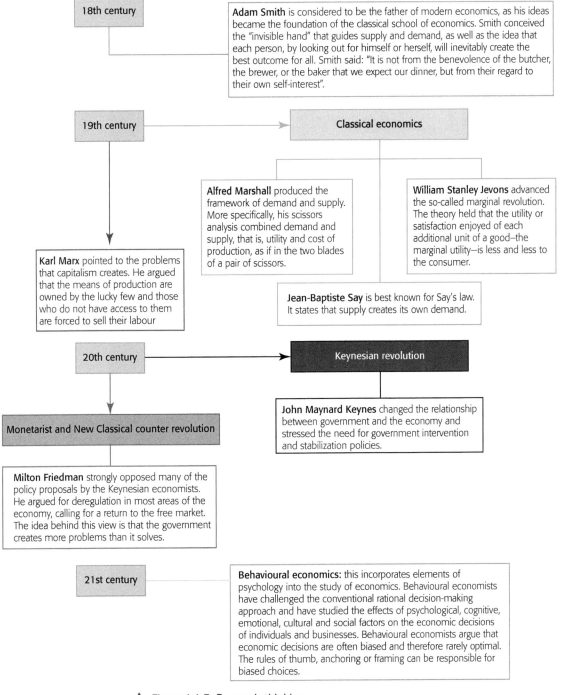

▲ **Figure 1.1.5** Economic thinking

Watch this

Search YouTube using these terms: Ariely control of our decisions TEDx. This video gives an insight into behavioural economics.

Search the web

For a more comprehensive timeline of economic thought, search using these terms: economics an illustrated timeline.

DP ready **ATL Thinking Skills**

Important economists

Which two of the people who have shaped economic thought over the centuries would you invite to dinner? Explain your answer.

Key terms—test yourself

Define these terms: scarcity, resources, opportunity cost, efficiency, social sciences, microeconomics, macroeconomics, leakages, injections, *ceteris paribus*.

Focus point

Economics is the social science that studies how societies make choices that lead to the best possible use of scarce resources, in an attempt to satisfy unlimited human wants. The production possibilities model and the circular flow of income model are representations of the economy. The production possibilities curve shows the possible combinations of two goods that an economy can produce in a given period of time. The circular flow model shows the interrelationships between firms and households in an economy. All models are built on the ceteris paribus assumption which is a key feature of economic methodology.

2 Microeconomics

Microeconomics focuses on the individual units of the economy: consumers, firms and markets. This section examines the goals of consumers and of firms. You will then learn how prices are determined as well as how governments often intervene in markets to affect outcomes. This section also shows how markets are responsible for the allocation of scarce resources; when and why markets are often successful, but also when and why they may fail.

In this unit you will learn about ...

→ demand and supply
→ the "invisible hand" and the "visible hand"
→ behavioural economics
→ elasticities

→ spillover effects
→ overuse of common pool resources
→ public goods
→ market power.

2.1   DEMAND AND SUPPLY: THE BOXING RING

In this section you will learn about ...

→ the meaning of the term "market"
→ the buyers' side: demand
→ the sellers' side: supply
→ putting the two sides together.

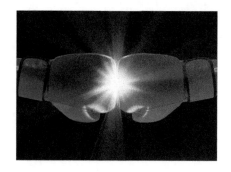

The issue

We have all heard or used the phrase "demand and supply", but what is its precise meaning? This section lays out the pieces that make up the demand and supply puzzle and puts them together to understand how markets work.

The meaning of the term "market"

A market is most commonly thought of as an open space where buyers and sellers of goods come together—but a market is not always found at a particular location. A market could be in a local neighbourhood, such as a fish market, but it could also be international, such as the world market for soybeans. The buyers and sellers of the market may never actually meet, just as in markets on the internet. Therefore, a **market** can better be defined as a mechanism that allows buyers and sellers to interact.

A market might be visualized as a boxing ring: on the one side there are the buyers (consumers) and on the other side there are the sellers (producers). Their "fight" is their interaction. The result is the price of the product.

The buyers' side: Demand

Demand refers to the quantities of a good that consumers are willing and able to purchase at various prices over a given period, *ceteris paribus*. Remember that **ceteris paribus** means that all other factors that may affect demand remain constant.

Think as a consumer. How many bananas would you buy per week? This depends on your willingness to buy bananas, which reflects your preference for bananas. Are you able to buy as many bananas as you are willing? This depends on their price and your income.

The law of demand

The law of demand states something simple: if the price of a good increases, the quantity demanded (*ceteris paribus*) decreases and vice versa—price and the quantity demanded change in opposite directions. This negative relationship is easy to understand. If something becomes more expensive, people will tend to buy less of it per period of time.

The negative relationship between price and the quantity demanded can be illustrated by a demand curve. Price is measured on the vertical axis and the quantity demanded per period is on the horizontal axis. Since the relationship is negative, the demand curve has a negative slope. This is shown in Figure 2.1.1.

If the price of bananas rises from P_1 to P_2, quantity demanded per period drops from Q_1 to Q_2, moving along the demand curve from point A to point B. Therefore, a change in the price of the good leads to a change in quantity demanded in the opposite direction, shown by a movement along the demand curve.

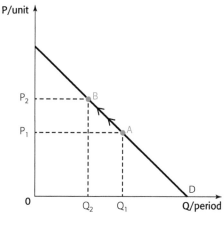

▲ **Figure 2.1.1** The demand curve

Non-price determinants of demand

Ceteris paribus requires that all other factors affecting quantity demanded when price changes remain constant. These other factors are referred to as "non-price determinants of demand". A change in any of these may cause demand for a good in a market to either increase or decrease. More specifically:

■ Income: if consumers' income increases, demand for most products is expected to increase. These are referred to as **normal goods**. However, demand for some products may decrease following an increase in consumers' income. These are known as **inferior goods**. They are usually lower quality products for which better quality substitutes exist. For example, Ting's salary has increased and she will now buy less tinned meat as she can afford fresh meat.

■ Tastes and preferences: if consumers find a good more desirable, demand for that good will increase and vice versa. This explains why companies spend millions on advertising.

■ Prices of **substitute goods**: two goods are considered substitutes if consumers typically buy one or the other because they satisfy the same need. A rise in the price of one such product may lead to an increase in the demand for the other. For example, Anwar may switch to eating bananas if apples become more expensive. So, the demand for a good will increase if the price of a substitute increases.

■ Prices of complement goods: **complement goods** are goods that are jointly consumed. Saanvi usually has a latte and a muffin for breakfast. Recently the price of lattes increased, which may cause the demand for muffins to decrease. So, the demand for a good will decrease if the price of a complement increases.

■ Expectations of a price change: if consumers expect the price of a product to increase in the near future, then demand for it now may increase.

■ The number of consumers: it is expected that an increase in the number of consumers will tend to increase market demand as the market demand is the sum of individual demands.

Illustrating the effect on the demand curve of a change in a non-price determinant

A change in the demand for a product on a diagram is illustrated as a shift of the demand curve. If a change in one of the above determinants of demand causes demand to increase, then at each price more quantity of the good is demanded and the original demand curve will shift to the right. If demand decreases then the demand curve will shift to the left, as shown in Figure 2.1.2.

As shown if the demand for bananas increases, the demand curve shifts to the right from D_0 to D_1. At each and every price, quantity demanded is greater. If the demand for bananas decreases, the demand curve shifts to the left

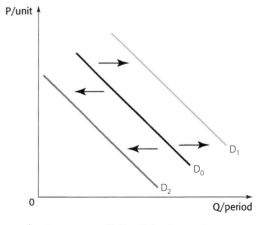

▲ Figure 2.1.2 Shifts of the demand curve

from D_0 to D_1. At each and every price, quantity demanded is less. Therefore, a change in one of the non-price determinants of demand, shifts the demand curve. But a change in price leads to a movement along the demand curve.

DP ready ATL **Thinking and communication skills**

Investigating demand

1. Prepare a large mind map, on screen or on a large piece of paper, that explains what you have learned about the concept of demand. Include diagrams and examples.

2. Working in a small group, identify different products for which you are aware that demand has changed. For example, think of what may have happened to the demand for rice or goji berries, GPS devices or luxury travel in your town, your country or the world. The time period of change may be a year or a decade. Explain the change in demand. Include fully labelled diagrams.

The sellers' side: Supply

Supply refers to the quantities of a good that producers are willing to offer at various prices over a given period, *ceteris paribus*.

Think as a producer. If you were a farmer with a given plot of land producing corn, how would your decision to produce and offer corn per period be affected by the market price of corn? How would you react if the market price of corn increased?

The law of supply

The law of supply states that if the price of a good increases then quantity supplied per period of time will increase, *ceteris paribus*, and vice versa. Price and quantity supplied move in the same direction. The reason is that at a higher price, profitability for the firm increases, so producers will have the incentive to produce and offer more units per period. Also, if producing more and more units of a good becomes more and more costly to the firm then it will be willing to produce and offer more only at a higher price.

The positive relationship between price and quantity supplied is shown on a diagram by the supply curve that has a positive slope. The supply curve is shown in Figure 2.1.3.

If the price of corn rises from P_1 to P_2, quantity supplied increases from Q_1 to Q_2, moving along the supply curve from point F to point Z. Therefore, a change in price leads to a change in quantity supplied in the same direction, shown by a movement along the supply curve.

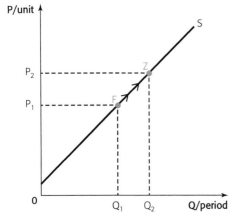

▲ **Figure 2.1.3** The supply curve

Non-price determinants of supply

Once again, *ceteris paribus* requires that all other factors affecting quantity supplied when price changes remain constant. These other factors are referred to as non-price determinants of supply. A change in any of these may cause supply of a good in a market to either increase or decrease. More specifically:

- Costs of production: a change in input prices or in technology can affect the costs of production. Amara owns a bakery and her specialty is apple pies. However, an increase in the price of the apples she uses as an input has caused her production costs to rise. This will lead to a decrease in the supply of Amara's apple pies. Dan, a herdsman, has converted his barn for the mechanical milking of cows. This has lowered his costs of producing milk. The supply of milk has increased.

  Costs of production will also change if the government imposes an indirect tax on a good or if it pays producers a subsidy. An indirect tax is usually a fixed amount of money to be paid to the government per unit of a good. The tax increases production costs, so supply will decrease. A subsidy is a payment by the government to firms; this decreases their costs of production and so increases supply.

- Prices of goods in **competitive supply**: goods are in competitive supply if they use, and therefore compete for the same resources. Masha is a farmer using her land to produce kiwis and avocados. If the price of avocados rises, she will change the use of some of her land from growing kiwis to growing avocados. The supply of kiwis will decrease.

- Prices of goods in **joint supply**: goods are jointly supplied if the production of one good automatically leads to the production of another. Emir farms sheep for cheese and wool production. If the price of cheese increases, Emir will buy more sheep in order to offer more cheese. At the same time, though, he will be able to supply more wool.

- Expectations of a price change: if producers expect the price of a product to increase in the near future, then they may decide to supply less now and take advantage of selling it at a higher price later.

- The number of firms: it is expected that an increase in the number of producers will tend to increase market supply as the market supply is the sum of individual supplies.

 Internal link

See section 2.5 for more on indirect taxes and subsidies.

Illustrating the effect on the supply curve of a change in a non-price determinant

If any of the non-price determinants of supply changes then the supply curve will shift. An increase in supply shifts the supply curve to the right whereas a decrease in supply shifts the supply curve left, as shown in Figure 2.1.4.

As Figure 2.1.4 shows, if the supply of corn increases, the supply curve will shift to the right from S_0 to S_1. At each and every price, quantity supplied is greater. If the supply of corn decreases, the

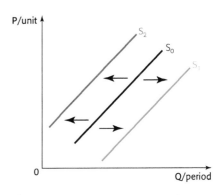

▲ Figure 2.1.4 Shifts of the supply curve

Investigating supply

1. Prepare a large mind map, on screen or on a large piece of paper, that explains what you have learned about the concept of supply. Include diagrams and examples.

2. As a class, discuss the following. How might the supply of agricultural products be influenced by the introduction of agbots (agricultural robots) in processes such as harvesting, fruit picking and soil maintenance? How will low-skilled workers be affected? Search online for relevant information.

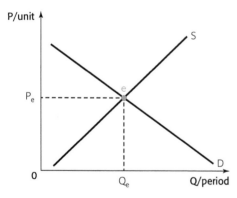

▲ **Figure 2.1.5** The market for avocados

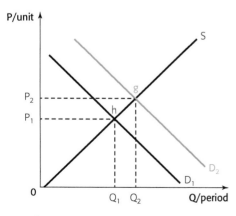

▲ **Figure 2.1.6** The market for kale

supply curve will shift to the left from S_0 to S_2. At each and every price, quantity supplied is less. Therefore, a change in any of the non-price determinants of supply shifts the supply curve. But a change in price leads to a movement along the supply curve.

Putting the two sides together

The two sides of the market (or boxing ring) have been separately examined. What remains to be seen is what happens when they are put together to fight. The fight (their interaction) will determine the price of the good.

When will the fight between consumers and producers stop? Most likely when they no longer have a reason to keep fighting; that is, when they have reached a point of balance. This point is referred to as market equilibrium. In market equilibrium the price of a good is referred to as the equilibrium price. It is the outcome of the fight. The fight ends here because when the **equilibrium price** is reached, the amount of the good consumers are willing and able to buy per period is equal to the amount producers are willing and able to offer per period; that is, quantity demanded equals quantity supplied. The market "clears". Consider the market for avocados, outlined below.

Figure 2.1.5 shows the market for avocados. Market equilibrium is formed at the intersection of the demand and supply curve, at point e. The equilibrium price is P_e and the corresponding quantity is the equilibrium quantity Q_e since at P_e, $Q_d = Q_s$. At any other price, either $Q_d > Q_s$ or $Q_s > Q_d$. If $Q_d > Q_s$ we say that there is excess demand in the market and the price will as a result tend to increase. (**Excess demand** is when, at some price, quantity demanded is higher than quantity supplied.) If $Q_s > Q_d$ we say that there is excess supply in the market and the price will as a result tend to decrease. (**Excess supply** is when, at some price, quantity supplied is higher than quantity demanded.)

Changes in market equilibrium

If any of the non-price determinants of demand or supply change there will be a shift in either the demand or the supply curve and the market will move to a new equilibrium.

Consider the market for kale. Kale is a green leafy vegetable, recently listed among the "superfoods" which has made it increasingly popular. As such, demand for kale has increased, which is shown by a rightward shift of the demand curve in Figure 2.1.6.

Initially market equilibrium was at point h with the market price of kale at P_1 and the corresponding equilibrium quantity at Q_1. Following the increase in demand, the demand curve has shifted to the right from D_1 to D_2. Market equilibrium is now at the intersection of the supply curve S with the new demand curve D_2, at point g. The increase in demand for kale has led to a higher market price ($P_2 > P_1$) and an increase in equilibrium quantity ($Q_2 > Q_1$).

Something similar has happened in the market for coconuts (see Figure 2.1.7). Weather conditions, droughts in particular, and farm diseases have negatively affected the supply of coconuts.

Initially, market equilibrium was at point j, with the market price of coconuts at P_1 and the equilibrium quantity at Q_1. The droughts and diseases reduced supply of coconuts and so the supply curve has shifted to the left from S_1 to S_2. Market equilibrium is now determined at the intersection of the demand curve D and the new supply curve S_2, at point h. The decrease in supply has therefore led to an increase in the market price ($P_2 > P_1$) and a decrease in equilibrium quantity ($Q_2 < Q_1$).

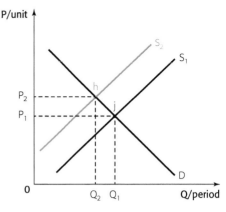

▲ Figure 2.1.7 The market for coconuts

DP ready ATL Thinking, research and communication skills

Demand and supply of agricultural products

1. Consider the following statements.

   a. "New methods of growing crops have caused bumper yields in the production of rice, causing a decrease in the price of rice."

   b. "The popularity of bananas is decreasing as consumers are switching to other fruit options."

   Explain, using the determinants of demand and supply, and appropriate diagrams, the changes in the market price and equilibrium quantity for rice and bananas. Can you think of any other factors that could affect the demand or the supply of these goods?

2. Agricultural product prices tend to be highly volatile. In a small group:

   a. examine the factors responsible for the fluctuating prices of agricultural products

   b. investigate the problems associated with volatile prices for countries that are dependent on agricultural exports.

Focus point

The interaction between consumers and producers in markets determines the price of the product. If there is excess demand price will rise. If there is excess supply price will fall. Price will settle at the equilibrium. The equilibrium price is the one that clears the market.

Key terms—test yourself

Define these terms: market, demand, supply, normal goods, inferior goods, substitute goods, complement goods, competitive supply, joint supply, equilibrium price, excess demand, excess supply.

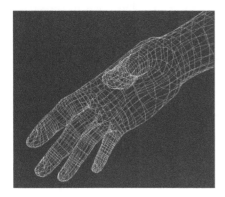

In this section you will learn about ...

→ the role of the price mechanism

→ market efficiency.

The issue

As you have seen, markets tend to find themselves at a point of balance, the equilibrium point. How is this happening? How do markets reach equilibrium following changes in demand and supply? The answer lies with the price mechanism or the "invisible hand" of the market, which will be explained in this section.

The role of the price mechanism

Changes in demand and supply cause changes in price. These changes in price act as both signals and incentives and the good is then rationed to consumers. Let's consider the example of the market for kale shown in Figure 2.2.1.

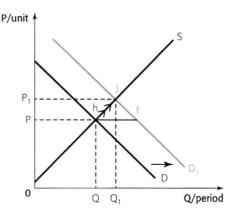

▲ Figure 2.2.1 The market for kale

Initially, the market is in equilibrium at point h, where the price of kale is at P and quantity is at Q. An increase in demand, due to a favourable change in tastes and preferences, is shown by a rightward shift of the demand curve from D to D_1. At P, there is now excess demand for kale equal to line segment (hf), since quantity demanded exceeds quantity supplied. This exerts upward pressure on price. The price of kale starts rising.

This increase in the price of kale is a signal to producers of kale. It contains information that consumers now demand more kale than before. This is the signalling role of prices in a market economy. The increase in the price of kale also has an incentive role. It creates the incentive to farmers to produce and offer more kale as it is now more profitable.

As the price of kale increases and producers increase quantity supplied, there is an extension along the supply curve, from point h to point j. The price will keep rising as long as there is excess demand in the market. It will increase to P_1. At P_1, quantity demanded is again equal to quantity supplied and a new equilibrium has been reached where more kale is produced.

Note that an equilibrium price also has a rationing function: all consumers who are willing and able to pay it, will end up with the good.

DP ready ⌇ATL Thinking Skills

The price mechanism

Let's say the demand for kale decreases.

1. How would the price mechanism (that is, the signalling and incentive functions of price changes) work following the decrease in demand?

2. How would the market move to a new equilibrium?

Resource allocation

An increase in the demand for a good will increase its price. Producers respond to the increase in price by increasing the amount offered. To do this they need more resources, such as land, labour and machines. Resources will have to be diverted away from other goods and this reallocation of resources is determined by the change in the price of the good. In a market economy, it is the price mechanism that continuously allocates and reallocates scarce resources.

> **DP ready** ATL **Thinking Skills**
>
> ### Reallocation of resources
>
> Consider what would happen if the price of kale decreased.
>
> **1.** How would producers respond?
>
> **2.** How would resources be reallocated following the decrease in price?

Market efficiency

What does demand also show?

Demand shows, at each price, how much consumers are willing to buy per period. If you read the demand curve vertically (that is, for each Q go all the way up until it meets the demand curve), it shows something most interesting. It shows how much people are willing to pay, at the most, for each additional unit of a good. Logically, this maximum cannot be greater than the additional benefit they enjoy from consuming that unit. So, the market demand also shows the **marginal benefit**—that is, the additional benefit enjoyed from each additional unit consumed.

Figure 2.2.2 shows the demand for coffee. We realize that for unit Q_1, say the 5th unit, consumers would be willing to pay P_1 dollars at the most. For unit Q_2, say the 9th unit, they would be willing to pay P_2 dollars at the most, while for unit Q, say the 20th unit, they would be willing to pay P dollars at the most.

Consumers will purchase additional units of a good per period of time only as long as the price they are prepared, at the most, to pay is greater than the market price charged. If the market price of coffee is P dollars, then consumers will buy all units up until unit Q, as for each of these units they were willing to pay at least or more than the market price.

The excess of what consumers would have been prepared to spend over what they actually spend for a given amount purchased is referred to as the **consumer surplus**. In Figure 2.2.2, the consumer surplus is shown by the shaded area below that demand curve and above the market price for the units consumed; that is, area Pfz.

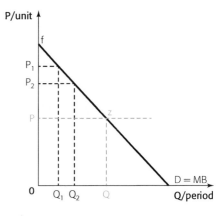

▲ Figure 2.2.2 The consumer surplus

What does supply also show?

Supply shows, at each price, how much firms are willing to offer per period. You can also read the supply curve vertically. Doing that shows the minimum firms require to be paid to offer each additional unit. That minimum must be the additional cost, which is known as the **marginal cost,** of producing each additional unit. The supply curve (S) also shows the marginal cost (MC) of producing the good.

Figure 2.2.3 shows the supply of coffee. Unit Q_1, say the 5th unit, will be offered if the price received is at least P_1 dollars. For unit Q_2, say the 9th unit, firms require at least P_2 dollars while for unit Q, say the 20th unit, firms require at least P dollars. It follows that if the market price is determined at P, then firms will be willing to offer all units up until Q: for each of these units the firms earn at least, or more than, the marginal cost of producing these.

The difference between what firms earn and the minimum they require is known as the **producer surplus**. In Figure 2.2.3, the producer surplus is given by the shaded area below the market price and above the supply curve for all units sold; that is, area PhJ.

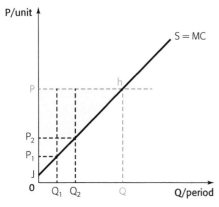

▲ Figure 2.2.3 The producer surplus

Optimum production from society's point of view

If the world market for coffee is illustrated in Figure 2.2.4, what is just the right amount of coffee from society's point of view? Should the 20th unit of coffee be produced? It should, because consumers would have been willing to pay (MB) more than the additional cost (MC) of producing it. What about the 65th unit? That unit should also be produced from society's point of view as again, for that unit, the MB is greater than the MC. This is true up until the 70th unit (Q) for which MB = MC.

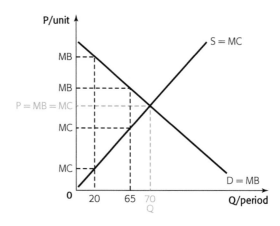

▲ Figure 2.2.4 The market for coffee

From society's point of view, Q units of coffee are just the right amount of coffee that should be produced. Market forces alone, demand and supply, without the need for the government to intervene, lead to a market price of P per unit of coffee and to just the right amount of coffee produced from society's point of view. The market achieves what is known as **allocative efficiency**.

If allocative efficiency is achieved then not only just the right amount of the good is produced, but also just the right amount of resources (land, workers and machines) are allocated in the production of each good. The **social surplus**—the sum of the consumer surplus and the producer surplus—is maximized. This is the miracle of Adam Smith's "invisible hand".

DP ready ATL **Thinking Skills**

Social surplus

What would happen to social surplus if for some reason more or less than the socially optimal amount was produced?

 TOK

Remember that demand refers to willingness but also to the ability of people to buy a good at each price. Ability is linked to income. If there is a lot of poverty in a country, is it morally justified to consider that the allocatively efficient level of output of any basic good is the best from society's point of view?

Focus point

The change in behaviour of market participants leads to a change in price and thus, more or less of a good is produced. A change in the allocation of resources follows. In this way, market forces alone lead to the optimal amount of the good produced and to the best possible allocation of resources.

Key terms—test yourself

Define these terms: marginal benefit, consumer surplus, marginal cost, producer surplus, allocative efficiency, social surplus.

In this section you will learn about ...

→ rational consumer choice

→ behavioural economics in action.

The issue

The goal of consumers is to maximize their utility from consuming goods and services. However, this may not necessarily be the case. Standard economic theory considers any difference in behaviour as irrational—but is it? This section explores how economic agents may actually "misbehave".

Rational consumer choice

The goal of the rational consumer is to maximize utility (or satisfaction) from consuming goods and services. More specifically, the rational consumer, acting on pure self-interest, will make the best choice (that provides maximum utility) by weighing up all information on relevant costs and benefits.

Consider Miranda, who received a surprisingly high winter electricity bill. One evening after work she decides to find out whether she could get a better deal with another energy plan or provider. Six hours later, Miranda finds the optimal solution—if she switches providers, she could save $50 this year. The rational consumer, like Miranda, is often referred to as a *homo economicus*: a self-interested agent who seeks optimal, utility-maximizing outcomes.

Behavioural economics

Behavioural economics has debunked the notion of a *homo economicus*; people are not the rational decision-makers that are assumed by standard economic theory.

If we suppose that Miranda's leisure time has a monetary value (say $10 per hour) then was it really worth six hours of her time to work out the energy saving? What if Miranda cannot be sure how much money she will save from switching? How much leisure time and effort would she need to sacrifice to arrive at a decision? Miranda's issue highlights the cognitive limits, time constraints and other barriers to optimal consumer decision-making. That is to say that people have **bounded rationality**, which refers to the restricted information, time constraints and cognitive limitations that people face, and which makes the idea of always choosing the "best" option prohibitively complex.

As a result of bounded rationality, people use **rules of thumb**, also known as **heuristics**, which are shortcuts to help them make judgments and decisions. However, these rules typically result in systematic errors.

TOK

Is the assumption of rational consumer choice realistic?

One example is **availability**, where people make judgments about the likelihood of an event based on how easily they can think of a similar example or case. This can lead to false decisions. For example, it has been found that there is an increased occurrence of the purchase of earthquake insurance following a major earthquake, even though the likelihood of re-occurrence in the near future is low.

Another example is anchoring. **Anchoring** takes place when people rely on a piece of information that is not necessarily relevant as a reference point when making a decision. For instance, in one experiment, participants were asked to write down the last three digits of their phone number multiplied by one thousand (for example, 576 = 576,000). They were then asked to estimate the prices of different houses. Results showed that participants with higher-ending telephone digits valued all the houses more highly. Anchoring works similarly in real world settings. For example, the first house shown to an individual by a real estate agent serves as an anchor and influences perceptions of houses presented next (as relatively cheap or expensive). This, of course, is known and exploited by businesses.

Besides bounded rationality and consequent rules of thumb, individuals can make decisions that are not optimal because of the framing effect. **Framing** refers to how options and opportunities are presented to people, which can significantly influence their choices. Of particular importance is whether people are presented with a negative or positive frame. Most people will choose the option that is presented in a positive way. Think of two fast food chains presenting their new burger. One uses the label "91% fat free" and the other uses the label "9% fat". Individuals will tend to prefer the first since it frames the burger as healthier despite the fact that both burgers contain the same amount of fat. The framing effect can therefore lead to a biased choice.

> **DP ready** | ATL **Thinking, research and communication skills**
>
> **Framing different options**
>
> In a small group, devise a number of simple but equivalent options framed differently. Present these options to other students and record which ones they choose. Does framing matter?

Behavioural economics in action

People's choices often end up being inconsistent with their preferences. Too often individuals are unable to appreciate what is in their own best interest. This opens the door for positive intervention in the decision-making process to motivate people to make choices in their best interest. Some examples follow.

Choice architecture

How a particular choice is presented—the choice architecture—can have a significant effect on the choice made. People tend to make default choices. The **default choice** is the option that a consumer "selects" if he or she does nothing. Default choices are therefore made automatically. The nature of the default option strongly affects consumers' behaviour.

The choice architect is whoever is responsible for organizing the context in which people make decisions. It is assumed that the choice architect knows more about what is in the individual's best interest. To encourage a particular behaviour that is assumed to improve welfare, the choice architect can set the desired outcome as the default choice. For example, if society would benefit from higher rates of organ donation, then the default choice can be set to everybody's organs being donated upon death. An individual may still choose to opt out of organ donation but that would not be the default. Similarly, to encourage pension scheme enrollment, workers can be automatically signed up for pensions. This is the default choice. A worker can still opt-out but that would not be the default.

Nudges

Another way to influence people's choices is through nudges. **Nudges** are small design changes capable of significantly changing people's behaviour. An expert can nudge people's choices in the direction the expert considers to be best. For example, nudging can be used to tackle the growing obesity problem. Sellers of goods and services can be nudged to display products or lists of products (such as on a menu) in a manner that induces people to buy healthier foods. One example could be putting fruit and vegetables in grocery stores at eye level.

Nudging can also be used to induce behaviour that is environmentally friendly. For instance, garbage bins to dispose of recycled material can be twice or even three times bigger than bins for regular waste. Having less room for general waste can nudge people to recycle more.

Defaults and nudges can but should not mislead people. This requires some intervention. Only with proper regulations is it more likely that the choices people make are better choices.

TOK

Debate the extent to which governments will nudge people in the right direction.

Search the web

Search using these terms: fly Schiphol nudge washington post. Professor Thaler is a leading behavioural economist and Nobel Prize winner. Read about his favourite example of "tweaking the environment" so that we change how we behave.

| DP ready | ATL Thinking, research and communication skills |

Choice architecture and nudges

Investigate how choice architecture and nudges influence decision-making in a particular context. Share this with your classmates.

Key terms—test yourself

Define these terms: bounded rationality, rules of thumb (heuristics), availability, anchoring, framing, default choice, nudges.

Focus point

Behavioural economists have challenged the traditional rational economic decision making. They have showed how economic agents are subject to bounded rationality and make biased choices which lead to sub-optimal decisions.

In this section you will learn about ...

→ price elasticity of demand (PED)
→ income elasticity of demand (YED)
→ price elasticity of supply (PES).

The issues

Price elasticity of demand (PED): Firms need to know how their revenues will be affected if they increase the price they charge. They need to find out what proportion of a tax imposed on the good or service they offer can be shifted on to consumers. A government would like to know, for example, how high to make a cigarette tax if the goal is to decrease smoking and not just to collect more tax revenues. This section explains why knowledge of price elasticity of demand (PED) helps with these and other related issues.

Income elasticity of demand (YED): Some firms are more likely to expand when the economy is growing. Also, over the long term, as economies grow and incomes rise, the agricultural sector shrinks, and farmers experience a relative decline in income. Growth leads to a rising share of manufacturing and especially of services. Income elasticity of demand (YED) helps to explain this.

Price elasticity of supply (PES): If demand increases, both the equilibrium price and the equilibrium quantity will increase, but the effect on price and quantity is not always the same. Price elasticity of supply (PES) helps us to understand why.

Price elasticity of demand (PED)

What is PED?

Think of tickling two friends. One looks at you expressionless, thinking that your behaviour is very odd. The other friend jumps up and cannot stop laughing. Obviously, they have responded differently.

PED tries to measure how the quantity demanded of a good will respond to a change in its price. More formally, PED is defined as the responsiveness of quantity demanded to a change in price. PED is measured as the ratio of the percentage change in quantity demanded over the percentage change in price.

$$PED = \frac{\% \Delta Qd}{\% \Delta P}$$

Since price and quantity demanded always move in opposite directions (the law of demand), PED is always a negative number. Usually the minus sign is ignored and PED is referred to as a positive number.

 Internal link

Turn to section 2.1 for more on the law of demand.

If PED is greater than 1 it means that the change in quantity demanded is proportionately bigger than the change in price: if the price of a good increased by 2% and its quantity demanded decreased by 3% then PED is 1.5 (ignoring the minus sign). This is known as **price elastic demand**.

If PED is between 0 and 1, it means that the change in quantity demanded is proportionately smaller than the change in price: if the price of a good increased by 2% and its quantity demanded decreased by only 1% then PED is 0.5 (again, ignoring the minus sign). This is known as **price inelastic demand**.

Extreme cases

- PED = 0 (perfectly inelastic; vertical demand curve). An increase in price will lead to no decrease in quantity demanded. This is highly unlikely in a market even if the good is vitally needed. For example, in some countries' health-care systems, even if the good is a very necessary medication, some lower-income uninsured patients will be priced out. If, however, we are focusing on individuals then demand for many goods may be perfectly inelastic if they have the necessary income.
- PED → ∞ (infinitely elastic; demand horizontal). Again, this is of rather theoretical importance. If the demand faced by a firm is horizontal at some price, then this implies that the firm is so small compared to the market that consumers will buy any quantity offered at that price, without the need for the price to decrease.
- PED = 1. This means that any change in price would lead to a proportionately equal (in the opposite direction) change in the quantity demanded. This is quite unlikely. Demand has a special shape. It is a "rectangular hyperbola".

Search the web

To find out more, search using these terms: rectangular hyperbola demand.

What does PED depend on?

Common sense helps us determine the factors that affect PED. Try to determine the relevant factors in the following examples.

- There are many close substitutes for good A. Consumers have fewer, if any, close substitutes for good B. The price of both goods increases. In which case will it be easier for consumers to switch to another good? Demand for which of the two goods will be more price elastic?
- The price of gasoline rises substantially. Drivers despair, but they still have to drive to work or the supermarket. After a while, though, wouldn't they consider other options, such using public transport or sharing car journeys with others? If the higher price lasts they may think of buying hybrid car or even moving closer to work. Will demand for gasoline be more price elastic in the short term or the long term?
- The price of fresh fish significantly increases. Eating fresh fish is considered a healthy choice. Now consider two individuals: a banker earning a high salary and an unskilled worker earning much less. Who will probably start eating frozen fish instead of fresh? Doesn't the expenditure on a good as a proportion of income also determine how responsive demand will be following a price change?

- Now let's consider demand for an addictive good—cigarettes. Will a small tax convince many smokers to quit?
- What about demand for everyday necessities—would you consider demand for these to be price inelastic or price elastic?

Illustrating PED

Perhaps surprisingly, PED is not the slope of a demand curve. PED is greater the higher the original price is. PED varies along a straight-line demand curve as shown in Figure 2.4.1. At the midpoint m, PED is equal to 1. At point a it tends to infinity and at point b it is equal to 0.

At higher prices (above point m) demand is price elastic (PED > 1) while at lower prices (below point m) demand is price inelastic (0 < PED < 1).

Of course, this makes sense. An increase in price when a good is already expensive will hurt consumers more than if the good was cheaper.

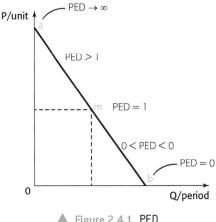

▲ Figure 2.4.1 PED

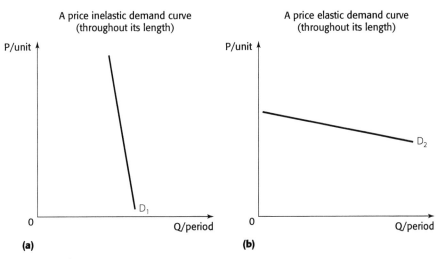

▲ Figure 2.4.2a Price inelastic demand b Price elastic demand

To illustrate a demand that is considered price inelastic, draw it far from the origin and steep, like D_1 in Figure 2.4.2a. To illustrate a demand that is considered price elastic, draw it far from the origin and flat, like D_2 in Figure 2.4.2b.

Table 2.4.1 summarizes information about elasticity of demand.

		Demand is considered:	
price elastic	if PED > 1	So %ΔQd > %ΔP	Draw flat but far from the origin
price inelastic	if 0 < PED < 1	So, %ΔQd < %ΔP	Draw steep but far from the origin
unitary elastic	if PED = 1	So, %ΔQd = %ΔP	Draw a curve that never touches either axis
perfectly elastic	if PED $\to \infty$	So, consumers will buy any amount at some price	Draw parallel to the Q-axis
perfectly inelastic	if PED = 0	So, when P changes, Qd does not	Draw vertical to the Q-axis

▲ Table 2.4.1 Elasticity of demand—a recap

PED and revenues

The question that a firm faces on what will happen to its revenues if it increases price can now be answered. Firms know that by increasing price, quantity demanded will decrease. By how much,

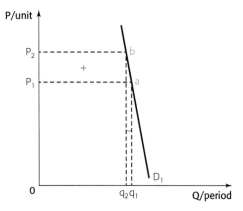

▲ Figure 2.4.3 Increase in price and decrease in demand

though? This is why firms would like to know PED for their goods or services. Would they prefer demand to be price elastic or price inelastic? The answer is price inelastic, so that the decrease in quantity demanded is proportionately less than the increase in price. For example, if a firm increased its price by 10% it would be happy if quantity demanded decreased only by 6%, so that PED is 0.6.

In Figure 2.4.3 price charged increased from P_1 to P_2 and quantity demanded decreased from q_1 to q_2. **Total revenues** (P times Q) collected will increase from area $0q_1aP_1$ to area $0q_2bP_2$.

Table 2.4.2 summarizes information about the relationship between price and demand.

Demand	when price increases	when price decreases
If demand is price elastic (so, PED > 1)	then, total revenues (TR) will ↓	then, TR will ↑
If demand is price inelastic (so, 0 < PED < 1)	then, TR will ↑	then, TR will ↓

▲ Table 2.4.2 Price and demand—a recap

PED and the government

Does a government care about the PED of products? Of course it does. If it imposes an indirect tax (a per unit tax on goods) and it hopes to collect a lot of money in taxes, will it prefer to tax a product with a price inelastic demand or a product with a price elastic demand? Tax revenues collected equal the tax imposed per unit times the number of units sold. Since the government would like quantity demanded to decrease as little as possible, it will prefer to tax goods with a price inelastic demand.

What if the goal of the tax is not so much to collect high tax revenues, but to decrease consumption of a product such as cigarettes. Could a high tax that would make cigarettes very expensive achieve this? Remember that PED is higher at higher prices and that how much consumers respond also depends on the proportion of their income that is spent on the good. Could this explain why cigarette taxes are in some countries relatively low while in others they are extremely high?

PED of primary products

Primary products include agricultural products, such as coffee or cotton, as well as metals and minerals, such as copper and zinc. Each of these has few, if any, close substitutes. Kellogg's cannot produce Corn Flakes using wheat. Consider cerium, a rare earth mineral. Cerium is necessary in the production of cars' catalytic converters as it enables them to run at very high temperatures. Does a manufacturer of catalytic converters have much choice if the price of cerium rises? What does this suggest about the PED of primary products?

PED of manufactured products

Demand for manufacturing sector products, such as cars or laptops, is more price elastic. This is because consumers face more and closer substitutes. If a consumer is considering buying a BMW, a Mercedes may be an alternative to consider. Also, expenditures on manufactured goods are often a big proportion of income for many consumers. That may explain why their demand is typically more price elastic.

DP ready ATL **Thinking and communication skills**

Analysing reasons for PED

Refer to the information in the table below.

Product or service	PED
Salt	−0.1
Gasoline, short run	−0.2
Physicians' services	−0.6
Gasoline, long run	−0.7

Product or service	PED
Restaurant meals	−2.0
Vacations abroad	−3.2
Ford cars	−3.4

▲ Table 2.4.3

In a small group, try to think of plausible reasons for each product's PED. Present your findings on a poster and share it with the rest of your class.

Income elasticity of demand (YED)

What is YED?

Income elasticity of demand (YED) is the responsiveness of demand following a change in consumers' income. It is measured as the ratio of the percentage change in quantity demanded over the percentage change in income.

$$YED = \frac{\%\Delta Qd}{\%\Delta Y}$$

Typically, YED is a positive number since income (Y) and quantity demanded (Qd) change in the same direction. If incomes are increasing, demand for most goods will be increasing and vice versa. These are the normal goods introduced earlier and their YED is positive.

If incomes in an economy are increasing, demand for some goods may increase faster. For example, incomes may increase by 5% and quantity demanded for a product may increase by 7.5%. Using the formula above, YED is $\frac{+7.5}{+5} = +1.5$. If YED is positive and greater than 1 then an increase in income has led to a proportionately greater increase in quantity demanded. This is known as **income elastic demand**. Demand for most services is income elastic.

In contrast, if incomes are increasing and demand increases but at a much slower rate, this is known as **income inelastic demand.** For example, if incomes increase by 5% and quantity demanded increases but only by 2% then YED is equal to $\frac{+2\%}{+5\%} = +0.4$. This is more likely for many food products like potatoes or salt.

DP ready ATL **Thinking Skills**

YED on services and on various products

1. Think of why demand for most services is income elastic while demand for many food items is income inelastic. Explain why the YED of inferior products is negative. Give examples.

2. Consider the YED for used cars in a city where consumers are poor, and contrast it with a city with high-income consumers. Do you think that the YED of a good is the same for all consumers across all income levels?

Table 2.4.4 summarizes information about YED.

Normal goods (YED > 0)	
0 < YED < 1	YED > 1
Income inelastic demand	Income elastic demand
Examples: farm products; food; basic day-to-day goods and necessities (kale, rice, canned tuna, pencils, haircuts)	Examples: most services; expensive (luxury) goods (beauty treatments, cruises, cars, dishwashers, iPhones, sail boats)
Inferior goods (YED<0)	
Examples: used cars, low-quality clothing, lower-quality food	

▲ Table 2.4.4 YED—a summary

Illustrating income elasticities

To illustrate differing income elasticities we use what are called Engel curves. In an Engel curve, income is on the vertical axis; quantity demanded of a good (or, more broadly, expenditures on the good) is on the horizontal axis. Normal goods have an Engel curve that is upward sloping: as income increases, quantity demanded also increases. If the demand is income elastic, the Engel curve must intersect the vertical axis (E_1), whereas if demand is income inelastic, the Engel curve must intersect the horizontal axis (E_2).

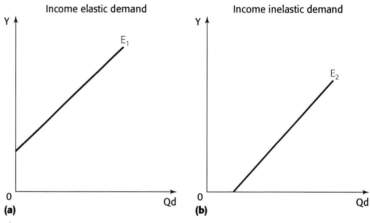

▲ Figure 2.4.4a and b Normal goods—differing income elasticities

Product or service	YED	Product or service	YED
Public transportation	−0.26	Furniture	1.42
Dining out	1.54	Foreign travel	3.01
Petrol (gasoline)	0.46	Food	0.16
Electricity	0.24		

▲ Table 2.4.5

As a result of the eurozone crisis that started in 2009, incomes decreased and unemployment increased in Spain, Portugal, Greece and Ireland. Given the YED values in Table 2.4.5, think about the impact of this crisis on the industries and activities listed. Do you think that in countries with incomes below the European Union (EU) average, YED for food will be higher or lower than for countries with much higher incomes than the EU average? Present your findings for discussion in your class.

Price elasticity of supply (PES)

What is PES?

Price elasticity of supply (PES) is the responsiveness of quantity supplied to a change in price. We measure it as the ratio of the percentage change in quantity supplied (Qs) over the percentage change in price.

$$PES = \frac{\%\Delta Qs}{\%\Delta P}$$

Since price and quantity supplied always move in the same direction (law of supply), PES is always a positive number.

If PES is greater than 1, it means that the change in quantity supplied is proportionately greater than the change in price: if the price of a good increased by 5% and its quantity supplied increased by 7% then PES is 1.4. This is known as **price elastic supply**.

If PES is between 0 and 1, it means that the change in quantity supplied is proportionately smaller than the change in price: if the price of a good increased by 3% and its quantity supplied increased by only 1.5% then PES is 0.5. This is known as **price inelastic supply**.

 Internal link

See section 2.1 for more on the law of supply.

Extreme cases

- PES = 0 (perfectly inelastic; vertical supply curve).

    An increase in the market price of a good will lead to no increase in the quantity supplied. Think of a fresh fish market where one morning there is an unexpected increase in demand for sardinella. The price will increase but the quantity of sardinella available for sale by sellers cannot change. The PES of sardinella at that market that day is zero. Supply is perfectly inelastic.

- PES →∞ (infinitely elastic; horizontal supply curve).

    A horizontal supply curve implies that no matter how much is demanded, sellers are willing to satisfy demand at that price. This means that producers are able to produce and supply more without any increase in their production costs.

- PES = 1 (unitary supply; any straight line through the origin).

    This is a rather theoretical case as it means that any change in price would lead to a proportionately equal change in quantity supplied. An increase in price by 3% leads to a 3% rise in quantity supplied. This is quite unlikely.

What does PES depend on?

Again, common sense will help you to determine the factors that affect PES. Try to determine the relevant factors in the following examples.

- A firm sells plastic flowers and stores significant stock. Contrast it to a firm that sells fresh flowers in the market. For which seller will it be easier to meet an increase in demand?

■ Two factories are producing cement. Factory A is fully utilizing its capacity. Factory B is not; it has plenty of spare capacity. For which factory will it be easier to meet an increase in demand for cement?

■ A firm supplying gardening services employs mostly unskilled workers. A medical research company requires very highly skilled and trained workers. Following an increase in demand, for which one of the two firms will expanding output be more difficult? Use the term "labour mobility" to answer this.

Most importantly, the time period determines PES. Three time periods are used: the momentary run, the short run and the long run. The distinction is criterion-based.

■ In the momentary run, all factors of production are considered fixed. Supply will be perfectly inelastic. Firms will not be able to meet an increase in demand.

■ In the short run, some factors can change but there is at least one factor that is considered to be fixed. A firm's premises are considered fixed (capital) but it can hire more labour, so to some extent it can meet an increase in demand.

■ In the long run, all factors of production are considered variable. A firm can change its scale of operations. An increase in demand can be met. PES is thus greater in the long run than in the short run.

Illustrating PES

Again, PES is not the slope of a supply curve. It can be shown that if supply cuts the vertical axis then it is price elastic (PES > 1), whereas if it cuts the horizontal axis it is price inelastic. Remember that we are talking about percentage changes of price and quantity supplied, and not absolute changes. Refer to Figures 2.4.5a and 2.4.5b.

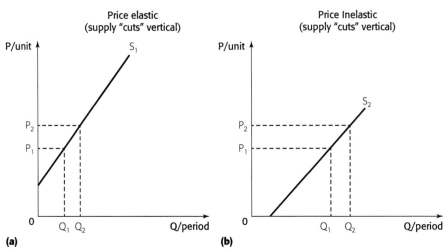

▲ Figure 2.4.5a and b Supply—price elastic and price inelastic

This is not proof, but it is quite clear that the percentage change in price from P_1 to P_2 is the same in Figures 2.4.5a and 2.4.5b but the percentage change in quantity supplied is much bigger in Figure 2.4.5a, as the change from Q_1 to Q_2 is roughly 50% of the initial quantity supplied Q_1.

Table 2.4.6 summarizes information about price elasticity of supply.

Supply is considered:			
price elastic	if PES > 1	so, %ΔQs > %ΔP	It must cut the vertical axis
price inelastic	if 0 < PES < 1	so, %ΔQs < %ΔP	It must cut the horizontal axis
unitary elastic	if PES = 1	so, %ΔQs = %ΔP	It must go through the origin (any slope)
perfectly elastic	if PES $\rightarrow \infty$	so, at that price, the firm is willing to offer as much as demanded	Draw it parallel to the Q-axis
perfectly inelastic	if PES = 0	so, when P changes, Qs does not	Draw it vertical to the Q-axis

▲ Table 2.4.6 Price elasticity of supply—a recap

So, how is PES responsible for the effect that an increase in demand has on P and on Q?

Given a shift of demand to the right, the more price inelastic supply is, the greater the (proportionate) effect on price. It makes sense as price inelastic supply means that firms will not be able to easily expand output, so it will be price that will mostly increase. If, however, supply was price elastic then output would expand proportionately more than price increased.

PES of primary goods and manufactured goods

Supply of primary products is typically price inelastic. Producing a product such as grapes typically takes months (from planting to harvesting) while increasing output in mining facilities requires extremely expensive mining equipment.

Typically, supply of manufactured products is price elastic, as a sudden increase in demand can usually be met by asking workers to work overtime or by hiring more labour. Of course, the firm must have other necessary inputs available and some unused capacity.

Focus point

Elasticities determine the extent to which:

- the quantity demanded changes following a change in price or in income
- the quantity supplied changes following a change in price.

Elasticities are therefore important influences on the decisions of firms and governments.

DP ready | ATL | Research and communication skills

Research what rare earth minerals are. Select a few and find out what they are used for. Explain to your classmates why we expect both PED and PES to be quite low in value.

Key terms—test yourself

Define these terms: price elasticity of demand (PED), price elastic demand, price inelastic demand, total revenues, income elasticity of demand (YED), income elastic demand, income inelastic demand, price elasticity of supply (PES), price elastic supply, price inelastic supply.

The issues

A **price ceiling** (or **maximum price**) is a form of price control that a government can impose in a market. Price ceilings refer to the highest possible price that can be charged for a good. The government's goal is to protect consumers against excessively high prices, but undesirable side effects usually arise.

A **price floor** (**minimum price**) is a form of price control that a government can impose in a market. Price floors act as the lowest possible price that can be charged for a good and are usually set in agricultural product markets. The government's goal is to protect producers, usually farmers, but in most cases, this comes at the expense of other stakeholders.

Indirect taxes are taxes on goods and services or on expenditures. They can be specific or *ad valorem*. **Specific taxes** (or unit taxes) are a specific "dollar" amount per unit of a good. ***Ad valorem* taxes** are a percentage of a good's price. Indirect taxes are imposed by governments for many reasons and they affect market outcomes, stakeholders and resource allocation. This section examines the consequences of indirect taxation.

Subsidies are also a form of government intervention in markets. They are payments by the government to firms. They may be successful in achieving certain goals of the government but they are costly and may have undesirable side effects. This section examines the effects of subsidies on markets and on stakeholders.

Price ceiling (maximum price)

Why do governments impose price ceilings?

A price ceiling is set by the government, which is below the price determined by the market. The price is then not allowed to exceed this level. Price ceilings have historically been imposed in many countries on basic goods, usually on food products such as milk or bread, but also on gasoline and heating fuel. In many cities around the world, authorities have also imposed **rent controls** in the rental housing market. Rent controls are examples of price ceilings. Price ceilings therefore aim to make certain basic goods and services cheaper and so more affordable to low income consumers.

Analysing the impact of a price ceiling

First, let's consider the case of a rent control. High rents make housing less affordable for many households. For example, in 2019 the average monthly rent for a two-bedroom apartment in London was over $2,000 and London is among the most expensive cities in the world to rent. Because of this, the Mayor of London may impose rent controls. Figure 2.5.1 illustrates the impact of rent control in the market for rented apartments in London.

The rent control (P_c) is set below the market-determined rent (P_e) and represents the highest possible rent landlords can legally charge.

At P_c the number of apartments now offered for rent is lower than the number of apartments tenants are willing and able to rent ($Q_s < Q_d$). The result of the price being set by authorities below the market equilibrium price is a **shortage**, as quantity demanded exceeds quantity supplied. This shortage of apartments available for rent is given by $Q_d - Q_s$ equal to line segment (Q_sQ_d) or distance (AB).

Are rent controls effective?

Rent controls make housing more affordable but they can also lead to the following issues.

■ Landlords will decide according to their own preferences who they will rent their property to. For example, to households without a pet or to households without young children. There is also a high risk of discrimination based on ethnic background or religion.

■ There may be long waiting lists for tenants who want to rent a property.

■ Landlords may demand unofficial payments in addition to the legal maximum rent or may demand large deposits.

■ The quality of rental property will deteriorate as landlords will earn less, and will not have the incentive to carry out maintenance on their properties.

■ Some landlords may switch to short-term rentals (such as through the company Airbnb). This decreases the number of available properties for longer-term leases.

■ There will be lower incentive for real estate developers to construct more housing units.

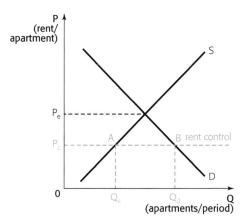

▲ **Figure 2.5.1** Impact of rent control in the rented apartment market in London

TOK

When rent controls are imposed, landlords have a larger choice of tenants wanting to rent their property. What are the ethical considerations of landlords' decisions about who can rent their property? Should the government enact laws that protect tenants from possible abuse?

Rental property

1. Explain whether it is always feasible for the government to plan and implement rent controls.

2. Describe the issues that arise if the rental housing market is informal and so largely invisible.

3. Search online using the word "gentrification". In which cities have neighbourhoods recently undergone gentrification? Is there a link between gentrification and rents? Collect relevant data. Share these with the rest of your classmates and hold a discussion on the role of city authorities in these cases.

4. In some cities, Airbnb is considered responsible for surging rents and for many tenants being evicted. Search for relevant information. Describe whether rent controls would help or worsen the crisis.

5. When a major company, such as Google or Alibaba, decides to open new offices in a city, rents are expected to increase. However, the increased economic activity will benefit many people. In pairs, consider these issues and discuss policies that you would recommend.

Price ceilings on basic goods

A price ceiling in the market for a basic food product or for fuel can be analysed in exactly same way as rent controls. The price ceiling would be set below the market determined price and would be the maximum price sellers can legally charge. As a result, the quantity of the good demanded would exceed the quantity of the good supplied, and so a shortage of the good would result.

Similar consequences to those arising after the introduction of rent controls may appear in markets for basic goods, such as bread, when a price ceiling is set. Sellers can choose who will buy their bread; they may prefer to sell to regular customers, attractive customers or even important customers. Queues are likely to develop outside grocery stores or bakeries as people will rush to buy bread before supplies run down. Parallel markets (known as "black" markets) may emerge as consumers who are unable to buy bread in legal markets may be prepared to pay a much higher price. In the long term, the quality of available bread may worsen as bakers could be tempted to use cheaper inputs.

Creativity, action, service

There may be areas or neighbourhoods in your hometown where there has been an increase in evictions. Various cities have tenants' protection or tenants' rights centres. Investigate whether such an organization exists in your city or town and consider volunteering your time. You may also organize a fundraising project to help the organization finance its expenditures.

Food price controls

In developing countries, spending on food takes up the biggest proportion of household income. Therefore, when prices rise, the effect on poorer families can be severe, forcing them to cut back on shelter, medicines, clothes and school books.

1. Explain why food price controls could help in such cases. Also consider whether they could worsen the crisis. Collect information from different online sources to support your opinions.

2. As a class, discuss your views.

Price floor (minimum price)

Why do governments impose price floors in agricultural markets?

A **price floor** is a price set by the government, or other authority, above the market determined price and the price is not allowed to fall below this level. Governments impose price floors in agricultural markets for the following reasons.

- There are fluctuations in prices and therefore also in farmers' incomes. The supply of agricultural products is affected by weather conditions, such as droughts or floods, which can reduce supply. These changes in supply result in price volatility, which leads to unstable incomes for farmers.

- The agricultural sector's share of national income is decreasing. As economies grow, the demand for agricultural products grows, but more slowly. Therefore, over time, farmers' incomes decrease relative to incomes in the manufacturing and service sectors.

- To protect employment in rural areas. Price floors support agricultural production, which may prevent local farmers from moving into the cities (urbanization). In this way, employment in rural areas will be preserved.

> **Internal link**
>
> There is more on income elasticity of demand in section 2.4.

Analysing the impact of a price floor

For a minimum price to be effective it must lie above the free market equilibrium price. Let's take an example from agriculture in India. The Indian government has imposed price floors on 23 crops including wheat. Figure 2.5.2 shows the Indian market for wheat.

Market equilibrium was at point k with the market price of wheat being P_e and respective quantity Q_e. The price floor is set above the equilibrium price. At P_{min}, farmers can offer Q_s units of wheat while consumers purchase Q_d units. A **surplus** occurs when, as a result of the price being fixed above the market equilibrium price, quantity supplied exceeds quantity demanded. In this case there is a surplus $Q_s - Q_d$ equal to line segment (Q_dQ_s) or distance (ab).

A surplus exerts a downward pressure on the price—so what does the government do? In order for the minimum price to be maintained, the government buys the surplus at the promised price (that is, at P_{min}). This artificially increases demand (D + government purchases). In 2017–18, the Indian government purchased approximately 35 million tonnes of fresh wheat.

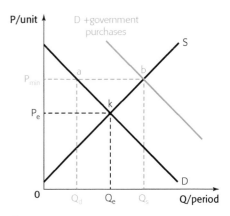

▲ Figure 2.5.2 **Effect of a minimum price in the Indian wheat market**

Winners and losers

Farmers are better off as their incomes are increased and stabilized. This can be particularly beneficial for small-scale farmers. Employment in rural areas may be protected, which is especially important for developing countries that have large agricultural sectors.

With the minimum price, buyers of the good or product pay more than they would otherwise, and enjoy less of the good. If the price-controlled product is used as an input in manufacturing firms, then production costs for these firms will be higher. This may lead to higher prices in their goods.

Governments are forced to spend heavily to purchase the surpluses. Specifically, the government must spend $(P_{min} \times ab)$; that is, the promised price floor times the amount of the surplus. In Figure 2.5.2, the Indian government would be forced to spend an amount equal to area $Q_d ab Q_s$. This implies that there is an opportunity cost involved, as financing this expenditure will require imposing new taxes now; or borrowing more now and imposing new taxes later; or cutting back expenditures on some other government project (such on building schools).

What can the government do with the surplus?

The government must make a decision about what to do with the surplus it purchases. Very often, these agricultural surpluses are simply destroyed. For example, millions of tons of surplus peaches have been buried over the years in northern Greece. A government may store the surplus (if they are non-perishable) and sell them later to avoid the price rising too much as a result of a crop failure. The disadvantage is that this gives rise to additional storage costs. Another option is to sell the surplus abroad. However, this exerts pressure to reduce the world price of the good, which hurts foreign producers, leading to international tensions.

TOK

Keeping in mind the consequences that come with a price floor, how can we know when the problem that the price floor intends to solve is significant enough to justify the intervention?

DP ready ATL **Thinking, research and communication skills**

Price floors on agricultural products

1. Research whether your government is imposing or has in the recent past imposed a price floor on the market for an agricultural product. Can you find information on what the government did with the surplus?

2. Government support for agricultural prices results in governments purchasing surpluses of agricultural products. Why do you think governments cannot simply give the products away to poor people? Discuss this question as a class.

Price floors in labour markets

A price floor in the labour market takes the form of a minimum wage. Many countries have wage laws that determine the minimum wage that employers must pay their workers. For instance, in 2019, the minimum wage in Luxembourg was set at 11.97€ per hour, in Greece at 3.94€ per hour and in Brazil at about $1.80 per hour. The aim is to guarantee a socially acceptable level of income to unskilled workers.

DP ready ATL **Thinking and communication skills**

Price floors in labour markets

1. Draw a labour market diagram with money wage (W) as the vertical axis and number of workers (L) as the horizontal axis.

2. Explain why a minimum wage policy is often criticized as leading to higher unemployment for unskilled workers.

3. In groups, discuss whether high employment for unskilled workers is a necessary consequence of a minimum wage policy. Think about the following questions.
   a. What if employers in some industries were able to keep wages at artificially low levels?
   b. Would employers be more likely to do that in industries where there is one employer, a few employers or many employers?

Indirect taxation

Why do governments impose indirect taxes?

■ To decrease consumption of certain goods such as sugar, alcohol or tobacco because consumption of these products harms not only consumers but also society at large. These goods are referred to as demerit goods.

Internal link

See section 2.6 for more on demerit goods.

- The UK government introduced a sugar tax in England in April 2018. The health risks for people who regularly consume sugar-sweetened beverages include a much higher risk of developing type 2 diabetes.

- Alcohol consumption costs the UK more than £55 billion annually and the US more than $250 billion.

- Smoking in England costs society roughly £12.6 billion annually.

■ To decrease use of fossil fuels by industry as the burning of fossil fuels leads to greenhouse gas emissions which are considered responsible for global warming and climate change. The devastating effects of climate change on economies, health and the environment are well documented.

■ To collect revenues and thus be able to finance government expenditures. Greece collects taxes of €1.02 for every litre of gasoline consumed and collected a total of almost €27 billion in 2017 from indirect taxes to finance government expenditures.

■ To decrease imports in certain industries and thus benefit domestic firms and employment. In 2018 the US collected more than $40 billion from taxes on imports.

Analysing the effects of an indirect tax

Figure 2.5.3 illustrates the market for sugar sweetened beverages. Initially, equilibrium market price was at P and equilibrium quantity at Q. An indirect tax increases the cost of production. An increase in production costs decreases supply, shifting it to the left or, better yet, vertically upwards by the amount of the tax, from S to S_t. Remember, the supply curve also reflects the marginal cost of production. The vertical distance between S and S_t (= ab) is the size of the tax.

Following the tax, the price consumers pay will rise from P to P_c and the quantity of sugar-sweetened beverages consumed will decrease from Q to Q'. Firms will earn P_p per beverage, which is equal to what consumers pay (P_c) minus the tax (ab = P_cP_p). The tax revenues collected by the government are equal to the tax per beverage (ab) times the number of beverages sold (Q'), thus area ($P_p$abP_c).

The proportion of the tax that consumers pay is $\dfrac{PP_c}{P_cP_p}$. This is referred as the incidence of the tax on consumers. The incidence of this tax on producers is therefore $\dfrac{PP_p}{P_cP_p}$.

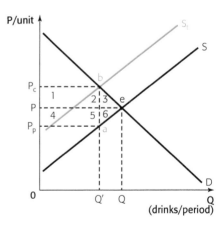

▲ Figure 2.5.3 Market for sugar-sweetened beverages

The impact on various stakeholders

Since consumers pay a higher price and consume less of the good, they are worse off. Consumer surplus decreases by area (1, 2, 3).

Not all consumers are the same—some will be rich, others poor. It is important to keep this in mind as indirect taxes are considered regressive: lower income individuals pay proportionately more. The "dollar" amount of the tax paid by two individuals may be the same but this amount will represent a greater proportion of the income of the poorer person. As a result, indirect taxes are considered unfair. Of course, if the goal of the tax is to reduce consumption of demerit goods, such as cigarettes or sugary drinks, then lower income households may benefit in the long run as they may not be able to buy the products and so will enjoy better health.

Producers are also worse off. They earn less per unit sold, they sell less, their revenues decrease and producer surplus also decreases by area (4, 5, 6). Remember that the production side includes not just the firms producing the taxed good but also other related firms, as well as workers.

Consumers and producers lose area (1, 2, 3, 4, 5, 6) but the state collects area (1, 2, 4, 5) in additional tax revenues which can be used to finance education and health services. Society therefore suffers a **welfare loss** equal to area (3, 6). Scarce resources are misallocated. However, the decrease in output may be "good" news for society if the tax is on polluting activities or on demerit goods.

The impact of PED on consumption, tax revenues and tax incidence

What is the role of PED in determining how much the consumption of a taxed good will decrease? If demand is relatively price inelastic, then an indirect tax will lead to a smaller decrease in consumption than if demand was relatively elastic. What does this suggest about the success of such a tax?

What if the goal is to collect high tax revenues? PED is once again crucial in determining the size of revenues collected. Tax revenues are the product of the size of the tax times the level of consumption following the tax. Given the size of the tax, the smaller the resulting decrease in consumption, the greater the tax revenues collected.

The **incidence of an indirect tax** depends on both the PED and the PES of the good. The side of the market which is more price inelastic will bear the bigger tax incidence. So, given PES, the more price inelastic demand is, the greater the incidence on consumers and vice versa.

DP ready ATL Thinking Skills

PED and PES

Consider two goods with the same PES but differing PEDs. Using appropriately drawn diagrams show:

1. the role of PED on consumption levels
2. the role of PED on the size of tax revenues collected
3. the role of PED, given PES, on tax incidence.

What if it is an **ad valorem** *tax?*

What if the tax was not a specific amount per unit but a percentage of the price (that is, an *ad valorem* tax)? The "dollar" amount of the tax would now depend on the price. The logic of the analysis is exactly the same, but the new supply curve would not be parallel to the initial supply curve, but steeper. All other results are identical.

DP ready | ATL **Thinking Skills**

Ad valorem tax

Draw a diagram showing the effect of an *ad valorem* tax on the market of a good.

Interconnectedness in economics

Figure 2.5.3 shows that a sugar tax could achieve the goal of reducing consumption of sugar-sweetened beverages. What about the effects of such a tax on sugar producers? The good that is taxed uses inputs that other firms produce. In this example, consider the firms involved in the production of sugar, an input in the production of sugar-sweetened beverages.

How will the level of sales and also of employment in these firms be affected? Also, what about retailers who sell beverages? The importance of interconnectedness in economics is evident. This is why policy-makers must assess the broader repercussions of any policy choice. We may need to assume *ceteris paribus* (that is, all other things being equal) to facilitate our analysis but in the real world not much remains constant.

An indirect tax on a demerit good, such as sugar or alcohol, may lead to a chain of substitutions. This means that some consumers of the taxed product may switch to substitutes. A tax on sugar-sweetened beverages may induce consumers to switch to other drinks that are even higher in sugar. An indirect tax on alcoholic beverages may induce some to switch to lower quality (and so cheaper) brands of alcohol. Policy-makers must consider all possible consequences on all related markets. Unintended consequences must be avoided.

 TOK

There is a lot of disagreement on the effects of a sugar tax. Search the terms "sugar taxes a briefing IEA" and then "taxes on sugary drinks WHO". How can you explain the largely opposing views that are given? What does this suggest about reason in economics?

Policy-makers often rely on indirect taxes as a source of tax revenues. Indirect taxes are regressive. Is there an ethical dimension that policy-makers should consider in relying on indirect taxes as a source of revenue?

In groups, reflect upon and discuss whether, or to what extent, a government has the right or the obligation to steer consumers away from consuming certain products.

Subsidies

Why do governments spend so much on subsidies?

- Governments want to ensure that certain groups of producers enjoy sufficiently high incomes. This has been an important justification of farm subsidies. However, farm subsidies also make farm products cheaper. This may lead to more exports or fewer imports of agricultural products for a country. Food also becomes cheaper and this benefits lower income households.

- Governments want to increase the consumption of goods that benefit not only the individual consumer but also society at large (merit goods). Think of vaccines or, more generally, health care and education. Subsidies lower their cost and make them more accessible. Health and education are referred to as merit goods.

- Public transport is also often subsidized as it reduces pollution and congestion.

- Green technologies are also subsidized as they become relatively cheaper than fossil fuels inducing firms to adopt them.

Analysing the effects of a farm subsidy

First, let's consider a farm subsidy. As a subsidy is a payment by the government to firms, it will lower their production cost. Supply of the agricultural good will increase and shift to the right or, better yet, vertically downwards by the amount of the subsidy. Remember the supply curve is also the marginal cost (MC) curve. Figure 2.5.4 illustrates the payment of a subsidy to rice producers in India.

Initially, the equilibrium was at point e with the price of rice at P per kilogram and the equilibrium quantity at Q kilograms per period. The vertical distance (fg) represents the per unit subsidy paid which lowered production costs and so increased supply to S_s.

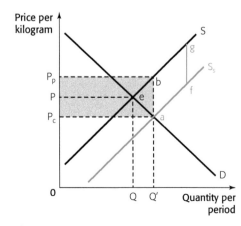

▲ Figure 2.5.4 Effect of a per unit subsidy to rice farmers in India

The new market equilibrium is at point a, with the price that rice buyers pay decreasing to P_c. Production and consumption of rice increases to Q' kilograms. Indian rice farmers will earn for each kilogram sold whatever buyers pay plus the subsidy. This is P_p, which is equal to P_c plus the vertical distance (ab) at the new quantity Q'. Government expenditure will equal the subsidy (ab) paid per kilogram times the number of kilograms produced (0Q), or its equal (P_ca). This is the area ($P_c$abP_p).

The rice subsidy increases production and consumption of rice. It makes rice more affordable and increases revenues for rice producers in India. The government must find the money to fund the subsidy. This may require imposing higher taxes now, or borrowing now and imposing higher taxes later, or perhaps some another government-funded project, for example, equipping public schools with smartboards, is cut. In other words, there is an opportunity cost involved.

DP ready **ATL Thinking Skills**

The impact of subsidies

"A farm subsidy (or, any subsidy) benefits both producers and consumers, as the former earn more (P_p) and the latter pay less (P_c). Since both sides are better off, a government should subsidize all producers."

1. Do you agree with the statement above?

2. In your opinion, what is the necessary condition for a subsidy to benefit society at large and so to be considered efficient?

3. The US has been paying large subsidies to its cotton producers. Find out which countries are the "Cotton-4 countries" in Africa. Examine the impact of US cotton subsidies on the population of these four countries. Present your findings to the class.

TOK

Many people think that agricultural subsidies help small farms that are family businesses. In many countries this is true. However, in many advanced economies, the primary beneficiaries typically include huge agribusinesses producing commodities such as wheat, cotton, corn, rice and soybeans.

Should low, or middle-income taxpayers in these countries pay higher taxes to subsidize such large-scale agribusinesses? If these agribusiness subsidies in advanced economies are eliminated, then "net-food importing" developing nations (countries that rely on food imports) may suffer. Can you see why? What is the ethical dilemma involved?

Rent subsidies

Rent subsidies are often paid to lower income families to make housing more affordable. The diagrammatic analysis is identical to the one above—it reveals that rents will decrease and so tenants will benefit. It also reveals that part of the subsidy will be captured by landlords: tenants are not the only beneficiaries.

Public transport subsidies

In many cities, public transport is heavily subsidized by the state, to make ticket prices lower. In this case, the law of demand suggests that the use of public transport services increases. It also suggests that use of cars, a substitute, becomes less attractive. Pollution and also congestion in the city decrease.

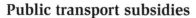

DP ready   ATL **Thinking, research and communication skills**

Subsidies—who pays, who benefits

A subsidy can be thought of as a transfer of income away from taxpayers to some specific population group. The number of taxpayers in a country will be greater than the number of beneficiaries of a specific subsidy. This means that the burden to each taxpayer is smaller than the help each beneficiary of a subsidy enjoys.

Describe what this suggests about which group will try to influence government decisions on whether to grant a subsidy.

Focus point

There are several ways in which the government intervenes in the operation of markets. It may set price ceilings or price floors, impose indirect taxes or grant subsidies. With all these forms of intervention, the government aims to meet certain objectives, but these come with consequences.

Key terms—test yourself

Define these terms: price ceiling (maximum price), price floor (minimum price), indirect tax, specific tax, *ad valorem* tax, subsidies, rent controls, shortage, surplus, incidence of an indirect tax.

2.6 SPILLOVER EFFECTS

In this section you will learn about...

→ market failure

→ negative production externalities and negative consumption externalities

→ positive production externalities and positive consumption externalities.

The issue

"Rapid human-induced warming has serious implications for the stability of the planet's climate."

"Excessive alcohol use is responsible for lost productivity, higher health care expenses, and motor vehicle crash costs."

"Education contributes to less crime and poverty and leads to new ideas and diffusion of technology."

There is one common thread in these statements: externalities (also known as spillover effects), which are a main source of **market failure**. With the tools of economics we can analyse why externalities arise and what policies can be devised to deal with them.

Market failure and externalities

What is market failure?

The "invisible hand" miraculously leads to allocative efficiency— but the invisible hand may not always be our friend. Sometimes, markets do not work to the best interest of society and lead to either too much or too little production or consumption of a good. When this happens, resources are misallocated, social surplus is not maximized and so the market fails.

Internal link

Find out more about allocative efficiency in section 2.2

What are externalities?

An **externality** can be viewed as a side effect of an economic activity that is not properly taken into account by the market participants. More specifically, an externality arises when the production or consumption of a good imposes costs on a third party for which the third party is not compensated, or creates benefits for a third party for which it does not pay. If costs are imposed on third parties it is the case of a negative externality. For example, Mr Kaplan, who drives to work every morning, adds to greenhouse gas emissions and traffic congestion. He is therefore imposing a cost on others, which he does not take into account. On the contrary, if benefits are created for third parties, it is a positive externality. Mr Kaplan also gets a flu shot every year, which reduces the risk of him becoming ill, but also reduces

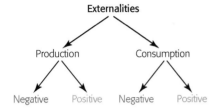

Externalities

Production   Consumption

Negative Positive Negative Positive

▲ Figure 2.6.1 The four externalities

the risk of spreading the disease to his fellow passengers on the train or his co-workers. He is therefore creating a benefit to others for which he is not compensated. Figure 2.6.1 shows the four types of externalities.

To analyse externalities fully, it is necessary to keep the following points in mind.

Remember that demand also shows the marginal benefit (MB). Since the benefit from consuming the good is enjoyed by the consumers who are buying the good, the demand represents the marginal private benefit (MPB). If there is an externality, the full benefit enjoyed by society is different from the private benefit. The **marginal social benefit** (MSB) includes the private benefit and any external effect that is not taken into account.

Remember that supply also shows the marginal cost (MC). Marginal cost is the cost to producers of producing one more unit of the good. This includes the costs of production that firms take into consideration, such as wages or the cost of raw materials. Supply therefore represents the marginal private cost (MPC). If there is an externality, the full cost to society differs from the private one. The **marginal social cost** (MSC) reflects the value of all resources that are used up in the specific production process. MSC consists of the MPC taken into consideration by the firm, and also any external cost not taken into account. Table 2.6.1 summarizes definitions of the relevant costs and benefits.

An externality creates a divergence between MPB and MSB, or between MPC and MSC. For example, think of Mr Kaplan. When he drives to work, is the MPB equal to MSB? The answer is no. Mr Kaplan enjoys the benefit of driving to work but he also imposes a cost on others: MSB < MPB. However, when Mr Kaplan gets the flu shot he benefits others and so, MSB > MPB.

Cost or benefit	Definition
Marginal private benefit (MPB)	The benefit to the consumer from each additional unit consumed
Marginal social benefit (MSB)	The benefit that is enjoyed by society from each additional unit consumed
Marginal private cost (MPC)	The cost to the producers of each additional unit produced
Marginal social cost (MSC)	The cost to society of each additional unit produced

▲ Table 2.6.1 Definitions of the relevant costs and benefits

Market failure when a negative production externality arises

Power plants in many countries burn coal to generate electricity. The burning of coal releases several greenhouse gases that contribute to global warming. Power-generating firms take into consideration their costs of production, such as input prices and wages, but do not take into account climate change costs. Therefore, the supply reflects MPC but the MSC is greater, as the cost of electricity generation to society exceeds the cost these firms consider.

Figure 2.6.2 shows the market for electricity in a country. Since there are no side effects (that is, externalities) from the consumption of electricity, demand is equal to both MPB and MSB. The supply though is only equal to MPC, as the MSC is greater. The difference between MPC and MSC reflects the costs of the environmental damage that the burning of coal causes (that is, vertical distance ab is the external cost of electricity generation). Market forces lead to output Q_m at price P_m where the demand equals supply (or, MPB $=$ MPC). However, the socially optimal level of output is Q* where MSC $=$ MSB. There is overproduction of electricity, which means that resources are overallocated. Why? It is because for all units between Q* and Q_m, MSC $>$ MSB, (that is, the cost to society is greater than the benefit gained by society from consuming them). All units past Q* should not have been produced from society's point of view; there is a welfare loss shown by the shaded area. The presence of the negative externality caused the market to fail.

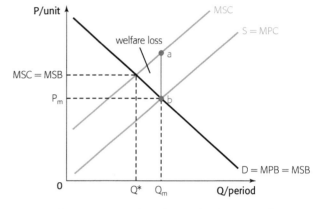

▲ Figure 2.6.2 Negative production externality

 Search the web

To find out more about pollution caused by industrial acivity, search for India pollution ft. Read the *Financial Times* article (11 December 2018).

Dealing with negative production externalities

Indirect taxation may be a possible way of dealing with negative production externalities. Remember that an indirect tax is an additional cost of production. In the case of a negative production externality the indirect tax placed must equal the external cost. In this way, the indirect tax will increase polluting firms' private costs. As a result, the MPC and MSC will become equal and the level of output will reach the socially optimal level. Unfortunately, the size of the necessary tax is difficult to determine because external costs are very difficult to estimate.

Watch this

Search in YouTube using these terms: China pollution under the dome. Watch the documentary about air pollution in China.

 TOK

What are the problems in knowing whether climate change is produced by human activity?

Alternatives to an indirect tax

Governments can impose a carbon tax, which is a charge on the use of fossil fuels, such as coal. The use of carbon taxes is spreading around the globe. The amount of the tax is dependent on the amount of carbon that is released when the fuel is burned. The higher the amount of carbon emitted, the higher the tax. Since the tax varies with carbon emissions, firms using fossil fuels have the incentive to switch to alternative energy sources that emit less carbon, or even no carbon. Therefore, the external costs of production decrease as a result of using cleaner fuels.

Search the web

Find out more about carbon taxes. Search for: carbon tax working nyt. Select the *New York Times* article (2 April 2019).

Governments may be reluctant to set very high carbon taxes as they hurt businesses. In many cases the carbon tax placed on power-generating firms has led to higher energy bills for households, which increases the cost of living and hurts lower income families.

DP ready ATL **Thinking and communication skills**

Taxing business activity

Indirect tax provides an incentive to firms to reduce output while carbon tax creates an incentive to firms to pollute less. Discuss the following in class.

1. Which type of tax do you think is more appropriate?

2. **a.** Will all firms face the same costs of reducing pollution?

   b. What does this suggest about carbon taxes?

Besides taxation another government response involves **tradable pollution permits**, also known as **cap and trade** schemes. The government decides on the maximum acceptable level of pollution in its country, say P*. It then issues pollution permits (or allowances), the total value of which is P*. Government then hands these permits over or auctions them to polluters such as heavy industry and power plants. These permits are tradable. This creates a system of incentives. Firms will have an incentive to reduce pollution if they can decrease their emissions at a lower cost than the cost of buying the necessary permits to pollute. On the other hand, firms that find it cheaper to buy permits than to decrease pollution will go ahead and buy permits. In this way, pollution will decrease by those firms which can do it with the least cost. In 2005 the EU-15 began implementing its Emissions Trading Scheme to reduce pollution from key industries. Since 2005 greenhouse gas emissions in Europe have been falling.

Watch this

Search YouTube using: EU ETS. You will find a short illustration of how the "cap and trade" principle works.

DP ready ATL **Thinking and research skills**

Reducing pollution

1. Describe how easy or difficult is it for the government to decide the maximum level of pollution allowed.

2. Find a country with a "cap and trade" scheme and research how effective the scheme has been in reducing pollution.

TOK

Is the optimal level of pollution zero? What knowledge issues are involved in assessing the optimal level of pollution?

Governments can also address the issue of negative production externalities through a command-and-control approach. This usually involves regulations such as limiting the emission of pollutants, limiting the levels of output of polluting firms, or requiring polluting firms to install technologies that reduce emissions. Regulations are usually easier to design and implement compared to taxation or tradable permits. Still, it may be costly for authorities to monitor the industries and enforce the regulations.

Market failure when a negative consumption externality arises

There are some goods that generate negative externalities when they are consumed. These are often referred to as **demerit goods**. Alcohol, for example, when excessively consumed often leads to violence, accidents, lower productivity in the workplace and health problems. The consumption of alcohol therefore imposes costs on third parties. However, consumers do not consider the external costs when deciding how much of the good to consume. The benefit gained by consumers is greater than the benefit enjoyed by society as a whole and so demand is only equal to MPB, as MSB is less. Figure 2.6.3 shows the market for an alcoholic drink, in this case vodka, where the MSB curve is below the D = MPB curve by the amount of the external cost of consumption. Note that since there are no external effects from production, supply is equal to both MPC and MSC.

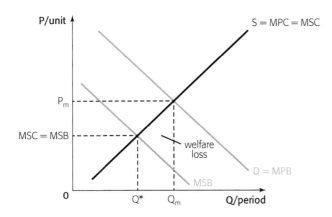

▲ Figure 2.6.3 **Negative consumption externality**

Consumers buy all units of vodka up to the point where demand equals supply. Consumption is therefore at Q_m and price P_m. At Q_m, MSC exceeds MSB. This means the cost to society from the consumption of the next unit of vodka is greater than the benefit society gains.

Figures compiled by the UK's Institute of Alcohol Studies and the Home Office showed that in the UK in the period 2009–2011 the excessive use of alcohol cost:

- £3.5 billion per year to the National Health Service
- £7.3 billion per year to the economy due to lost productivity resulting from alcohol abuse
- £11 billion per year to society because of alcohol-related criminal acts (www.ias.org.uk).

The socially optimal level of consumption is at Q* where MSC = MSB. All units past Q* should not have been consumed from society's point of view. There is overconsumption of the good and a welfare loss shown by the shaded area. The market for the alcoholic drink fails.

Dealing with negative consumption externalities

The policy aim in the case of a negative consumption externality is to reduce the consumption of the good generating the external costs. Indirect taxes are one option. In most countries around the world there are taxes on tobacco products. Recently, in some countries, taxes have also been placed on sugary drinks and perhaps a tax on red meat may soon follow. Given that the tax raises costs of production and reduces supply, it leads to a higher market price. The consumer is forced to pay more for the good, which can then reduce consumption and the associated external costs.

Is it that simple?

Remember that addictive goods tend to have low price elasticity of demand (PED). Tobacco, alcohol, sugar and even junk food are addictive—so consumers may not be very "sensitive" to price hikes. This means that a very high tax may be necessary in order to reduce consumption of these goods. However, this may lead to "a chain of substitutions". For instance, smokers may switch to e-cigarettes or heating tobacco devices that have been also proven to be harmful. Moreover, consumers may seek to buy the good in a black market where no tax is paid to the government. Therefore consumption falls by much less than desired and the external costs remain high, while the government receives much less in tax revenue. For example, the tax increases on tobacco products that successive governments in Greece have implemented, have contributed to a loss of 690 million euros in revenues. Also, remember that indirect taxes are regressive, so consumers earning relatively low incomes will be affected the most.

Are there any alternatives?

Another option for governments is legislation and regulation aimed at preventing or reducing the consumption. This may involve a ban, such as the ban on smoking in public spaces that exists in many countries. It may involve setting a minimum age at which a person can legally consume a good. For instance, in Egypt the minimum age at which someone can purchase or drink alcohol is 21.

Another approach to reducing consumption of certain demerit goods are packaging warnings. Manufacturers of, for example, tobacco products and alcoholic drinks, are forced by law to include health warnings on their products. Australia was the first country to introduce the plain packaging law, which demands that packaging removes all branding (colours, corporate logos and trademarks) and allows manufacturers to print only the brand name in a standardized font, in addition to the health warnings. All these laws and regulations aim to reduce demand towards MSB and therefore allow consumption to get closer to the socially optimal level.

Another way authorities could decrease the demand for goods with negative externalities is through advertising. For example, there is the Children's Food Campaign in the UK. Its goal is to raise awareness of the external costs associated with such consumption and, in turn, reduce demand for the goods. However, given the addictive nature or, habitual consumption of goods such as cigarettes, alcohol and even sugary drinks, existing consumers may not be incentivized to reduce their consumption. It may be that persuasion will actually prevent those that have not yet "taken up the habit", and especially the young. Nevertheless, the effectiveness of advertising and persuasion can only be seen in the long term.

In some cases a price floor may also be used to tackle consumption. For instance, the Scottish government has set a minimum price for a "unit of alcohol" at 50p. The unit of alcohol is determined at 10 millilitres of pure alcohol. The minimum price of each alcoholic beverage is determined by the number of units of alcohol it contains—that is, the number of units times 50p. This has made all types of drinks and all brands with the same number of units of alcohol equally expensive, and so consumption may decrease.

Search the web

To find out more about public health policy, search using these phrases: WHO tobacco; WHO alcohol. (WHO is the World Health Organization).

DP ready ATL **Thinking and communication skills**

Become a policy-maker

Imagine you are a policy-maker and have to deal with a negative consumption externality of your choice.

1. Explain which policy you will choose and why.

2. Present the issue and your chosen policy to your class.

TOK

To what extent can a government interfere in the freedom of its citizens to consume?

Market failure when a positive production externality arises

Firms producing certain goods may generate positive externalities. For instance, firms in the finance industry offer extensive training to their workforce. These firms incur a private cost associated with training. But when a worker leaves to join another firm, that firm enjoys the benefit of the trained workers without paying for it. This means there are external benefits created by the original firm that are enjoyed by third parties who do not pay for. In such cases, the MPC incurred by the firm is greater than the MSC.

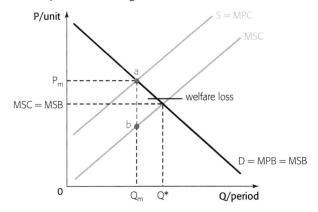

▲ Figure 2.6.4 Positive production externality

Figure 2.6.4 shows the market for financial services in Singapore. Supply is only equal to the MPC curve and the MSC curve lies below it by the amount of the external benefit. Since there are no external effects from consumption D = MPB = MSB. Market determined output is at Q_m and at price P_m, where demand equals supply. At Q_m MSB exceeds MSC, because at Q_m the benefit to society gained from the next unit produced is greater than the value of the resources used to produce it. The socially optimal level of output is Q* where MSC = MSB. For all units Q_m to Q* MSB > MSC, which means that from society's point of view these units should have been produced. There is underproduction of the good and the shaded area shows the associated welfare loss. The free market fails because not enough resources are allocated to the production of the good.

DP ready   ATL **Thinking, research and communication skills**

Search the web

Search using this phrase: Bilbao effect. Collect relevant information and analyse this it with the economic tools you have just learned.

Give a brief presentation to your class.

Dealing with positive production externalities

Despite the fact that benefits are created there is still underproduction of the good and a misallocation of resources. Policy-makers therefore aim to encourage production and increase output levels.

This can be achieved with the granting of subsidies. Remember that a subsidy is a payment by the government to firms that lowers their cost of production. The subsidy increases supply and the level of output. If the subsidy is equal to the external benefit of production then the MPC will become equal to MSC and the level of production will reach the socially optimal level.

Is it that simple?

As with external costs of production, external benefits are difficult to assess. Therefore the subsidy may not be enough to correct market failure and ensure allocative efficiency or indeed the subsidy might lead to overproduction of the good. Also, a subsidy is associated with the opportunity cost of the funds needed to pay for the subsidy.

Are there any alternatives?

Another government response could be direct provision: that is, the government may itself provide the good that has positive externalities associated with its production. For example, the government could provide training for workers through government-run training schemes. However, governments may not have the expertise required for successful intervention. Also, there may be significant opportunity costs associated with direct provision.

Market failure when a positive consumption externality arises

The consumption of some goods creates positive externalities. These goods are often referred to as **merit goods**. For example, education is a merit good because its consumption not only benefits the individual receiving it, but also benefits society in the form of higher productivity, less criminality and/or poverty and greater social cohesion. Figure 2.6.5 shows the market for university education in the US.

There are no external effects from production, so S = MPC = MSC. However, given that consumption creates external benefits the MSB is higher than the MPC and so the MSB curve lies above the MPB curve. Market equilibrium is at P_m, Q_m. At this level of consumption MSB exceeds MSC. This means that society benefits from the consumption of each additional unit of the good—each additional university enrollment is greater than the cost to society. The socially optimal level of consumption is at Q* where MSB = MSC. Therefore, all units from Q_m to Q* should have been consumed from society's point of view. There is underconsumption of university education. The shaded area shows the associated welfare loss. The market fails.

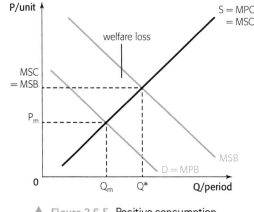

▲ Figure 2.6.5 Positive consumption externality

Educating girls is perhaps the single most valuable investment in the developing world. The benefits extend beyond increasing overall economic productivity. An educated mother will have fewer children. Her children will be healthier and more likely to be educated thus creating a virtuous circle.

Watch this

Search in YouTube using these terms: Ntaiya empower a girl TED. Watch the video of the talk on the importance of women's education.

 DP ready ₃₃ **Thinking and research skills**

Merit goods—education and health care

Given the significant benefits of education and health care (which is also a merit good), why do you think these are still underconsumed?

🌐 **Search the web**

Find information on the web about the anti-vaccination movement. What is taking place? What may be the impact on the market for vaccines?

Dealing with positive consumption externalities

When positive consumption externalities arise, policy-makers aim to encourage consumption. One way of doing this is through subsidies. A subsidy increases supply which then lowers the market price of the good. The lower price induces a higher level of consumption. For instance, if the US government subsidizes higher education institutions, tuition fees would be lower and more students may be able to enroll.

Is it that simple?

There is an opportunity cost associated with subsidies. The tax revenue used to subsidize the industry cannot be used to provide other goods and the government needs to have enough tax revenue to be able to raise consumption in this way. This is particularly important for developing countries. Developing nations have relatively low income levels and therefore low tax revenue, so it may be difficult to subsidize merit goods. As a result, such countries may be unable to enjoy the benefits created by the consumption of education and health care that are most crucial for their development.

Are there any alternatives?

Governments may also try to increase consumption of goods with positive externalities through legislation. For example, many countries have legislation that makes education compulsory up to a certain age. Similarly, in many countries there are laws that require children to be vaccinated against certain types of disease.

In cases where the external benefits are very large, such as education and health care, governments directly provide these goods. That is to say that some governments choose to provide education and health care free at point of delivery. Still, direct provision may be a significant burden on the government's budget. The state must run schools and hospitals equipped with trained professionals, or purchase and distribute vaccinations for free. All these government expenses therefore fall on taxpayers.

DP ready ATL **Thinking Skills**

1. What do you think happens when the government is forced to cut back on its spending?

2. In some cases, state schools have overcrowded classrooms, or hospitals have no available beds or even not enough medical equipment. What do these facts suggest?

Creativity, action, service

The use of e-cigarettes and other similar devices has spread, especially among the young. These devices are perceived as healthier alternatives to cigarettes but recent data suggests that health risks persist. Organize a campaign to raise awareness in your local community about the effects of using e-cigarettes. You can design several posters to inform the public. You may also organize a fundraising event to support teams or non-profit organizations helping those who are trying to quit smoking.

Focus point

Key terms—test yourself

Define these terms:
externalities, demerit goods, merit goods.

Externalities are spillover costs or benefits. If there are external costs, the market will lead to a level of production and consumption above the socially optimal level. If there are external benefits, the market will lead to a level of production and consumption below the socially optimal level. As a result, the market fails and government intervention may be required.

2.7   ARE WE DOOMED?

In this section you will learn about...

→ **common pool resources**

→ **measures to control overuse of common pool resources.**

The issue

Overfishing is depleting oceans across the globe, with 90% of the world's fisheries fully exploited or facing collapse. This issue relates to the overuse of common pool resources like fisheries, forests or even the atmosphere, that often leads to their depletion, posing a significant threat to sustainability. This section explores why common pool resources such as fisheries tend to be overexploited and how this problem could be addressed. If it is not, maybe we are not doomed, but it certainly doesn't look good for you and your children!

Common pool resources

Common pool resources are resources that are not owned by anyone but are available for anyone to use without payment. Examples include wildlife, irrigation systems (groundwater), and some fisheries, forests, hunting grounds, pastures and lakes. Note that since the atmosphere has been used as a "sink" of many anthropogenic pollutants, it is also considered a common pool resource.

Common pool resources share two characteristics: they are non-excludable and their use is rival (that is, their consumption by one person limits the amount available for others). For example, fishing vessels in unregulated fishing areas can catch as many fish as they are able to, as no one can be excluded from fishing in these waters. Of course, if one vessel catches a ton of fish there will be one ton less for all other vessels. One person's use of a common pool resource diminishes the amount available for others.

The result is an overuse of common pool resources. This is why fish stocks in many parts of the world are severely depleted or why many forests are disappearing. A resource that is commonly accessed is usually overused and this is known as the "tragedy of the commons". **Sustainability** can be defined as meeting the needs of the present without compromising the ability of future generations to meet their own needs. Sustainability is therefore threatened by overexploitation of resources currently available.

 TOK

Is it possible to have knowledge of the future?

Watch this

Search in YouTube using these terms: deforestation revolution world issue. Watch the video by Rob Stewart on deforestation and its effects.

The simplest way to analyse the overuse of common pool resources is in terms of externalities. Consider Lipet's Seafood Company. It fishes in the Gulf of Mexico, a common pool resource. Its fishing activity reduces the stock of fish available for all other vessels. Lipet's Seafood Company is therefore imposing a cost on all other fishing vessels in the area as they will have to fish longer and harder to catch the same amount of fish. This is an external cost as Lipet's Seafood Company does not take this cost into account.

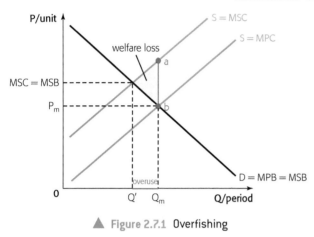

▲ Figure 2.7.1 Overfishing

Figure 2.7.1 refers to overfishing, but can be used to illustrate the overuse of any common pool resource as a negative production externality.

The MPC curve represents the private costs incurred by the fishing companies that fish in open oceans. The external costs reflect the depletion of the stock of fish and the resulting environmental damage. Fishing fleets will fish up to Q_m while the socially optimum is lower at Q^*. The line segment (Q^*Q_m) reflects overfishing.

Controlling overuse of common pool resources

In some cases, regulation by governments may prove effective in controlling overuse of common pool resources. Setting fishing quotas is an example. Fishing quotas are catch limits (usually expressed in tonnes) that are set for most commercial fish stocks. The EU has set fishing quotas for the managing of fisheries and for preventing depletion of fish stocks. However, even with fishing quotas, there may still be issues. For example, a shipping company of a certain nationality is only subject to its national government's fishing quota. If its fleet is registered in a different country it is no longer subject to the quota.

Search the web

Search using these terms: China fisheries brink NYT. You will find a *New York Times* article (30 April 2013) on overfishing and the possible effect on developing countries.

Search the web

To find out more on overfishing and fishing quotas, search for: mackerel plunder collapse nyt. Read the *New York Times* article (25 January 2012) on overfishing. The article reports how an EU shipping company has managed to evade the EU quota.

DP ready ATL **Thinking Skills**

Depleting fish stocks

In the article featured in "Search the web" opposite, Eric Pineda, a Chilean dock agent recognizes the declining catch, and states that he needs to increase his fishing activity before there is nothing left at all.

Explain what Pineda said, using the relevant framework and terms.

Other regulations may involve restrictions regarding hunting seasons, issuing licences or permits for particular activities (such as hunting or fishing), the establishment of protected areas for endangered ecosystems, as well as emission standards. Such regulations often involve costs of monitoring to detect violations.

Regulations are typically imposed by national governments. However, the overuse of common access resources often has international consequences, in which case international cooperation of governments is necessary.

Educating, especially the young, about the importance of adopting environmentally conscious behaviour may be most significant way of controlling overuse of common pool resources.

DP ready ATL **Research and communication skills**

 Search the web

Search using these terms: international agreements UN. Add "fisheries" then "forests".

1. Working in small groups, find information on international agreements that aim to limit the sustainability risks associated with the overuse of common pool resources. Keep in mind that the atmosphere is also a global commons. Make sure you include information about the Paris Agreement of 2015.

2. Present your findings to your class.

Collective self-governance

A different approach is the self-governance of the commons as proposed by Elinor Ostrom, the winner of the Nobel Prize in Economics in 2009. The idea is that a group of users of a resource can devise frameworks of use under certain conditions. These frameworks effectively regulate access to the common resource and balance resource use and resource renewal.

 Search the web

Search using these terms: Ostrom Nobel prize facts. You will find out about the first woman to receive a Nobel prize in economics.

Creativity, action, service

Despite the growing concern about environmental sustainability there are still many who are unaware of the long-term effects of several human activities on the environment. Organize a campaign to increase awareness in your school about these issues. You may also use social media to approach a greater audience. A fundraising CAS project may help support groups that work towards protecting wildlife. Also consider organizing a day trip where you can actively participate in beach cleaning or tree planting or any similar activity needed by your local community.

TOK

Collective self-governance implies that people cooperate. How could reason and emotion affect their decisions?

Focus point

Common pool resources are likely to be overused, since people do not take into account the effect of their use of such resources on others. This poses a threat to sustainability and so their overuse needs to be controlled.

Key terms—test yourself

Define these terms: common pool resources, sustainability.

In this section you will learn about...

→ public goods
→ why public goods are a case of market failure.

The issue

What do lighthouses, national defence, traffic lights and law and order have in common? They all share the characteristics of a public good. This section explores what public goods are and why they are a case of market failure.

Public goods and market failure

Do not let the term "public" confuse you here; it does not simply refer to any good provided by the state. In fact, a **public good** is one that has the following two characteristics: it is non-excludable, and its consumption is non-rival. Non-excludability implies that once the good becomes available to one person, it automatically becomes available to all. Non-rivalry implies that consumption by one person does not diminish the amount of the good available for others.

Here are some examples.

■ National defence or security—once national security is provided to one citizen it is impossible to stop others from enjoying its benefits. If one citizen enjoys the benefits, this does not diminish the amount available to others.

■ Law and order—if one citizen is enjoying safety through enforced laws, then all other citizens are also enjoying it. And, if one citizen is enjoying safety, this does not reduce the amount of safety available to others.

■ Traffic lights—traffic lights on the street are automatically available to all drivers. The use of the traffic light by one motorist does not diminish the amount available for other drivers.

■ A lighthouse—when a lighthouse is operating no one can be excluded from its benefits. If the lighthouse is used by one ship the same amount of its service is available to all other ships.

One issue is that if people cannot be excluded from enjoying the benefits of a good, they have no incentive to pay for it. They behave as free riders; enjoying the benefits of a good without incurring a cost. If public goods are left to the market, because of the free-rider problem there will be no output, since private firms will have no incentive to produce and offer such goods. This means that no resources will be allocated to the supply of the public good, leading to market failure.

Search the web

Search using these terms: public good lighthouse. Investigate whether lighthouses have ever been privately owned.

DP ready ATL **Thinking Skills**

DP ready ATL **Thinking Skills**

Broadcasting

Research some examples of over-the-air television and radio broadcasting, based on the following questions.

1. Do over-the-air stations have the properties of a public good?

2. How can these television and radio stations be privately owned?

3. How do these stations earn money?

4. What is the difference between over-the-air broadcasting and cable television or Netflix?

Public goods and market failure

The government must provide public goods using tax revenue. Note, though, that the government is not necessarily producing the public goods. For example, traffic lights are not produced by the government but by private firms who are contracted by the state. Still, there are opportunity costs associated with such expenditure on public goods—this expenditure must be financed either by higher taxes now, or by borrowing now and higher taxes later, or by reducing some other government expenditure.

 TOK

On the basis of what knowledge criteria do authorities weigh the costs and benefits of each public good and decide which to provide?

Focus point

Public goods are underprovided by the market. The problem is that they are non-excludable and their consumption is non-rival. Therefore, without government intervention it would not be possible to prevent people behaving as "free riders".

Key terms—test yourself

Define the term public goods.

In this section you will learn about...

→ maximizing profits
→ the meaning of economic costs
→ when economic profits are zero
→ homogenous and differentiated products
→ entry barriers

→ perfect competition
→ monopoly and oligopoly
→ concentration ratios
→ abuse of market power.

The issue

In this section we will initially focus on the firm. The concept of economic costs will be explained and the idea of profit maximization will be analysed. Following that, we will investigate market structures. The meaning of market power will be also examined and a discussion will follow on the possible risks as well as the possible advantages arising from its presence using real world examples.

Zooming in on firms

We typically assume that firms aim to maximize profits—but what does profit maximization really mean? **Profits** (π) are defined as the difference between the total revenues (TR) collected and the total costs (TC) of production: $\pi = \text{TR} - \text{TC}$.

The meaning of economic costs

An important point to remember is that in economics, since resources are scarce, **economic costs** include the value of all resources employed and are therefore sacrificed, whether the firm makes a payment or not. For example, consider Hana, a sushi restaurateur who owns the restaurant premises she uses. Her economic costs include not only the wages she pays her chef and other staff (explicit costs) but also the rent that she would have earned if she had rented her property to someone else (implicit cost).

However, economic costs must also include the minimum return (that is, the money) that Hana needs to earn from her sushi restaurant in order it to keep operating as it is and not to switch to her next best alternative, perhaps offering another cuisine or locating elsewhere. Entrepreneurial capital is also scarce, since it refers to funds that if used in one business, are automatically not available for use in another. The minimum return Hana requires is equal to what she could have been earning in the next best alternative with the same risk. This minimum return has a strange name, **normal profits**, and if it is not earned a firm will shut down. Normal profits are therefore also an element of economic costs, and part of the firm's implicit costs.

Marginal and average and their relationship

The term "marginal" in economics means "additional". Marginal cost (MC) is the additional cost of producing one more unit. Marginal revenue (MR) is the additional revenue from selling an additional unit. Average cost (AC) is the cost per unit of output produced (thus TC/Q) and average revenue (AR) is revenue collected per unit of output, (thus TR/Q which is the price at which the good is/was sold, so P and AR are always equal.

You will be aware of the relationship between marginal and average. For example, if after five quizzes your average score is 70% and on the sixth quiz (the "additional" quiz) you score 80%, your average will increase; whereas if you score 60% on your sixth quiz, your average will decrease.

Output required to maximize profit

How much output should a firm choose to produce in order to maximize profits? The answer is simple. As long as the additional revenue from producing and selling one more unit is bigger than the additional cost incurred to produce it, the firm should keep on producing more and more units per period because its profits will be increasing.

- As long as MR > MC a firm should continue producing units as profits will be increasing.
- Profits will be maximized when, for the last unit produced, MR = MC.

Illustrating with pencils

You are a craft producer of pencils. You have just made five pencils. Let's say that the profits earned from producing and selling these five pencils is $14. Now consider making an additional sixth pencil. If the additional revenue collected from selling it is $4.00 and the additional cost of producing it is $1.00, would you produce and sell that sixth pencil? Yes, as your profits would increase to $17.00. What if the additional revenue (MR) from one more pencil, the seventh, was still $4.00 but the additional cost (MC) of producing it was $3.99? What would your profits be from producing and selling seven pencils per day? They would increase and be equal to $17.01. You should be realizing that, as long as MR > MC your profits will increase by increasing output, up until that pencil for which MR = MC. At that point, your profits will be maximized.

What if economic profits are zero?

If a firm's economic profits are zero, its owners will be happy. Assume that a firm producing, for example, ice cream rolls requires at least $10,000 to stay in business. Remember, this $10,000 is referred to as normal profits and forms part of economic costs.

Let's say the firm's total revenues (TR) are $80,000 per month and its total economic costs are also $80,000 per month (within which though we have included the $10,000 normal profits since normal profits are also a production cost from the economist's viewpoint). The firm is making zero economic profits, but will remain in the ice cream rolls business because it is still earning $10,000 per month and the owner, Ed, deposits that amount in his bank account. The firm is making only normal profits. If TR are $95,000 while total economic costs are still $80,000, the firm is making $15,000 **supernormal profits** (excess profit above the minimum return necessary to keep the firm in business) and $25,000 is deposited in the bank. However, if TR drop to $76,000 per month and economic costs are still $80,000, then Ed is making **economic losses** (negative economic profits) of $4,000 per month. Ed may be able to deposit $6,000 per month in his bank account but that is not enough for him to remain in business.

Zooming out of firms and in on markets

Think of the market for corn or cotton; the market for hair salon services or restaurants in your city; the market for cell phone services and the market for electricity distribution. They all differ in many respects.

- The market for corn or cotton (or many farm products) is considered a perfectly competitive market. **Perfectly competitive markets** have very many small firms, selling a homogeneous product and there's nothing to prevent entry of new firms into the market. **Homogeneous products** are products that consumers consider perfect substitutes (identical).

- The market for hair salon or restaurants is considered monopolistically competitive. Monopolistically competitive markets have many small firms and there's nothing to prevent entry into the market of new firms; but these firms sell a differentiated product. **Differentiated products** are products consumers consider close but not perfect substitutes.

- The market for cell phone services is typically **oligopolistic**. These markets have few interdependent firms and there are barriers preventing new firms from entering. The product may be either homogeneous (such as cement or steel) or differentiated (cell phones or banks).

- The market for electricity distribution is a **monopoly**. In a monopoly market there is one firm dominating the market and there are barriers preventing new firms from entering.

Entry barriers

An **entry barrier** can be anything that deters entry of new firms into a market. The state may erect barriers by granting a limited number of licenses (for example, to operate a television station) or patents (for a pharmaceutical company's new drug). Firms try to erect barriers to limit competition and to be able to keep any supernormal profits. Common barriers to protect a firm's position include heavy advertising and brand name creation, offering multiple variations of their product (for example, Kellogg's) or continuously developing new improved versions of their products (think of the car industry). Lastly, natural barriers exist leading to a so-called natural monopoly when the production technology of the good is such that only one large firm can profitably operate.

Perfect competition

Why is perfect competition "perfect"? Firms in perfect competition have no market power. This means that there are so many firms operating, and each is so small compared to the market, that any one of them cannot affect the price that market forces determine— each of these firms is a "price taker".

Think of the world coffee market. There is a world demand for coffee and a world supply of coffee. The world supply includes many small coffee producers from many countries. Market forces (demand and supply), determine the equilibrium price of coffee. Amadi is a small coffee producer in Harrar, Ethiopia. He cannot affect the world price of coffee—because whether he produces and offers more or less coffee to the world market, the world market supply for coffee will not be affected. Coffee is a homogeneous good, so if Amadi tries to sell his coffee beans at a higher price, no buyer will buy his coffee. As he is such a small producer, he can sell all he wants at the market determined price for coffee. The price is therefore both his average revenue (AR) and his marginal revenue (MR). The typical, profit-maximizing firm will choose that output level for which MR is equal to MC.

If Amadi (or the typical firm) starts to make supernormal (abnormal) economic profits, there is an incentive for others to enter this market. They can enter it because, in perfect competition, there are no barriers. If the typical firm was making economic losses, then firms would exit the market. In the short run the typical firm can make supernormal profits (like Amadi), zero economic (normal) profits or even economic losses. In the long run, though, the typical firm will necessarily make zero economic profits; that is, only normal profits. Entry and exit will ensure this outcome.

The long run in perfect competition

As more producers enter the world coffee market, the world supply for coffee will increase and put pressure on the world coffee price to decrease. Entry of new producers will stop when supernormal economic profits are competed away and driven down to zero, (that is, to normal profits only), so that each coffee producer is making just enough money to remain in the business and not move to the next best alternative, for example, to producing maize. Symmetrically for the case of economic losses: firms will exit, the market supply will decrease, the market price will increase and this process will stop when there is no reason for more firms to exit; that is, when the typical firm is making zero economic (normal) profits. Remember that is just enough money to stop an entrepreneur from switching to the next best alternative with the same risk.

Perfect competition is not "perfect" solely because of lack of any market power. There is another important reason. In a perfectly competitive market, allocative efficiency is achieved because, for the last unit produced, P = MC and social surplus is maximized.

In perfect competition, P is equal to MR and, for maximum profits, MR is equal to MC. It therefore follows that the perfectly competitive firm will produce where P = MC, guaranteeing allocative efficiency.

Perfect competition may be quite unrealistic but it is still useful because it serves as a benchmark to evaluate the performance of actual markets. We will see that if market power exists (and it very often does exist) then prices are higher for consumers and allocative efficiency is not achieved.

The invisible hand

Is the invisible hand invisible because it doesn't exist? In most markets, firms are able to set their price. Agricultural markets, such as the world coffee, soybean or corn markets, are the exception. In other cases, Netflix and Spotify can set their rates for subscribers, Emirates Airline can set airfares, the power company in your city can set the price it charges for electricity and your neighbourhood hair salon owner can set the price for his haircuts. So, most firms are "price makers".

Firms such as Amazon, Google, the owner of the electrical grid in your country and the sole gasoline station in a village are considered monopolies. Not only are they price makers but the degree of market power they enjoy is quite substantial and that could prove a problem for society. Cell phone service providers, such as Verizon, AT&T, T-Mobile and Sprint in the US, and the big four UK supermarkets operate in oligopolistic markets. They can set rates and prices while their market power is substantial, especially if they collude and agree to fix prices together. Restaurants in Rome or in Hong Kong and beauty salons in Mumbai operate in monopolistically competitive markets. They can also set prices for their services but the market power each of these firms enjoys is quite limited. Too many close substitutes exist for consumers and colluding is not possible.

In all of these imperfectly competitive markets (consisting of monopolistically competitive markets, oligopolies and, of course, monopoly markets), the outcome is often not the most desirable for society. It deviates from the outcome achieved when markets are perfectly competitive. We say that there is a market failure.

Internal link

To remind yourself about allocative efficiency and social surplus turn to section 2.2.

Internal link

There is more on market failure in sections 2.6 and 2.8.

The miracle of markets is not present. Firms in imperfect markets produce and offer less than the socially optimal quantity, so allocative efficiency is not achieved, and the price faced by buyers is higher than the competitive ideal. That is why, for some economists, the invisible hand is invisible simply because it doesn't exist. However, markets where firms have significant market power, may sometimes provide society with some important benefits.

Monopoly

A monopoly faces very little, or even no competition. Whether it is Google or Amazon or the sole gasoline station in a remote area, it dominates the market. Monopolies face the market demand curve and so can charge a higher price by restricting the output they sell. If a monopoly makes supernormal profits, it will be able to maintain these in the long run as there are high **barriers to entry**. Monopolies are thus allocatively inefficient and this leads to a welfare loss.

What is natural about natural monopoly?

Why does it make total sense to have only one railway network, one electrical grid, one water supply company or one natural gas distributor in an area? In these cases, the set-up costs are huge because large-scale infrastructure is required. Imagine if there were two companies where you live, each with its own underground network, that offered subway services or, two separate electrical grids that distributed electricity to households. If one company served the whole market, the cost per unit (AC) would be much lower than if two companies were operating. There are huge economies of scale (EOS). EOS exist if a larger firm can produce a good at a lower unit (average) cost compared to smaller firms. If EOS are so huge that only one company can profitably operate in a market, then there is a **natural monopoly**. Huge EOS can form a barrier for other firms to enter. It makes sense in such cases to have a monopoly. However, since the products and services offered by natural monopolies are vital, natural monopolies are typically regulated, with governments setting prices.

Monopolistic competition

In between perfect competition and monopoly are companies such as your neighbourhood restaurant. In fact, monopolistic competition is a lot closer to perfect competition since, in monopolistically competitive markets, there are many small firms and virtually no barriers for other firms to join. The product is differentiated, though. For example, the restaurant "Gaspar food n' mood" in Athens does not offer the dining experience you can enjoy in "Nolita". These restaurants are located on the same busy street, next to each other, but they are not considered to offer identical services.

Internal link

Sections 2.1 and 2.4 cover demand and price elasticity in depth.

All monopolistically competitive firms face negatively sloped demand curves because if they raise price they will lose some, but not all, customers. However, if restaurants in an "up and coming" neighborhood enjoy supernormal profits, then more entrepreneurs will be attracted; and since there are no barriers, more firms will enter. That means that the demand that Nolita faces for its restaurant experience will "shrink and tilt"—demand for its services will shift slowly to the left because its market share decreases, and it also becomes flatter (more price elastic), as more and closer substitutes will be available for diners in Athens.

Entry of more firms will stop when the typical firm earns only normal profits, so that there is no incentive for more firms to enter, or for any of the existing firms to exit.

Now consider a neighbourhood where things are going badly and some restaurants are suffering losses. How will equilibrium be achieved in the long term? We simply need to describe the reverse process. Firms will exit, and demand for the remaining firms will increase. Firms will stop exiting when economic profits are zero (only normal profits).

Nolita is also a market failure, but is that a problem? The restaurant is allocatively inefficient as it can also restrict output to charge a higher price. Diners in Athens, however, have a tremendous variety of restaurants to choose from. This may more than compensate for the inefficiencies of monopolistic competition. In cities, consumers can usually find the exact cuisine they want and can choose to buy fuel from the most convenient gas station. The availability of many close substitutes implies that prices cannot be much higher than in perfect competition. Lastly, such firms engage in some kind of non-price competition: we are sometimes offered dessert for free at a restaurant or given a toy Ferrari as a gift at a gasoline station.

Oligopoly

"Oligos" is a Greek word that means "few". An oligopoly is a market with only a few firms, where barriers to entry do exist (otherwise there would be more firms). The good or service offered can be either homogeneous or differentiated. Many markets, in many countries, are becoming more and more concentrated (see below).

Concentration ratios

Market concentration is measured with concentration ratios. The **concentration ratio** of a market is the proportion of total market sales accounted by the "n" largest firms, where "n" is usually, but not necessarily, the four largest firms in terms of sales. For example, in the US in 2018, the market share of the four largest cell phone service providers (expressed as the 4CR) was 98%. Verizon accounted for 35% of total sales, AT&T 34%, T-Mobile 17% and Sprint 12%.

DP ready | **Research and thinking skills**

Market concentration

Search the web

Search using these terms: America's concentration crisis.
Find data and news articles on the trend of concentration in the US.

Analyse the implications of the concentration in markets in the US. To what extent should the US government have concerns?

Interdependence in oligopolistic markets

The key to whether a market is oligopolistic or not is to determine whether there is interdependence between that market's firms. **Interdependence** exists if the outcome of any action of one firm depends on the reaction of rival firms. Think of two firms in a market, firm A and firm B. If firm A cuts its price, it cannot be sure what will happen to its sales—that depends on how its rival, firm B, will react. The outcome will be different depending on whether firm B also decides to cut its price or maintains its current price.

Interdependence in oligopolistic markets implies greater uncertainty and the risk of a **price war** when firms compete by successively cutting price. This is rare, but possible. Oligopolistic firms may start a price war to force a rival out of business—although price wars often hurt all firms in the market.

Search the web

Search using the terms: UK supermarket price war.
Find out what had happened in the UK when the major supermarkets engaged in a price war.

The risk of a price war gives oligopolistic firms the incentive to collude. **Collusion** exists when firms agree to fix prices and engage in other anti-competitive behaviour. This is generally illegal as it undermines the most basic benefit of free markets, that of competition. Competition leads to lower prices and faster rates of innovation. Also, when firms collude, income is transferred from the many consumers (as they are forced to pay higher prices) to the few colluding firms and their shareholders.

How do oligopolistic firms compete?

Since collusion implies an agreement to coordinate prices, prices do not often change when collusive agreements exist. Even if there is no collusive agreement, oligopolistic firms still do not compete through price cuts to avoid a risky price war. Instead, oligopolistic firms often adopt non-price competition. They try to increase their sales and their market share in various ways: a soft drinks manufacturer increases advertising, an electronics firm offers extended guarantees on its products, a cosmetics company offers volume discounts on shampoo, a radio station organizes competitions.

Is "big" beautiful?

When "big" is beautiful

Larger-in-size firms with significant market power (referred to as monopoly power) can often produce goods at a lower unit cost. They may enjoy economies of scale (EOS). This enables them to sell at a lower price, which benefits consumers. Consumer surplus is higher. Also, the barriers to entry in monopoly and oligopoly allow these firms to maintain supernormal profits. This allows them to invest, often enormous amounts of money, in research and development (R&D) leading to innovations that benefit society in many ways. R&D expenditures by Daimler (Mercedes Benz) rose in 2017 to more than 8 billion euros. These expenditures were aimed at developing new autonomous driving, safety and assistance systems, low-resistance tyres and new vehicles, among other goals.

Search the web

Search using these terms: Scania Volvo collusion EU commission. Also search using: yogurt France collusion Newsweek. These cases show why fines may not be enough to deter collusion.

When "big" can be ugly

Market power allows firms to raise price. The fact that EOS enables firms to produce at a lower unit cost does not necessarily mean that they will pass on the saving to the consumer. They may choose simply to enjoy higher profits. The outcome depends on whether they face any current or potential competition.

Abuse of market power

Matters become worse if in a market a firm's dominant or monopoly position leads to abuse of that position. A dominant position does not in itself constitute a reason for governments or competition authorities to intervene. However, abuse may be present if it is suspected that a firm acts with the intention to eliminate competitors or to prevent entry of new firms.

Focus point

The lack of any market power by perfectly competitive firms leads to low prices for consumers and to allocative efficiency. In the real world though, most firms do have some degree of market power. Prices are therefore often, but not always, higher. Large firms may enjoy economies of scale as a result of their size and may invest in R&D, which leads to innovations. But when firms abuse their market power and eliminate competitors or block entry of new firms, then welfare decreases.

Watch this

Search online using these terms: TED talks Vestager. Watch the talk about market dominance.

 Search the web

Search using these terms: podcast capitalisn't regulating facebook. You will find a three-part discussion about whether tech giants should be regulated.

Key terms—test yourself

Define these terms: profits, economic costs, normal profits, supernormal profits, economic losses, perfectly competitive markets, oligopolistic market, monopoly, natural monopoly, homogeneous products, differentiated products, interdependence, entry barrier, concentration ratio, price war, collusion.

3 Macroeconomics

Macroeconomics focuses on the economy as a whole. Initially, this unit presents the tools of aggregate demand and aggregate supply, which are used to analyse an economy. You will learn the meaning of phenomena that feature in the daily news, such as inflation, unemployment and economic growth, as well as how these are measured. Their causes and consequences are then examined. Finally, policies available in the macroeconomics toolkit are explained and evaluated.

In this unit you will learn about:

→ measuring economic activity

→ aggregate demand (AD) and aggregate supply (AS)

→ Monetarist (New Classical) versus Keynesian views

→ macroeconomic objectives

→ inequality and poverty

→ macroeconomic policies.

3.1 MEASURING ECONOMIC ACTIVITY

In this section you will learn about:

→ gross domestic product (GDP)

→ gross national income (GNI)

→ the business cycle.

The issue

Most countries have a system of national income accounting in order to measure economic activity and then assess the performance of their economies. This section looks in detail at gross domestic product (GDP) and related national income statistics. GDP is the most often used measure of economic activity. However, it is not always the most appropriate measure, especially when assessing well-being.

Gross domestic product (GDP)

GDP is the total *value* of all *final* goods and services produced *within an economy* over a period of time, usually a year. Let's look closely at this definition's wording. The "value" of a good or a service is simply its quantity multiplied by its price. "Final" goods and services are those ready for use. Intermediate goods, which are inputs to the production of final goods and services, are excluded to avoid double counting. For example, steel is an input to the production of cars and so it is an intermediate good while cars are the final good. Steel is already included in GDP as part of cars. Considering it separately would only lead to counting it twice. "Within an economy" means that the goods and services are produced within the physical borders of the country.

How is GDP measured?

There are three ways to calculate GDP. Government statisticians use all three methods.

- The **output approach:** this method adds up the value of all the final goods and services produced by each economic sector, such as agriculture, manufacturing, transport and banking.

    GDP = sector 1 + sector 2 + sector 3 + … + sector n

- The **expenditure approach:** this method measures the total amount spent on domestic output. Total spending includes:
  - consumption spending (C): spending by households
  - investment spending (I): spending by firms
  - government spending (G)
  - net exports (X – M): spending by foreign consumers on domestic goods and services (exports) minus domestic spending on foreign goods and services (imports).

    GDP = C + I + G + (X – M)

- The **income approach:** This method adds up all the income generated in the production process and by the factors of production in the economy.

    GDP = rents + wages + interest + profits

The three methods described above are equivalent and, with some minor adjustments, all three methods give the same result. Why is this the case? Remember the circular flow—in an economy the value of goods and services produced is equal to the expenditures made to purchase these goods and services. These expenditures did not disappear, they were received as income by all those who were responsible for the production of these goods and services.

 Internal link

The circular model is explained in section 1.1.

Gross national income (GNI)

GNI is a variation of GDP. The definition of GDP states that it measures the value of output produced "within an economy"— GDP focuses on what is produced within the boundaries of an economy independently of the nationality of the factors of production involved. In contrast, **GNI** focuses on the nationality of the factors of production involved and the incomes they earn independently of their location. Consider a British firm operating in India. Since production is taking place in India, it will not be included in the UK's GDP. Yet, the profit created by the British firm in India is sent back to the UK. It will be included in the UK's GNI since the income generated from the production in India is received by British shareholders. GNI includes the income of a country's citizens and corporations regardless of where they are located in the world.

> GNI = GDP + factor income from abroad – factor income sent abroad

Nominal versus real values

Remember that the value of a good or service is the quantity multiplied by price. Nominal value is value measured in terms of prices that exist at the time of measurement, so nominal GDP or nominal GNI are expressed in terms of current prices. Now consider the following. If GDP was $10 million in 2017 and 10% more in 2018 (that is, $11 million), we cannot know whether the higher figure was due to an increase in output produced. It could be that output was the same but prices increased by 10%. To measure actual changes in output, we need a modified version of GDP which is adjusted for price changes, known as real GDP. **Real GDP** and **real GNI** are measures of economic activity after eliminating the effect of changes in prices.

Per capita figures

Dividing GDP or GNI by the population of a country gives **per capita GDP** and **per capita GNI** respectively. Per capita figures provide an indication of average or per person output or income in the economy.

What do these statistics tell us?

The most important use of GDP or GNI is as a measure of the size of the economy. GDP or GNI can show whether an economy is doing better or worse compared to a previous year and can be used to compare the performance of one economy against others. Also, national income statistics help policy-makers devise appropriate policies if an economy is performing poorly and are used for evaluating the extent to which the policies adopted were successful. Of course, for comparisons over time, real GDP and real GNI are used to isolate the effect of price changes. Per capita income figures are also used as a measure of the standard of living in a country as they provide a very rough indication of the access to goods and services that the population of a country has. Beyond that, per capita income statistics have to be used with care.

Per capita income leaves a lot to be desired as a measure of living standards.

- As an average, per capita income provides no information about the distribution of income in a country. Per capita income of a country may be high because the top 1% of the population earn extraordinarily high incomes but the bottom 99% earn very little.

- Per capita income may be rising but at a huge cost to the environment. The effect of increased production on the environment is ignored. If per capita incomes double over a decade but at a cost of epic pollution and environmental degradation, is it safe to conclude that living standards have also doubled?

- Per capita income statistics fail to include the value of leisure. Leisure is an important dimension of people's well-being, but its importance is not accounted for. Per capita income level may be the same in two countries, but it makes a difference whether people work 60 or 35 hours per week.

- Living standards are not only affected by current income but also by the stock of wealth of the population. The house or the car a family owns provide services that significantly contribute to the family's well-being.

- The level of public health care and public education available to citizens may differ between two countries with the same per capita income, greatly affecting living standards. High-quality health care and education, available free at the point of delivery, allow families to spend more on other goods and services.

- Certain expenditures may also show up as positive contributions to economic activity and thus to income, although they have been made to counteract activities that have caused harm. For example, the expenditures for cleaning up the oil spill in the Gulf of Mexico in 2010 were an addition to GDP with no adjustment made for the environmental catastrophe.

For all these reasons, alternative measures to assess well-being have been developed.

The Better Life Index (BLI)

The BLI has been developed by the Organization for Economic Cooperation and Development (OECD). It is designed to produce an overall well-being index that brings together internationally comparable measures of well-being. It includes the following dimensions: income, wealth and inequality, jobs and earnings, housing conditions, health status, work and life balance, education and skills, social connections, civic engagement and governance, environmental quality, personal security and subjective well-being (peoples' satisfaction with their lives). For instance, according to the BLI, the US—despite having a higher per capita GDP than many other countries (much higher compared to the OECD average)—is faced with significant income inequality and ranks below average in terms of work and life balance.

The Happy Planet Index (HPI)

The HPI has been developed by the New Economics Foundation of London and is designed to assess whether each country is able to

National statistics and measures of well-being

Visit your country's national statistics web page (or the World Bank's web page) and record GDP and GNI (nominal and real) data as well as income per capita figures for the past five years.

1. Is there a difference between nominal GDP and GNI? If so, explain what could be the reason for this difference.

2. Is there a difference between nominal GDP and real GDP in any of the years recorded? If so, explain what could be the reason for this difference.

3. Describe the overall trend in these indices over the five-year period. Explain what you can infer about the performance of your economy. Discuss this with the rest of your class.

4. Find your country's BLI or HPI scores or ranking. In groups, discuss your findings in terms of the factors you consider important for well-being, and which factors you think should be improved so as to achieve higher scores in the near future.

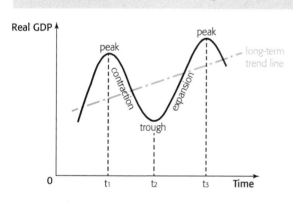

▲ Figure 3.1.1 The business cycle

Economic growth and the business cycle

1. Search for and record the growth rate of the economy in your country over the past five years.

2. Which phase of the business cycle do you think the economy is in at present?

Key terms—test yourself 🔑

Define these terms: gross domestic product (GDP), gross national income (GNI), real GDP/GNI, per capita GDP/GNI.

promote the well-being of its residents. It is made up of three variables: average life expectancy, average subjective well-being and ecological footprint (the amount of land required to provide a country's inhabitants with all their natural resources and assimilate their wastes). Surprisingly, the top five countries in the HPI ranking have GDP per capita levels below $10,000. Costa Rica ranked top, with Costa Ricans having a significantly higher well-being than the residents of many rich nations.

The business cycle

Economic activity does not continuously increase over time. Typically, periods of expansion are followed by periods of contraction. The **business cycle**, illustrated in Figure 3.1.1, refers to these short-term fluctuations of an economy's real GDP over time.

Between time t_1 and t_2 the economy is contracting since real GDP is decreasing. This is described as a recession (technically for two consecutive quarters of declining real GDP). At t_1 the economy was at a peak and just about to enter recession. The major characteristic of a recession is rising unemployment. At t_2 the economy is in a trough and just about to enter recovery. Between time t_2 and t_3 the economy is growing (in expansion) since real GDP is increasing.

This economy is also growing over the long term as the trend line is upward sloping. The trend line is the average annual long-term growth of the economy.

An economy is growing when real GDP is increasing, and it is contracting when real GDP is decreasing. The growth rate of an economy is the percentage change of real GDP between two years. If the percentage change in real GDP is positive, then real GDP is increasing, suggesting that the economy is growing. However, if the growth rate is negative, then real GDP is decreasing, and the economy is in recession. Note that if the growth rate is positive but decreasing (from, say, 2.1% to 0.8%) real GDP continues to increase but at a slower rate. The economy is not yet in recession.

Focus point

National income statistics help in evaluating economic performance through time, across countries as well as in devising and evaluating policies. When it comes to assessing well-being, per capita income statistics can be employed. However, they have to be used with care as they can be misleading.

3.2 AGGREGATE DEMAND AND AGGREGATE SUPPLY

In this section you will learn about:

→ **aggregate demand (AD)**
→ **aggregate supply (AS)**.

The issue

Phrases such as "weakened demand" or "negative demand shock" often appear in the news to describe an economy-wide decline in demand. This economy-wide demand is called aggregate demand (AD) and will be introduced in this section together with aggregate supply (AS).

Aggregate demand (AD)

Aggregate demand (AD), where aggregate means total, refers to the total planned spending on domestic goods and services at different average price levels per period of time.

Spending on domestic goods and services can originate from households, firms, the government and the foreign sector. AD therefore includes **consumption expenditures (C)** (spending by households on durables and non-durables), **investment expenditures (I)** (spending by firms on capital goods), government expenditures (G) and exports (X). Since some of the expenditures that households, firms and the government make are on foreign goods, we must subtract imports (M). So:

$$AD = C + I + G + (X - M).$$

If this looks familiar, it is because GDP measured by the expenditure approach is the same sum. However, GDP and AD are not at all the same concepts. GDP is actual output produced, say in 2019, in a country, whereas AD shows the planned level of spending at different price levels in that country.

On a diagram, AD is illustrated by the AD curve. The horizontal axis shows real GDP and the vertical axis shows the average price level, an index of the average of the prices of all final goods and services in the economy. The AD curve is negatively sloped because at a higher average price level, planned spending on domestic goods and services decreases, as in Figure 3.2.1.

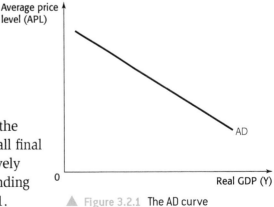

▲ Figure 3.2.1 The AD curve

Why is the AD curve downward sloping?

You might think that the downward slope is a consequence of the law of demand. However, when we consider the AD curve, we are considering an increase or a decrease in all prices, not just in the price of one good. To understand why the AD curve slopes downward, we need to understand why a rise in the average price level (APL) reduces spending. Reasons include the following.

- The wealth effect: if the APL rises then the real value of bank deposits and of bonds decreases. $100,000 in the bank buys less. People feel poorer and they tend to spend (C) less. So, if the APL rises then C falls, leading to a downward sloping AD curve.

- The trade effect: if the APL rises then exports become more expensive while imports seem relatively cheaper. Exports will tend to decrease and imports to increase so NX decreases. So, if the APL rises then NX falls, leading to a downward sloping AD curve.

- The interest rate effect: if the APL increases, then people need to hold more money to buy the same goods and services. The demand for holding money (cash and checking accounts) increases. If the supply of money by the central bank is constant, then the "price" of money (which is the interest rate), rises. However, higher interest rates decrease consumption and investment expenditures as people and firms borrow from banks to buy durables (such as houses) and capital equipment (such as factories). So, if the APL rises then C and I decrease leading to a downward sloping AD curve.

Changes in the APL cause movements along the AD curve. There can also be shifts of the AD curve. As shown in Figure 3.2.2, an increase in AD means that there is a shift of the AD curve to the right from AD_1 to AD_2. A decrease in AD means that the AD curve shifts to the left from AD_1 to AD_3.

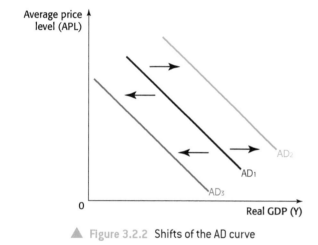

▲ Figure 3.2.2 Shifts of the AD curve

These shifts of the AD curve can be caused by changes in its components, which are explained below.

Factors affecting the components of AD

Consumption expenditures (C)

This is spending by households on durables, non-durables and services and it depends on the following.

- Interest rates: the **interest rate** is the price paid for borrowing money for a period of time expressed as a percentage. Households usually borrow to buy durables such as cars or houses. Higher interest rates make borrowing more expensive. People borrow less and so spend less, shifting the AD curve to the left. The reverse is seen following a decrease in interest rates.

- **Consumer confidence:** this is a measure of how optimistic households are and how secure they feel about the future. If they are confident, they are likely to spend more, shifting the AD curve to the right. If they are afraid of losing their job, they will cut back on their spending, shifting the AD curve to the left.

- Household **wealth:** this refers to the value of what households own, such as stocks, bonds, deposits or real estate, minus what they owe. An increase in household wealth due to, for example, a rise in property prices, leads to more spending, which shifts the AD curve to the right. If stock prices fall, wealth decreases and so will consumption.

- Personal income taxes: these determine the level of disposable income, which is the income left after taxes are paid. If the government raises income taxes, disposable income falls, spending drops and the AD curve shifts to the left, and vice versa.

- Household **indebtedness:** this refers to how much money households owe from taking out loans or from using credit cards. If they owe a lot, they will cut back on their spending as they will first try to decrease their debt. The AD curve will shift left.

Investment expenditures (I)

This is spending by firms on capital goods (such as machines) and it depends on the following.

- Interest rates: if interest rates increase, then the cost of borrowing from banks will increase. Businesses will borrow less and so spend less on capital goods, as these expenditures are typically financed by borrowing. The AD curve shifts to the left. Decreases in interest rates have the opposite effect: the AD curve shifts to the right.

- **Business confidence:** this refers to how businesses feel about their future sales and about the economy. If they are optimistic, they are more likely to invest and so the AD curve shifts to the right. Business pessimism, though, results in a decrease in investment spending and to a leftward shift in the AD curve.

- Technology: industries in which technology advances quickly will witness more investments, causing increases in AD and a rightward shift in the AD curve.

- Business taxes: these affect firms' profits. A decrease in business taxes increases the profitability of investment projects. More investment projects will be approved so investment spending will tend to increase. The AD curve will shift to the right. An increase in business taxes may result in decreased investment and a leftward shift of the AD curve.

- Corporate indebtedness: if firms have high levels of debt because of past borrowing, they will be hesitant to take out more loans and make investments as they will first try to decrease debt. AD decreases and the AD curve shifts to the left.

Government expenditures (G)

Government expenditures are affected by the government's political and economic priorities. Governments spend to provide public and merit goods such as national defence, education and health services. For example, if it is a political priority to equip all public schools with fast internet connections and smartboards, or to build more regional health centres, then government expenditures will increase. However, as shown later in this unit, governments spend to increase AD. This is referred to as fiscal policy.

 Internal link

Section 3.6 covers fiscal policy in detail.

Any increase in government spending will increase AD and shift the AD curve to the right. A decrease in government spending will shift the AD curve to the left.

Net exports

The **net exports** figure is the difference between foreign spending on domestic output (export revenues) minus domestic spending on foreign output (import expenditures): net exports = (X – M). It depends on the following.

- Income of trading partners: if the income of our trading partners increases, their level of spending will increase. Part of their increased spending will be on imports, which are our exports. The exports of an economy will tend to increase if the income of its trading partners increases, shifting the AD curve to the right, and vice versa.

- Exchange rates: an exchange rate is the price of one country's currency in terms of another country's currency. If the exchange rate decreases, then exports become cheaper and more competitive abroad while imports become pricier and less attractive domestically. As a result, net exports increase, shifting the AD curve to the right. An increase in the exchange rate will have the opposite effect; net exports decrease, shifting the AD curve to the left.

- Trade policies: this refers to restrictions to international trade, often imposed by governments. If the government of one country decides to impose restrictions on the imports of another country, then imports will fall and so net exports will rise, shifting the AD curve to the right. Relaxing trade restrictions will have the reverse effect.

DP ready ⊏ **Thinking, research and communication skills**

AD and confidence indicators

1. Prepare a large mind map, on screen or on a large sheet of paper, that explains what you have learned about AD. Include diagrams and examples.

2. Visit your country's national statistics webpage. Find the consumer and business confidence indicators and record the trend in these indicators for the past 10 years. Analyse whether there is a pattern.

3. Discuss in class what factors could have recently affected the level of consumer confidence in your country.

 TOK

Consumer and business confidence affect the level of AD. What knowledge issues arise in attempting to measure confidence?

 Internal link

Find out more about the Monetarist (New Classical) and the Keynesian views of economics in section 3.3.

Aggregate supply (AS)

Aggregate supply (AS) is defined as the planned level of output domestic firms are willing to offer at different APLs per period of time. Note that AS is not the same as real GDP. AS shows how much firms are planning to offer at different APLs. As with AD, AS can be shown by a diagram of the AS curve. However, unlike the AD curve, the shape of the AS curve is rather controversial as it reflects the views of the two main schools of thought: the Monetarist (or New Classical) view and the Keynesian view.

The Monetarist (New Classical) view of AS

Monetarists (and New Classical) economists make a distinction between the short run and the long run. As a result, there is a short-run AS (SRAS) and a long-run AS (LRAS).

The SRAS

Within the AS framework, the short run is the period during which money wages are fixed. The money wage is basically what is written on a paycheck: the dollars (or equivalent) earned per time period. Money wages are usually determined by labour contracts. This means that if the price level in the economy changes, as long as contracts are in effect, money wages will not adjust to match the change in the price level.

The reason money wages are closely related to AS is that they account for the largest part of firms' production costs. As long as money wages remain fixed, the biggest part of firms' production costs remains unchanged. If the APL increases, firms enjoy greater profitability, which induces them to offer more output. The opposite holds if the price level decreases. The SRAS curve is therefore upward sloping, as shown in Figure 3.2.3 where real GDP is on the horizontal axis and the average price level is on the vertical axis.

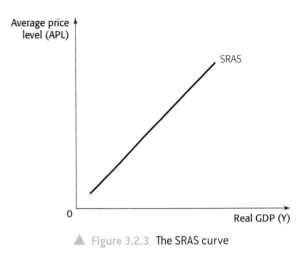

▲ Figure 3.2.3 The SRAS curve

In the short run, changes in the APL cause movements along the SRAS curve. There can also be shifts of the SRAS curve. As shown in Figure 3.2.4, an increase in SRAS means that there is a shift of the SRAS curve to the right from SRAS$_1$ to SRAS$_2$. A decrease in SRAS means that the SRAS curve shifts to the left from SRAS$_1$ to SRAS$_3$.

▲ Figure 3.2.4 Shifts of the SRAS curve

Changes in SRAS are mainly caused by changes in production costs. Note that these would have to be changes in costs of production that will simultaneously affect most firms in the economy, not just firms of a particular market. The SRAS curve will shift if the following changes occur.

- Changes in money wages: money wages can change if, for example, there is a change in the minimum wage. If money wages increase, firms' costs of production rise, resulting in a leftward shift in the SRAS curve. If wages decrease, the SRAS curve shifts to the right.

- Changes in energy prices: for example, changes in the price of oil affect the SRAS curve in the same way as changes in wages. An increase in the price of oil shifts the SRAS curve to the left; a decrease shifts it to the right.

- Changes in business taxes: business taxes affect costs of production. Higher taxes increase production costs and so shift the SRAS curve to the left. Lower taxes reduce production costs and shift the SRAS curve to the right.

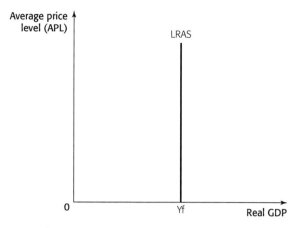

▲ Figure 3.2.5 Figure 3.2.5 The LRAS curve

Internal link

Unemployment is covered in more depth in section 3.4.

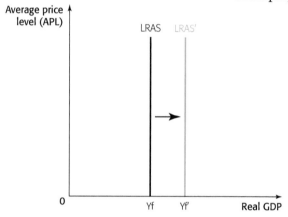

▲ Figure 3.2.6 Shifts of the LRAS curve

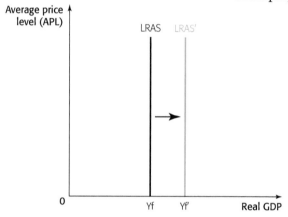

▲ Figure 3.2.7 The Keynesian AS curve

The LRAS

In the long run, money wages are flexible. They adjust fully to changes in the APL—if the APL rises by 2.4% then money wages will also increase by 2.4%. As a result, firms no longer respond to increases in the APL by increasing their level of output. That is because money wages match the increase in prices and so firms' profitability isn't changing. The LRAS curve is therefore drawn vertical to show that, in the long run, the level of output does not change even if the APL changes. This is shown in Figure 3.2.5.

More specifically, the LRAS curve is vertical at the level of **potential output**, Yf, since, in the long run when all adjustments have been made, an economy produces whatever its resources and technology allow it to produce. At this level of potential output there is full employment. Take care how you interpret this. Full employment does not mean zero unemployment. At the full employment level of output there is still some unemployment, which is referred to as natural unemployment.

If the LRAS increases and the curve shifts to the right then this implies that the potential level of output has increased, meaning that the economy's productive capacity has increased.

An increase in LRAS can be a result of the following.

■ An increase in the quantity of factors of production: for example, an increase in the quantity of labour due to immigration means that the economy is capable of producing more real GDP and so the LRAS curve shifts to the right.

■ An improvement in the quality of factors of production: for example, greater levels of education and skills improve the quality of labour. Workers become more productive and the LRAS curve shifts to the right.

■ Improvements and innovations in technology: these can lead to improved machines and equipment that are able to produce more output and so the LRAS curve shifts to the right.

■ Increases in efficiency: when an economy makes better use of its resources, it can, as a result, produce a greater quantity of output. Therefore, the LRAS curve shifts to the right.

■ Institutional changes: improvements in the **institutional framework** increase the economy's productive capacity. A reduced amount of bureaucracy facilitates economic activity and can increase the output produced, so the LRAS curve shifts to the right.

The Keynesian view of AS

In the Keynesian view there is no distinction between the short run and the long run and so there is only one AS curve. It has three sections, as shown in Figure 3.2.7.

Let's start backwards. Section III is vertical at the full employment level of output, Yf. In the Keynesian framework this full employment level of output is usually considered as a "wall", implying that there is no unemployment in the economy. Real GDP cannot increase beyond Yf. Section I, at the other end, is horizontal. The economy is operating significantly below the full employment level of output Yf, which means that there is huge spare capacity (that is, very high unemployment). This could be an economy in deep recession. Higher levels of output can be produced without the APL rising.

The in-between section, section II, illustrates an upward sloping AS curve. This relates to the fact that some industries in the economy reach full employment sooner than others. This situation is referred to as bottlenecks in production: spare capacity in some industries coexists with full employment in other industries. Real output may continue to rise, but because of the full employment conditions in some industries, less labour is available, wages may rise and so will the APL.

DP ready | **ATL Thinking, research and communication skills**

Prepare a large mind map, on screen or on a large sheet of paper, that explains what you have learned about AS. Include information about the Keynesian view and the Monetarist (New Classical) view. Also include diagrams illustrating each view.

 TOK

Keynesians and Monetarists (or New Classicists) have different views on the shape of the AS curve. Is there a "right" or a "wrong" view? What are the factors that need to be considered? In which other area(s) of knowledge are there different views on the same issue?

Focus point

Aggregate demand (AD) refers to the total planned spending on domestic goods and services at different average price levels per period of time, and includes consumption expenditures (C), investment expenditures (I), government expenditures (G) and net exports (X – M). It is illustrated by the AD curve which is downward sloping. Aggregate supply (AS) refers to the planned level of output domestic firms are willing to offer at different average price levels per period of time. The shape of the AS curve differs between the schools of economic thought.

Key terms—test yourself

Define these terms: aggregate demand (AD), consumption expenditures (C), investment expenditures (I), wealth, interest rate, net exports, aggregate supply (AS).

3.3 THE MONETARIST VS. THE KEYNESIAN TAKE

In this section you will learn about:

→ macroeconomic equilibrium
  — the Monetarist (New Classical) view
  — the Keynesian view.

The issue

Section 3.2 explained what makes up AD and AS. This section uses them together in order to determine macroeconomic equilibrium and to analyse variations in economic activity.

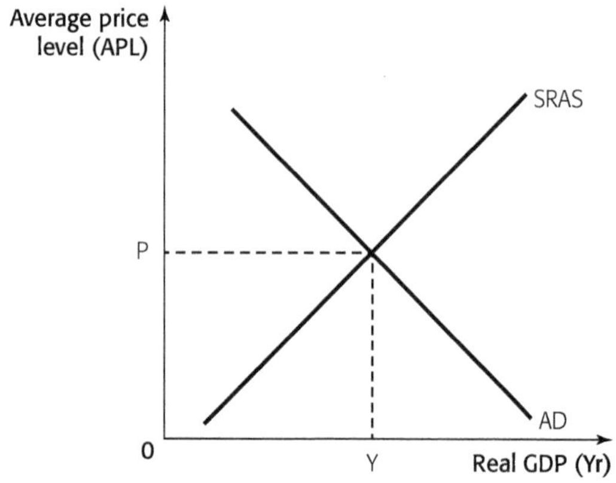

▲ Figure 3.3.1 Short-run equilibrium

Macroeconomic equilibrium

The Monetarist (New Classical) view

Short-run equilibrium

In the short run, macroeconomic equilibrium exists at the level of real GDP where AD and SRAS are equal, as shown in Figure 3.3.1.

The equilibrium level of real GDP is Y and the average price level is P, determined at the intersection of AD and SRAS. A shift in either AD or SRAS will cause a change in the equilibrium level of real GDP as well as the average price level.

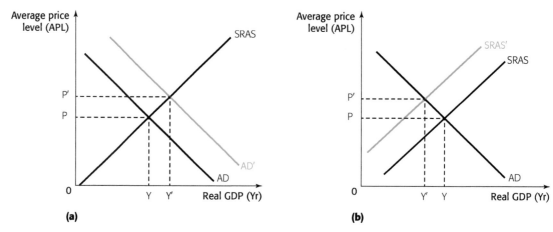

▲ Figure 3.3.2 a and b Changes in short-run equilibrium

As shown in Figure 3.3.2a, a reduction in interest rates has increased AD which has shifted to the right from AD to AD'. As a result, real GDP increased from Y to Y' and so did the average price level from P to P'. Similarly, in Figure 3.3.2b a rise in costs of production caused by higher business taxes has decreased SRAS, which has shifted to the left from SRAS to SRAS'. This led to a decrease in real GDP from Y to Y' and to an increase in the average price level from P to P'.

Long-run equilibrium

In the long-run, macroeconomic equilibrium will necessarily be at the economy's potential or full employment level of output. Short-run equilibrium may differ from the potential level of output but this is only temporary. In the long-run, the economy will always return to the full employment level of output, as a result of money wages fully adjusting.

Refer to Figure 3.3.3. The economy is at equilibrium at the potential level of output, Yf. The APL is at P_1 (see point a on Figure 3.3.3). Now, say that business and consumer confidence in the economy decrease. AD decreases shifting the AD curve to the left from AD_1 to AD_2 and the price level drops from P_1 to P_2. Remember that in the short-run money wages are fixed. With the decrease in the APL, firms' profitability decreases and so firms will reduce output, moving along SRAS1 from point a to point b. This means that real GDP falls to Y_2. When the equilibrium level of real output is below the full employment (or potential) level of output, it is known as a **deflationary (or recessionary) gap**. In this case, it is equal to Y_2Yf.

> **Internal link**
>
> See section 3.6 for more information on managing the economy.

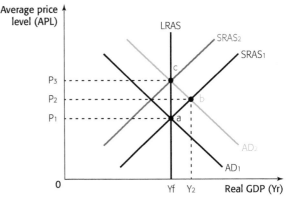

▲ Figure 3.3.3 Returning to full employment following a decrease in AD

However, according to the Monetarists, in the long-run money wages are flexible, which means that they will decrease to match the decrease in the APL. Remember that money wages is a shift factor for SRAS. Hence, SRAS increases and shifts to the right to $SRAS_2$. Equilibrium is back to the full employment level of output Yf; at a lower price level P_3. The economy has therefore moved on its own at point c.

According to Monetarists, an economy will recover (that is, the deflationary and recessionary gap will close) only through the adjustment of money wages. There is no need for the government to intervene. Something similar happens if there is an increase in AD. Again, initially the economy is at equilibrium at the potential level of output, Yf, with the APL at P_1. That is point a, shown in Figure 3.3.4. Now, say that a reduction in interest rates leads to an increase in AD, which shifts to the right from AD_1 to AD_2 and the APL rises from P_1 to P_2. Since money wages are fixed in the short run, the increase in the APL increases firms' profitability and induces them to increase output, moving along $SRAS_1$ from point a to point b. Real GDP is now at Y_2. This is a case of an **inflationary gap**: the equilibrium level of real output exceeds the full employment (or potential) level of output; in this case, Y_2Yf. Money wages will now restore the full employment level of output. In the long run, money wages will increase to match the increase in the APL. As such, the SRAS decreases, shifting to the left to $SRAS_2$. Equilibrium is back to the full employment level of output Yf; at a higher APL of P_3. The economy has therefore moved on its own to point c.

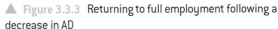

▲ Figure 3.3.4 Returning to full employment following an increase in AD

Again, according to Monetarists, an inflationary gap will close only through the adjustment of money wages. There is no need for government intervention.

To recap: in the Monetarist (New Classical) view, because of the adjustability of money wages in the long run, a deflationary or

> **TOK**
>
> Referring to the Keynesian and the Monetarist (New Classical) models of macroeconomics: in your opinion, what factors may influence a person's preference for one view over the other?

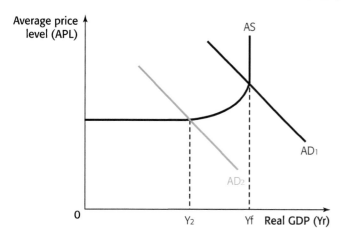

▲ Figure 3.3.5 The deflationary (recessionary) gap

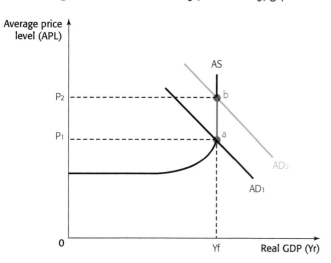

▲ Figure 3.3.6 The inflationary gap

an inflationary gap will automatically close and the economy will always return to the full employment (potential) level of output.

Now let's turn to the Keynesian view on macroeconomic equilibrium.

The Keynesian view

The deflationary gap

Consider the economy shown in Figure 3.3.5, initially operating at full employment. A collapse in business and consumer confidence causes a decrease in AD, which shifts the AD curve to the left from AD_1 to AD_2. Equilibrium real GDP Y_2 is below the full employment level of output Yf. The result is a deflationary (recessionary) gap equal to Y_2Yf.

Will the economy return to full employment on its own? According to Keynesians, the answer is no. According to the Keynesian view, money wages are "sticky downwards", in the sense that they may increase but they do not easily adjust downwards. As such, there is no automatic adjustment mechanism to push the economy back to the full employment level of output. Therefore, an economy may remain stuck in a **deflationary** or **recessionary gap** (that is, at a level of real GDP that is below the full employment level).

Is there a way out? Yes—the government must intervene in order to increase AD. This can be achieved either through expansionary fiscal policy or loose monetary policy.

The inflationary gap

Figure 3.3.6 shows an economy at the full employment of output Yf. A rise in business and consumer confidence now causes AD to increase which shifts the AD curve to the right from AD_1 to AD_2. Real GDP will remain at Yf (remember the "wall"). The APL will though rise from P_1 to P_2. Distance ab is referred to as the inflationary gap. Unlike in the Monetarist view, the gap is now on the vertical axis—because in a strict interpretation, full employment in the Keynesian model implies no unemployment.

Focus point

Macroeconomic equilibrium is determined at the intersection of AD and AS. Long run equilibrium in the Monetarist or New Classical model will always be at the potential (full employment) level of output. Short run equilibrium output in the Monetarist or New Classical model can be either below or above the potential (full employment) output, but only temporarily. The flexibility of money wages will guarantee that the economy will always return to its long run potential output. In the Keynesian model the economy can get stuck at a level of output below potential (full employment) output as wages are "sticky downwards". There is no automatic adjustment mechanism to restore full employment. There is a need for government intervention.

3.4 MACROECONOMIC OBJECTIVES

In this section you will learn about:

→ what we mean by economic growth

→ short-term and long-term growth

→ measuring economic growth

→ consequences of economic growth unemployment: different types of unemployment; the economic costs of unemployment

→ inflation, disinflation and deflation.

The issues

This section focuses on the issues of economic growth, unemployment and inflation. Economic growth can and has lifted millions out of poverty. The release by any government of the latest economic growth data of the country makes headlines in the news. Initially, this section explains the term "economic growth", distinguishing between short-term and long-term growth and how each may be achieved. Then the consequences of economic growth—which are not all necessarily positive—are explored.

The section moves on to focus on unemployment. How unemployment is measured is explained, as well as the related difficulties. Causes of unemployment are then explored and finally the costs of unemployment on the economy, on communities and on individuals.

The exploration of inflation includes why a low and stable rate of inflation is a major macroeconomic goal. The terms disinflation and deflation are also introduced. How inflation is measured, and the difficulties involved, are discussed. Possible causes of inflation and deflation are presented, along with the consequences of both.

▲ Unemployment during the Great Depression

What do we mean by economic growth?

At the simplest level economic growth means that an economy is getting larger. By "an economy" we mean output. Since an economy's total output is measured by real GDP, **economic growth** is defined as an increase in the real GDP of a country over time.

Short-term growth

Growth over the **short term** refers to growth that is a result of greater use of existing resources. Potential (or full employment) output does not increase. Aggregate demand (AD) is increasing, and this leads to increased real GDP (that is, growth). AD may be increasing for a variety of reasons. Any factor that increases any component of AD can cause this. For example, during the first two years of the Trump presidency, US stocks in the New York Stock Exchange were booming and house prices were

A focus on growth

1. Describe one factor that would increase government expenditures and so AD, leading to growth.

2. Describe some types of government expenditure that may also increase potential output.

3. Give examples of economies that have greatly relied on increased exports to drive their growth.

rising. These developments improved consumer confidence and business confidence and increased the wealth of US households. Increased wealth and confidence increased US consumption and investment expenditures and so AD. The US economy continued to register strong growth rates.

Illustrating short-term growth

How can we show growth over the short term on a diagram? It may be easiest to use a Keynesian AS curve and shift the AD curve to the right, as this would lead to higher real GDP (see Figure 3.4.1a). Will the effect of an increase in AD also depend on where the original AD intersects the Keynesian AS curve? Could the increase in AD prove ineffective in generating growth?

We also use a production possibilities curve (PPC) to show short-term growth (see Figure 3.4.1b). Think of an economy initially located at a point inside the PPC and then moving towards the north-east, closer to the boundary. Such a movement would indicate more being produced of both goods. Total output would be greater and since the production possibilities boundary would not have shifted outwards, this growth would have been the result of greater use of existing resources and not of more resources or better technology becoming available.

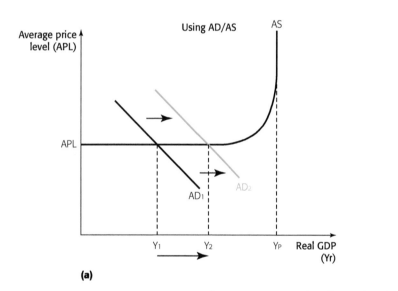

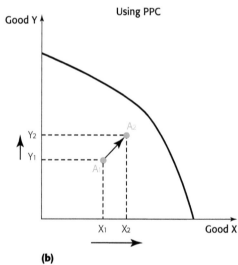

▲ Figure 3.4.1 a and b Illustrating short-term growth

Long-term growth

Long-term growth refers to growth that is a result of more or better resources becoming available and/or of improved technology. If more labour becomes available (perhaps because skilled migrant workers enter the country), or if past investments in human capital (in education and in health care) increase labour productivity (output per worker), then the economy's potential output will increase. Remember also that investment spending (I) is defined as spending by firms on capital goods (factories, machines, and so on). So, if investment spending by firms increases, AD will increase in the short term, and so will real GDP. But, since the economy will have a greater stock of capital (for example, more factories), the economy's potential output in the long term will also increase.

Improved institutions may lead to an increase in potential output and so long-term growth. Better laws and regulations may reduce the cost of economic activity so that more can be produced by fully utilizing the same resources and output increases. Historically, though, the main drivers of long-term economic growth are technological advances. Advances in technology in agriculture, in industry and in health services have been responsible for dramatic improvements in the potential output of all economies in the past two centuries. In recent years, advances in information and communication technologies are considered to be the driving force for further dramatic increases in potential output.

Illustrating long-term growth

How can we show growth in the long term on a diagram? It is perhaps easiest to use a monetarist LRAS curve and shift it to the right from $LRAS_1$ to $LRAS_2$ (see Figure 3.4.2a), which would illustrate an increase in potential output. Long-term growth can also be illustrated by "stretching out" a Keynesian AS curve so that the new full employment level of real output (Yp_2) is to the right of the initial one (Yp_1)—see Figure 3.4.2b. You could also illustrate long-term growth by an outwards shift of the PPC curve from A_1A_2 to B_1B_2 as shown in Figure 3.4.2c.

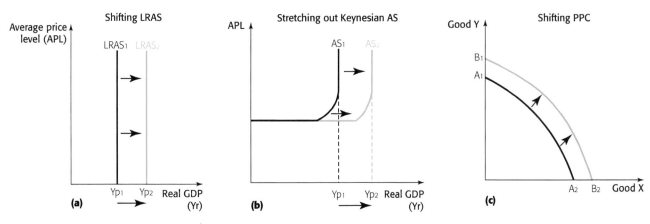

▲ Figure 3.4.2 a, b and c Illustrating long-term growth

Measuring economic growth

To measure economic growth, you simply need to calculate the percentage change in the real GDP of a country between two time periods such as two years, or perhaps two quarters. For the US, if real GDP in 2019 was $18,907 billion and in 2018 it was $18,323 billion, then the US growth rate between 2018 and 2019 was:

$$\frac{18907 - 18323}{18323} \times 100 = 3.19\%$$

China's economy grew by 6.6% in 2018, the slowest since 1990. This means that China's real GDP increased between 2017 and 2018 by 6.6%. The growth rate figure for Argentina in 2018 was −2.5%. This means that Argentina's real GDP decreased between 2017 and 2018, so the Argentinian economy was in recession.

Recent economic growth in five countries

Research and determine the most recent economic growth rate for your country as well as for four more countries of your choice. Try to select countries from different regions of the world.

1. Find annual real GDP figures for all five countries for the most recent five-year period. Calculate the four annual growth rates but also the growth rate for the five-year period.

2. Decide whether these growth rates are satisfactory. Explain why is it perhaps difficult to decide. Explain what factors you have to consider.

3. Try answering question 2 again after you have read to the end of this section.

Consequences of economic growth

Does economic growth improve living standards?

Economic growth means that an economy's total output (its real GDP) is rising. Given that the value of an economy's total output (its real GDP) is the reverse-side of the income generated in the production process (so, the country's national income) the following should be true. If an economy is growing faster than its population, then income per person (known as per capita income) is rising. For example, if an economy is growing by 5% per year but the population is increasing by 1% per year then, on average, income per person is increasing.

Higher per capita income levels allow increased average levels of consumption of goods and services. Individuals enjoying higher incomes have greater access to goods and services. Living standards for these individuals improve. This explains why the release of growth statistics make headlines in most countries.

Per capita is just an average

We should realize that when we divide GDP or GNI by population to arrive at per capita income, the result is just an average figure. There is a saying that if your head is in the oven and your feet are in the freezer then on average you are fine—but, of course, this is not true. This is why the term "inclusive growth" is appropriate in discussions about policy objectives. Economic growth must permit "all boats to rise in the tide". There is research suggesting that economic growth does not always lead to an increase in happiness. This is referred to as the Easterlin paradox. Some researchers advance the idea that rising income inequality may help explain this.

Search the web

Visit the site www.countryeconomy.com. You will find many variables for any country you may be interested in. You can, for example, see the evolution of GDP and per capita GDP for any country and for many years.

Watch this

Search YouTube using these terms: TED see how the rest of the world lives Rosling. You will see a photographic journey of how families in more than 50 countries around the world and across all income levels live.

Search the web

Search using the terms: happiness site:www.ft.com before:2014. You will find article on the potential importance of real income.

You might also like to watch an entertaining excerpt from Frans de Waal's TED Talk on moral behaviour in animals. It shows the reaction of capuchin monkeys to inequity. Search using the phrase: two monkeys were paid unequally: TED talk.

DP ready **ATL Research and thinking skills**

Countries with similar per capita incomes

Carry out online research to find pairs of countries with similar per capita income levels.

a. To what extent can you be sure that living standards in these countries are also similar? Describe the concerns you have about making an accurate analysis.

b. What other information would you need to have in order to investigate the extent to which living standards are similar or not?

Does economic growth affect income distribution?

How does economic growth affect income distribution? There is no single correct answer—it depends. Income distribution can both improve and worsen in a growing economy. Economic growth can decrease income inequality because of the fiscal dividend the government collects: growth implies higher incomes which lead to higher taxes paid and collected. Higher tax revenues allow a government to adopt policies that alleviate poverty. More can be spent to create or improve social security, such as setting up or improving a pension system, or paying unemployment benefits or granting cash transfers to the disabled and other destitute groups. Such short-term programmes could decrease income inequality. More importantly, growth allows a government to embark on longer-term programmes that lift people out of poverty and decrease income inequality. Growth over the long term enables a government to invest, for example, in policies to increase agricultural productivity, improve sanitation and basic infrastructure, especially in rural areas of the country. It allows economies to invest heavily in education and health care programmes that favour the poor, improving their "human capital" and increasing their productivity. What does this mean on a practical level? These investments increase the income-earning capacity of the poor and so decrease income inequality.

However, income inequality has often increased in growing economies. First, the fiscal dividend resulting from growth allows, but does not force governments to adopt policies that decrease income inequality. There is no guarantee that the benefits of growth are shared by all, no guarantee that these benefits will be fairly distributed. Growth may be driven by only a handful of industries or it may be concentrated in certain regions of a country (often, the coastal regions). It may rely only on certain skills, often of the more educated. Most importantly, it may be the result of market-based supply-side policies, such as trade liberalization and deregulation, that aim at accelerating growth but often also increase income inequality.

Does economic growth affect the environment?

Economic growth may prove beneficial to the environment. When, as a result of growth, a country reaches a high level of per capita income, then people demand a cleaner environment to live in. The

Search the web

Search for: ostry growth inclusion June. Find the article "The Economics of Promoting Inclusive Growth" by IMF economist Jonathan Ostry (June 2018). It looks at why growth is fragile when it is not inclusive. You could instead listen to Ostry by including the word "podcast" in the search terms.

economy has more resources available to spend on adopting cleaner technologies. This may hold true for "local externalities", such as indoor household pollution from cooking using polluting open fires. It does not seem to hold true for "dispersed externalities", such as carbon emissions. Economic growth is a result of increased levels of production, but increased production often relies on the use of fossil fuels or on the use and depletion of common access resources. Growth that neglects the impact on the environment is not sustainable. It is the younger generations that may realize the bitter truth behind this assessment.

Unemployment

What do we mean by unemployment?

If Ambroos does not have a job, he is not necessarily considered unemployed. **Unemployment** refers to when someone is actively searching for a job but unable to find one. If an individual is not actively searching for a job, that person is not considered unemployed.

The unemployment rate of a country is the number of unemployed individuals expressed as a percentage of the labour force. The labour force is not the population. It is not even the population of working age. The labour force only includes the employed and the unemployed, no one else. The unemployment rate is calculated as follows.

$$\text{Unemployment rate} = \frac{\text{Number of unemployed}}{(\text{Employed} + \text{Unemployed})} \times 100$$

Difficulties in measuring unemployment

Measuring unemployment accurately is not easy, for the reasons outlined below.

- Underestimation: the official figure may underestimate true unemployment because of **hidden unemployment**. This includes individuals who work part time but would prefer a full-time job; and **discouraged workers**—individuals who have searched for a job for a long time, have not found employment and decided to stop searching. They are not counted as unemployed, but if they were offered a job they would gladly accept.

- Overestimation: the official unemployment figure may overestimate true unemployment. Some individuals may claim to be unemployed even though they have a job. Possible reasons are that they want to continue collecting unemployment benefits or they are involved in illegal work.

- The official unemployment figure for a country is just an average. Unemployment rates may differ widely between geographical regions, and between genders, ethnicities and age groups. For example, unemployment is typically higher in rural areas than cities; it is often higher for women or minorities because of discrimination; and it is always higher for those aged between 18 and 25. For instance, at some point during Greece's economic crisis, youth unemployment figures exceeded 50%.

DP ready ATL **Thinking skills**

An example of US unemployment

Unemployment in the US had reached 10% in October 2009 and remained above 8% until August 2012. In April 2018 it had decreased below 4% and continued to decline.

 Search the web

Search the web for: workers hardest recession recovery nyt.
Read the *New York Times* article (3 August 2018) on one aspect of unemployment in the US manufacturing sector.

1. The *New York Times* article mentioned that a substantial number of "workers … on the sidelines" were gradually coming back to work. Describe who these workers were. Explain why they were rejoining the labour force.

2. What does the article suggest about the reliability of published unemployment statistics?

Reasons for inaccuracies in the official figure	Causes
Underestimation	Hidden employment: involuntary part-timers, discouraged workers, workers overqualified for their job
Overestimation	Workers claiming to be unemployed: to collect benefits or because their work is illegal
The official figure is an average	Significant differences may exist between: regions, genders, ethnicities, age groups

▲ Table 3.4.1 Problems when measuring unemployment—a recap

Types and causes of unemployment

Typically, unemployment is categorized as four types: seasonal, frictional, cyclical and structural.

- **Seasonal unemployment** is particular to the time of the year. For example, Lachlan works in construction in Toronto. Every winter, there are periods of time when construction workers are asked to stay away from work because of the job risks relating to freezing temperatures—so Lachlan experiences seasonal unemployment.

- **Frictional unemployment** refers to people who are between jobs for a limited time. There are always people in search of better jobs or people who have no work having moved location. For example, Ethan met Mia and decided to quit his job in Canberra to follow Mia to Sydney. It will take Ethan some time to find a job in Sydney even though job vacancies do exist and his skills are appropriate.

- **Cyclical unemployment** is related to the recession phase of the business cycle when businesses shrink or shut down. For example, in 2012–13, when the Italian economy was in a deep recession, many gyms in Milan shut down and Giuseppe lost his job as a trainer. When the Italian economy recovered, Giuseppe found a new job, as gyms re-opened or expanded.

Illustrating cyclical unemployment

Think of the best way to illustrate cyclical unemployment in a diagram. Remember that a decrease in AD leads to a deflationary gap.

Draw your diagram on screen or on paper.

■ **Structural unemployment** is of a more long-term nature than the other types of unemployment. It persists way past economic recovery. Two words explain the causes of structural unemployment: mismatch and rigidities.

Mismatch describes the situation where job vacancies exist but the skills of the unemployed are not the skills that employers demand. Consider Rainer, a truck driver in Austria. The introduction of driverless trucks could mean the Rainer's driving skills will not be in demand anymore. There may be available jobs in software development, but Rainer does not have the necessary training. Technological advances are a main cause of structural unemployment. Artificial intelligence may lead to redundancies in many industries.

Rigidities refers to labour laws and regulations that do not permit the labour market to adjust to changing market conditions. Some unemployment may result from a high minimum wage, and from laws that require firms to pay for the insurance of their employees or that make it difficult to dismiss workers. High unemployment benefits may also induce some people to reject low-paid work.

Types of unemployment and summary description	
Seasonal: related to the time of the year	Cyclical: related to a downturn of the business cycle (or recession)
Frictional: refers to people between jobs	Structural: results from a mismatch between the skills of the unemployed and the skills firms demand; or from labour market rigidities

▲ Table 3.4.2 Types of unemployment—a summary

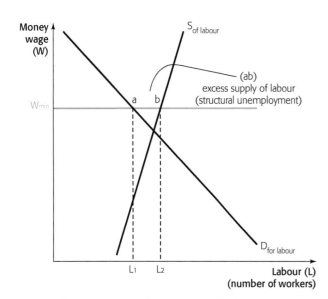

▲ Figure 3.4.3 Market for unskilled workers

Illustrating structural unemployment

One way to illustrate structural employment is to show a labour market diagram in which a minimum wage leads to fewer workers being demanded by firms than the number willing to work at that minimum wage level. This is shown in Figure 3.4.3.

At the minimum wage W_{min} firms are willing to hire L_1 workers while L_2 individuals are offering to work. There is excess supply of labour equal to L_1L_2 or (ab), which represents a type of structural unemployment.

Another way to illustrate structural unemployment is shown in Figure 3.4.4. This shows a particular labour market, in this case the market for truck drivers. There is a decrease in the demand for truck drivers because of the advent of driverless trucks.

Before the new technology, the market employed L truck drivers. The arrival of driverless trucks will decrease the demand for truck drivers to L'. Trucking firms will now only need to hire L' truck drivers for any trucks in a fleet that has not adopted the new technology. As a result, the new technology leads to L'L truck drivers losing their jobs.

The natural rate of unemployment (NRU)

The **natural rate of unemployment (NRU)** refers to the unemployment that exists when the economy is operating at its potential level of real GDP. The NRU reflects the fact that some unemployment is unavoidable and will always exist. There will always be some people who are seasonally or frictionally and, most importantly, structurally unemployed. The NRU does not include any cyclical unemployment.

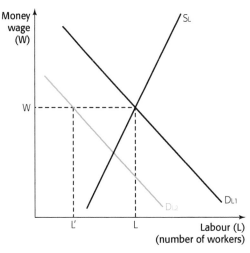

▲ Figure 3.4.4 Market for truck drivers

Costs of unemployment

An important goal of policy-makers is to ensure that high levels of employment are achieved or, in other words, to achieve and maintain low levels of unemployment. This is an important goal because, as explained below, high unemployment imposes significant costs on the economy, on individuals and on communities.

Economic costs

- Unemployment means that the economy is operating inside its production possibilities curve; it implies "lost output forever"; higher unemployment is associated with a loss in GDP.

- Rising unemployment decreases the tax revenues the government collects. It also increases government expenditures in many countries, for some period of time, as the government pays unemployment benefits.

- If unemployment is high and extends for a long period of time then income inequality widens.

- If unemployment is high, and has been for long period of time, then many workers may decide to emigrate to other countries in order to find employment. This is often referred to as a "brain drain". If the young and the educated leave, then the country's human capital is eroded, and this decreases its future growth prospects.

Search the web

Search the terms: self-driving vehicles truck drivers. You will find an informative article on the role of automation in certain types of jobs, including truck driving.

DP ready   ≥ **Research and thinking skills**

Youth unemployment

  Search the web

Search Google news for articles about high youth unemployment in Greece following the 2010 debt crisis. Include in your search the words "after:" and "before:" with specific dates. For example, use: Greece youth unemployment after:2010 before:2014. Then change your search text to: "after:2014" and "before:2019" to gain information about the issue through recent times.

1. Record the changing youth unemployment figures in Greece for as many years as you can find from 2010 onwards.

2. Describe what might be the consequences for the Greek economy of high youth unemployment.

Private costs

- Losing your job means losing your income from working. Even if unemployment benefits are available, they will be less than what you earned while working and they will only be paid for a limited period of time.

- If someone remains unemployed for long, job-related skills may be lost and this will negatively affect job prospects.

- Businesses with vacancies tend to prefer to hire a person currently working elsewhere rather than someone who is unemployed. They cannot be sure why the unemployed person lost their job, or is no longer working.

- Unemployed people often suffer family breakdown, alcohol or drug abuse, inability to pay debts, homelessness, loss of self-esteem or depression. Some even commit suicide.

Social costs

- In cities and regions with high and prolonged unemployment, crime and violence often increase.

- Drug and alcohol abuse may also increase, creating costs for businesses, law enforcement and the judicial system, as well as on the health care system.

DP ready ATL **(Thinking and communication skills)**

Unemployment and drug abuse

 Search the web

Search using these terms: job loss drug use Atlantic.
You will find an article from *The Atlantic* (19 July 2017) reporting results from international studies on the relationship between rising unemployment and drug abuse.

1. Discuss in groups whether there is a role for the state in minimizing the likelihood of drug abuse by individuals who are distressed because they have lost their job.

2. Implementing the ideas raised in your discussion may require increased government expenditure. Is it possible that in the long term this extra expenditure could be recovered?

TOK

Are there ethical considerations in firing a worker? Should the decision to terminate a worker's employment be based only on profit related criteria? Should a company decrease wages on all workers to contain costs in a downturn instead of firing some workers?

DP ready ATL **Thinking and communication skills**

Unemployment facts and issues

1. Prepare a mind map, on screen or on a large sheet of paper, that presents what you have learned about unemployment. Try to illustrate your points with real-world examples.

2. Share your ideas with the class.

Inflation, disinflation and deflation

Inflation is defined as a sustained increase in the average price level (APL). If there is a tendency for prices of goods and services in a country to be rising, then there is inflation. **Disinflation** refers to cases where prices are still rising but at a slower rate than before. **Deflation** refers to periods when the APL is decreasing.

Measuring inflation, disinflation and deflation

We need to measure the average price level of a country every year. We use the **Consumer Price Index (CPI)** to do this, which is an average of the prices of the goods and services that the typical consumer of a country buys. The goods and services that are included in the CPI are determined through extensive surveys that take place every few years. This APL for the country is calculated for every year (even for every month) and is expressed as a pure number; that is, a number without units of measurement. Once the CPI of a country for a number of years is known, the inflation rate is simply the percentage change in the CPI from one year to the next. So, if the CPI for 2017 was found to be 136.45 and the CPI for 2018 was equal to 142.22 then the rate of inflation for 2018 would be:

$$\frac{142.22 - 136.45}{136.45} \times 100 = 4.23\%$$

Now it is easier to see what disinflation and deflation actually mean. Table 3.4.3 shows Japan's actual rate of inflation for three years.

Year	Rate of inflation	Comment
2014	2.76%	Prices in Japan increased by 2.76% between 2013 and 2014. There was inflation in Japan
2015	0.80%	Prices in Japan in 2015 continued to increase but slower than they did in 2014: they increased but only by 0.80% which is less than the 2.76% inflation rate in 2014. There was disinflation in Japan
2016	−0.12%	Prices in Japan decreased in 2016 by 0.12%. The inflation rate was negative. There was deflation in Japan.

▲ Table 3.4.3 Rate of inflation in Japan 2014–2016. For more information see www.inflation.eu/inflation-rates/japan/

Difficulties in measuring inflation

The difficulties in measuring inflation are all related to shortcomings of the CPI (the average of the prices of all the goods and services that the typical consumer of a country buys).

- Who is this "typical" consumer? The simple answer is no one—the "typical" consumer is just an average of all of us. Therefore this consumer is both a bit old and a bit young, rich and poor, lives in a city but also in the countryside and is both a man and a woman. Actual buying patterns of any particular group, say young urban couples with an average income, are not measured.

Search the web

Search YouTube using the phrase: top 10 countries by inflation rate.

You will see a video of the countries with the top 10 inflation rates between 1980 and 2018. Note that extremely high inflation is referred to as hyperinflation.

- Improvements in quality are not sufficiently accounted for. If Milton bought a set of car tyres last year for $100 and this year he had to pay 10% more ($110) for a new set, but the old set lasted for 40,000 kilometres whereas he can drive 60,000 kilometres with the new set (50% more kilometres), then the new set is effectively cheaper. The published inflation rate may thus overestimate true inflation. This is referred to as the quality bias.

- New products enter our lives almost daily but are included in the CPI only after a long delay. For example, many consumers in Italy subscribe to Netflix and to Spotify but neither services are yet included in Italy's CPI. This is referred to as the new product bias.

- Every month, the statistical agency of a country sends off many young employees to collect the prices of the products included in the CPI. In many countries, though, more and more people buy more and more goods online, where prices are usually lower. If the statistical agency mostly collects prices from actual ("brick and mortar") stores, then the published inflation rate will tend to overestimate true inflation. This is referred to as the new retail outlet bias.

Causes of inflation

The easiest way to recognize the reasons prices may start increasing in a country is to recall the simple AD/AS diagram. Prices may start rising if AD is increasing and shifting to the right, especially as the economy is approaching full employment (potential) output. This is aptly referred to as **demand-pull inflation**. However, the APL may also be rising because AS decreases and shifts to the left. This is referred to as **cost-push inflation**.

Demand-pull inflation

Demand-pull inflation is shown in Figure 3.4.5.

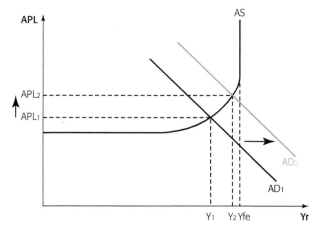

▲ Figure 3.4.5 Demand-pull inflation

As AD increases and the AD curve is shifting to the right, the APL is rising faster and faster the closer to the full employment output level (Yfe) the economy is. AD will increase when any of its components increases—remember:

$$AD = C + I + G + NX$$

The most common causes of demand-pull inflation include the following.

- Profligate government spending—"profligate" is the word used to describe excessive spending by a government. Governments often increase spending to maximize their re-election chances, as even a temporary boost of economic activity will serve this purpose. Government expenditures (G) are a component of AD, so if G rises, then AD will increase and shift to the right, potentially proving inflationary.

- Optimistic households and firms may spend excessively in the expectation that good times will persist. Since C and I are components of AD, AD will be increasing and shifting to the right, potentially proving inflationary.

- A surge in exports may also prove inflationary if the economy is operating near full employment.

- Inflationary expectations may also increase inflation as households prefer to spend now before prices rise even more, thus leading to higher AD.

- Perhaps more importantly, inflation results when too much money is chasing after too few goods. If too much money is pumped into an economy by the country's central bank, it will be spent and inflation could follow.

Cost-push inflation

Cost-push inflation is a result of AS decreasing and shifting to the left as in Figure 3.4.6. Note that the AS curve can be an SRAS or the upward sloping section of a Keynesian AS curve. In the case of cost-push inflation, not only are prices rising but growth also slows down (real GDP may even decrease) so that unemployment also rises.

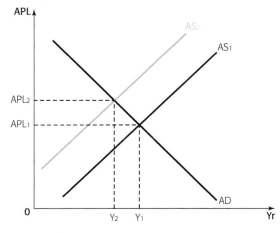

▲ Figure 3.4.6 Cost-push inflation.

The most common causes of cost-push inflation include the following.

- Historically, sustained and significant increases in the price of oil. Oil is still the predominant form of energy used in most production processes and if its price increases, production costs for most firms will increase. AS will decrease, and shift left leading to rising prices but also to slower growth (or even a decrease in real GDP) and rising unemployment.

 Search the web

Search using these terms: oil crisis 1970s inflation Britannica.
Read the short history of cost-push inflation in the 1970s.

- More generally, an increase in the price of **commodities** (raw materials used in manufacturing) may also lead to cost-push inflation.

- Powerful labour unions, successful in achieving higher money wages for their members, have been responsible for cost-push inflationary pressures. An increase in wages will also decrease AS.

- A **depreciation** of the exchange rate may lead to cost-push inflation if the country imports a lot of raw materials and intermediate products. A depreciation of the currency makes imports more expensive so production costs for many firms increase.

Why is inflation feared?

Price stability is another macroeconomic goal and it is the responsibility of central banks to achieve it. The European Central Bank and the US Federal Reserve define price stability as inflation below, but close to, 2%.

DP ready | ATL Thinking skills

Inflation rate

1. Why do you think that the goal is to maintain the rate of inflation close to 2%?

2. Explain what kind of risk the economy would face if the measured inflation was at 0.2%. Consider the role of the quality bias, the new retail outlet bias and the substitution bias. Revisit this question when you have also studied the costs of deflation.

Costs of inflation

- Inflation makes income distribution more unequal. There are two reasons for this.

  — The purchasing power (real income) of those earning fixed money incomes, such as wage earners and pensioners, decreases. If Joey earns $1000 per month, then what Joey can buy with this income decreases if prices increase. This is not the case for those who can adjust their earnings (such as lawyers or consultants). Income inequality widens.

— Low-income families, if they are able to make any savings, usually place them in bank accounts. If the interest rate paid on such an account is 3% but inflation is 5% their savings are worth less at the end of the year. The **real interest rate**, defined as the interest rate minus the rate of inflation, is negative. Higher income households can buy, often through borrowing, assets such as a house or land, the price of which is expected to increase faster than inflation. The poor often cannot borrow. In a sense, inflation transfers income from the poor to the rich.

 Inflation hurts the exports of a country because they become more expensive and so less competitive in foreign markets. This adversely affects growth especially if growth in the country is export-driven.

 Inflation makes it more difficult for businesses to decide whether an investment will prove profitable. If inflation is 4% this year it does not mean that it will be 4% next year. It could be 6% or 3%. Also, if inflation is 4%, it does not mean that the prices of all goods have increased by 4%. Some prices will have risen by more and other prices by less—4% is an average. Inflation is both variable and unbalanced and this increases the uncertainty that firms face. More uncertainty means less investment as it is difficult to judge whether an investment will prove profitable. Long-term growth is adversely affected.

 Inflation is "noise". It distorts the signalling power of relative price changes responsible for resource allocation in a market economy. If the price of kale rises, this sends a signal to producers that people want more kale. If all prices are rising as a result of inflation, the signal is not clear anymore and producers cannot be sure that people actually do demand more kale. Inflation leads to misallocation of resources.

 Inflation may induce people to save less. People will choose to buy goods, especially durables, before they become even more expensive, so people spend more and save less. As the real interest rate is often negative during inflationary periods, saving decreases.

Deflation

Deflation is negative inflation, meaning that prices on the average (measured by the CPI) are decreasing. Typically, deflation is a result of a collapse in AD. Households cut back on their spending and this forces some firms to cut prices in a desperate attempt to increase sales. On a diagram this can be shown by shifting AD to the left. Technically, deflation can also result if AS shifts to the right. Firms expecting AD to increase, make investments to expand capacity. If the expected increase in AD does not materialize then firms will be forced to cut prices. Sometimes this is referred to as "good deflation", as the economy has more factories. But this is misleading. Deflation is always bad for an economy because once it starts, it is difficult to stop.

Why is deflation bad for an economy?

- Deflation creates more deflation. A "deflationary spiral" may begin as people who expect prices to continue to fall postpone purchases. This further decreases AD. Prices and economic activity continue to decrease and (cyclical) unemployment continues to increase.

- Firms dismiss workers as a result of shrinking sales, which increases (cyclical) unemployment and decreases consumers' confidence.

- Firms that have borrowed will owe more in real terms. If a pen manufacturer borrowed $200,000 from a bank when the firm sold pens at $2.00 each, it is as if it owed the bank 100,000 pens. When the firm is forced to decrease the price of pens to $1.60, it is as if it owes the bank 125,000 pens. The debt expressed in terms of goods (the firm's real debt) has increased. The firm will avoid borrowing more and investing, preferring to decrease its debt first. AD will fall further. Prices will fall further, economic activity will decrease even more and (cyclical) unemployment will rise.

- Since many households and firms will not be able to pay off their debts, banks will accumulate non-performing ("bad") loans. If these are extensive, a banking crisis may follow.

- If an economy becomes caught in a deflationary spiral, policy-makers may not have many policy tools available. Monetary policy may be ineffective as interest rates could already be very close to zero. Using expansionary fiscal policy may not be an option if there are debt constraints.

- Uncertainty that businesses face is higher, as it also is with inflation, which decreases investment further.

- Just as with inflation, relative price changes lose their signalling power, leading to misallocation of resources and inefficiency.

DP ready   ATL **Thinking skills**

Low and stable inflation

Low and stable inflation is a macroeconomic goal.

1. Explain why:

   a. governments want low inflation

   b. policy-makers do not aim for a zero or a close-to-zero inflation rate.

2. Describe the costs of high inflation.

3. Explain why policy-makers do not want deflation.

4. Policy-makers may aim at stable inflation. Explain:

   a. what happens if inflation is variable rather than stable

   b. what kind of issues variable inflation presents to the economy.

Which is worse—inflation or unemployment?

As you may have expected, it depends. First, it depends on who you are. For wealthy households, with much of their wealth in fixed-income assets, such as bonds, inflation is worse. The bonds earn a fixed-interest income every year, say $100,000, which inflation would damage, as the annual return would be worth less and less. For workers whose primary concern is keeping their job, unemployment is much more costly. Even if these workers have some savings the value of which is eroded by inflation, it is more important for them to keep their job and continue earning a living wage.

More generally, it depends on your ideological leanings. Monetarists, such as Milton Friedman, considered inflation as the true enemy of an economy. Inflation leads to inefficiency and slows down growth. If price stability is achieved and maintained, the economy will grow faster and, in the long term, more jobs will be created. The economy will eventually return to full employment and to the natural rate of unemployment while more investments increase the economy's potential level of real output.

Independently of who you are or your ideological leanings, which one is more costly to the economy depends on the particulars. High and prolonged unemployment destroys the social fabric of the economy, may induce the youngest and the brightest to emigrate, which compromises future growth, and leads to higher income inequality. So it may be considered costlier than inflation. The opposing view is that accelerating inflation will also prove costly as investments would slow down, adversely affecting growth. Runaway inflation can severely damage savings, leading to social unrest. Policy-makers at each point in time, and in each economy, have to carefully weigh the costs of inflation against the costs of unemployment. Policy-making is perhaps both a science and an art.

 TOK

American President Harry Truman famously once asked for a "one-handed economist" because he was frustrated by his economic advisers always telling him "on the other hand …" and continuing "on the other hand…". If you are not familiar with this saying, search for it on the internet.

What does Truman's comment suggest about economics as compared with natural sciences?

DP ready ᴬᵀᴸ **Communication skills**

Inflation and deflation

In a small group, prepare two mind maps. One should focus on inflation and the other on deflation. Combine the two mind maps into one as a poster. Explain the structure of your mind map poster to fellow students.

Focus point

Economic growth must be inclusive and sustainable. Non-inclusive growth that leads to increased income inequality is referred to as ruthless whereas growth that leads to environmental degradation is referred to as futureless. When we read that an economy is growing, we must pause before celebrating.

Some unemployment, the natural unemployment, may be unavoidable but high and persistent rates of unemployment are very costly for an economy and, of course, for the unemployed individuals and the communities they live in.

Price stability is also a major goal for policymakers because both inflation and deflation are also costly to an economy, to businesses and to households.

Whether unemployment or inflation is worse, is a subject of significant debate. In any case, policymakers try to achieve price stability and high levels of employment, a combination that is not always easy to attain.

Key terms—test yourself

Define these terms: economic growth, short-term growth, long-term growth, unemployment, hidden unemployment, discouraged workers, seasonal unemployment, frictional unemployment, cyclical unemployment, structural unemployment, natural rate of unemployment, inflation, disinflation, deflation, CPI, demand-pull inflation, cost-push inflation, real interest rate, commodities.

3.5   INEQUALITY AND POVERTY

In this section you will learn about:

→ **equality and equity**

→ **the meaning of economic inequality and measuring inequality**

→ **the meaning of poverty and measuring poverty**

→ **the causes of economic inequality and poverty**

→ **the impact of economic inequality**

→ **progressive, proportional and regressive taxation**

→ **reducing inequality—the role of taxation and of other policies.**

The issue

Inequality is becoming one of the most contentious concerns in the world today. Some people have incomes way above what they need to maintain a luxurious lifestyle, while others struggle to acquire even the basic necessities. This section examines why some people are poor while others are rich, and examines how inequality and poverty can be measured and reduced.

Equality and equity

The ideas of equality and equity often arise in relation to the distribution of income. Equity means fairness, which is not the same as equality. Yet, these terms are often used interchangeably, since a more equitable distribution of income is typically interpreted as a less unequal income distribution.

The meaning of economic inequality

Economic inequality relates to the unequal distribution of income and of wealth. Remember that household income is generated from the payments received per period of time for the use of factors of production. Wealth consists of what households own—that is, their assets at some point in time minus what they owe (their debt). Assets include bank deposits, shares and bonds, as well as houses, cars or boats. Households can use wealth to consume more than their income, or may consume less than their income and add to their wealth.

The wealth and income distributions may be different in a country. Across the OECD countries, wealth inequality is twice the level of income inequality on average. Wealth inequality is highest in the US followed by the Netherlands and Denmark. In the US the top 10% of households own 80% of total wealth and the bottom 40% own just over 2% of total wealth. Wealth inequality is lowest in Japan, Poland, Greece and Belgium where the top 10% of households own slightly over 40% of total wealth. Interestingly, countries with high wealth inequality, such as the Netherlands and

 TOK

To what extent is equity an elusive concept?

Denmark, where households at the bottom 60% owe more than they own, are countries with a very equitable income distribution. Also, households with low net wealth are not necessarily poor in terms of their income and some may own substantial wealth but combined with high levels of debt.

Measuring inequality

The degree of income inequality in an economy can be measured through the use of the Lorenz curve and the Gini coefficient.

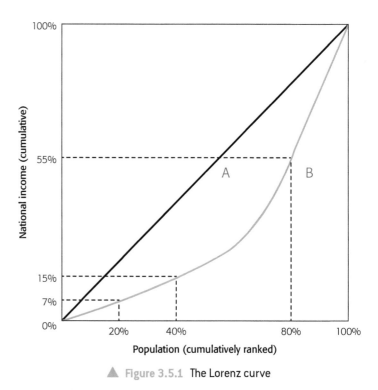

▲ Figure 3.5.1 The Lorenz curve

Population is represented on the horizontal axis of the graph, in cumulative percentages, from the lowest to the highest income households. On the vertical axis, the percentage of national income received cumulatively by each percentage group of the population is represented. So, in Figure 3.5.1 the poorest 20% of people receive only 7% of national income, the poorest 40% of the population receive 15% of national income while the richest

20% receive 45% of national income. The diagonal line is the line of perfect income equality, where the "poorest" 20% of people earn 20% of income and the "poorest" 40% earn 40% of national income. As the Lorenz curve shifts further to the right of the diagonal, the distribution of income becomes more and more unequal. So, more income inequality is shown by a shift of the Lorenz curve further to the right of the diagonal and less income inequality by a shift towards the diagonal.

The Gini coefficient can also be used to measure the degree of income inequality. The Gini coefficient is defined as the ratio of the area between the Lorenz curve and the diagonal over the area of the half square:

$$\text{Gini coefficient} = \frac{\text{area (A)}}{\text{area (A + B)}}$$

The Gini coefficient can vary from 0 (perfect equality—each person receives the same income) to 1 (perfect inequality—one individual earns all the income).

DP ready | ATL **Thinking and research skills**

Gini values

Visit the World Bank webpage and search for the Gini index by country.

1. Find your country and determine the Gini coefficient.

2. **a.** Find countries with high Gini values and countries with low Gini values.

   b. Outline possible reasons why income inequality is higher in some countries and lower in others.

The meaning of poverty

Poverty refers to the inability to cover minimal consumption needs. There is a distinction between absolute and relative poverty. **Absolute poverty** refers to the situation when a household does not have sufficient income to meet basic needs. **Relative poverty** compares the income of a household with the median national income. The more unequal the distribution of income within the total population, the more significant is the degree of relative poverty. The idea behind relative poverty is that people may still be poor, even if they can buy basic necessities, when they cannot afford the typical lifestyle in their society.

Measuring poverty

To measure absolute poverty, a minimum income level called the poverty line is identified. That is the minimum income needed in order to sustain a family in terms of food, housing, clothing and medical needs. Once the poverty line is defined, the amount of poverty can be measured by taking the percentage of the population who earn an income below the poverty line. A poverty line can be set at both a national and an international level. The World Bank sets the international poverty line. In 2015 the threshold was set to $1.90 per day—households living on less than $1.90 a day are in absolute poverty.

Relative poverty can be measured by specifying a percentage of median income, usually 50%. Households earning less than 50% of the median income are considered relatively poor. For example, let's say the median annual household income in an economy is $20,000. Taking 50% of this, we have $10,000. Any household for which annual income falls below $10,000 is considered poor in relative terms. The poverty line and minimum income standard described above measure absolute and relative poverty on the basis of income. They are single indicators.

However, poverty is multidimensional as it includes a range of human experiences such as hunger, malnutrition, illness, lack of shelter, lack of education, illiteracy, unemployment, insecurity and vulnerability, which are not captured by single indicators. For this reason the Multidimensional Poverty Index (MPI) has been constructed.

The MPI is a composite indicator of poverty. Oxford Poverty & Human Development Initiative (OPHI) as well as the United Nations Development Programme (UNDP) developed this index in 2010 in order to determine poverty beyond measures that are only based on income. It covers over 100 developing countries and helps to determine the most vulnerable people among the poor in different societies around the globe. The MPI captures the acute deprivations that each person faces with respect to education, health and living standards. These three dimensions are assessed by 10 indicators: child mortality, nutrition, years of schooling, school attendance, cooking fuel, sanitation, drinking water, electricity, housing and assets. If someone is deprived in three or more of these indicators, the index identifies them as "MPI poor", and the intensity of their poverty is measured by the percentage of deprivations they are experiencing.

DP ready | ATL **Thinking and research skills**

A survey of poverty

1. Find data on absolute and relative poverty in your country. Has poverty been increasing or decreasing over the recent years?

2. Visit the webpage Our World In Data. Scroll down to the topic "Growth & Inequality". Choose "Global Extreme Poverty".

   a. What is the number of people living in poverty across the world?

   b. Has the number been increasing or decreasing over time?

   c. Describe other trends in world poverty that you notice.

3. Visit the United Nations Human Development Reports website and go to "2019 Multidimensional Poverty Index" under the "Data" tab.

   a. Identify the key findings reported.

   b. Explain which dimension of this index you consider to be the most important.

Causes of economic inequality and poverty

The following are possible determinants of inequality and poverty.

- Inequality of opportunity: this occurs when people living in the same society do not have access to the same opportunities. High levels of inequality of opportunity mean that people's circumstances at birth such as their gender, the place where they were born, their ethnicity or their parental background determine to a large degree the educational qualifications they obtain, the type of job they get and, ultimately, their level of income.

- Different levels of resource ownership: income depends on the payments households receive by selling the factors of production they own. A highly unequal ownership of the factors of production would lead to a highly unequal income distribution.

- Different levels of human capital: human capital refers to the skills, education and experience of labour. Workers with less skill, education or experience earn lower wages.

- Discrimination: this entails treating people differently because of certain characteristics, such as ethnic or racial background, religion or gender. When discrimination occurs, individuals' freedom to choose and pursue their aspirations is restricted without regard for ability.

- Difference in power: inequality can also arise when there are disparities in market power and social power. Significant market power concentrated in the hands of a few firms may lead to economic inequality. Also, certain social groups may be granted exclusive privileges and preferences. This could boost their earnings and wealth, widening inequality.

- Degree of government support: the greater the support for the low income or poor, the lower will be the level of inequality in the economy.

The impact of economic inequality

Economic inequality may have a negative impact on economic growth. In fact, in OECD countries, the average increase in inequality of 3 Gini points over the past couple of decades is estimated to have cut GDP by around 8.5%. Growth is suppressed because of lower levels of human capital. Lack of funds to access health care and education can lead to lower human capital and so to lower labour productivity, which results in slower economic growth.

Moreover, with high inequality, the overall rate of savings in the economy tends to be lower, because the highest rate of savings is usually found among the middle classes, which are usually "squeezed" by inequality. High-income individuals typically will buy expensive houses and spend much of their income on imported luxury goods, jewellery and foreign travel. They may also seek safe havens abroad for their savings in what is known as capital flight. Therefore, when savings are low, the level of investment is low. Productive resources do not increase or improve and this limits economic growth. High inequality also facilitates "rent seeking" which refers to actions such as excessive lobbying, large political donations and bribery. When resources are allocated to such rent-seeking behaviours, they are diverted from productive purposes that could have led to faster growth.

The higher the inequality is, the smaller the fraction of the population that qualifies for a loan or other credit. When individuals with low incomes cannot borrow money, they may not be able to educate their children or start and expand a business. The result of these factors can be slower growth.

Inequality also undermines social stability. High inequality is associated with higher crime rates. Extreme inequality may result in upheavals and civil conflict that can cost lives and set back any progress. High inequality may also lead those on low incomes to support populist policies that can prove to be damaging. The political power of the rich and hence their bargaining power are strengthened by high inequality. Usually, the rich use this power to encourage outcomes favourable to them. Even worse, high inequality makes weak institutions very difficult to improve, because the powerful few are likely to view themselves as worse off from a socially efficient reform, and so they have the incentive and the means to resist it.

Progressive, proportional and regressive taxation

Taxes are distinguished into direct and indirect.

Direct taxes are directly paid to tax authorities by taxpayers and include personal income taxes, corporate income taxes and wealth taxes. Personal income taxes are paid based on all forms of income of a household such as wages, rental income, interest income and dividends. Corporate income taxes are taxes on the profits of a corporation. Wealth taxes are imposed on the ownership of assets. They include property taxes and inheritance taxes.

Indirect taxes are taxes imposed on goods and services. They are called indirect because consumers pay them indirectly through the sellers of the good or service being purchased.

Taxes can be progressive, proportional or regressive depending on the relationship between income and the percentage of income paid as tax. The percentage of income paid as tax is referred to as the tax rate. To explain the difference between these types of taxes we need to define the **marginal tax rate** (MTR) and the **average tax rate** (ATR). The MTR is additional tax paid as a result of additional income earned, or, the percentage taken on the last "dollar" earned. The ATR is the ratio of the tax paid over the tax base. The tax base refers to whatever is taxed so it may include income, expenditures, profits or wealth.

- A tax is **progressive** if, as income increases, the percentage of income paid in taxes (the ATR) also increases. Since the ATR increases, the MTR is greater than the ATR. Under progressive

Watch this

Search YouTube using these terms: Wilkinson Inequality harms societies TEDx. Watch the video on the consequences of economic inequality.

MTR	ATR
$MTR = \dfrac{\Delta T}{\Delta Y}$	$ATR = \dfrac{T}{Y}$

▲ Table 3.5.1 MTR and ATR

taxation, individuals or households with higher incomes pay a bigger proportion of income as tax than the ones with lower incomes.

- A tax is **proportional** if, as income increases, the percentage of income paid in taxes remains constant. The ATR therefore remains constant so the MTR is equal to the ATR. In a proportional tax system, all individuals or households pay the same proportion of income as tax regardless of their level of income.

- A tax is **regressive** if, as income increases, the percentage of income paid in taxes decreases. The ATR thus decreases, so the MTR is less than the ATR. In a regressive tax system poorer individuals or households pay a bigger proportion of their income in taxes.

Table 3.5.2 shows how a progressive income tax system works.

Income ($)	Tax rate
0–10,000	10%
10,001–30,000	20%
30,001–55,000	30%
55,001 and above	50%

▲ Table 3.5.2 Example of a progressive income tax system

Using Table 3.5.2, let's calculate how much tax an individual earning $60,000 per year would pay. The tax paid will be 10% for the first $10,000 of this income; 20% on income between $10,001 and $30,000; 30% on income between $30,001 and $55,000; and finally 50% on income between $55,001 and $60,000. So:

$$(0.1 \times \$10,000) + (0.2 \times \$20,000) + (0.3 \times \$25,000) + (0.5 \times \$5,000) =$$
$$\$1,000 + \$4,000 + \$7,500 + \$2,500 = \$15,000$$

The total tax paid on the $60,000 earned is $15,000.

If income taxes were proportional then everyone earning an income, regardless of the amount, would face the same tax rate, say 20%. Income taxes are never regressive, but indirect taxes are. Let's see why. Consider two individuals that have bought the same good. Both individuals have paid the same "dollar" amount of, say value added tax. Yet, since they do not have the same level of income, the amount of tax paid is a greater percentage of income for the poorer individual.

Reducing inequality

The role of taxation

Taxation can play a key role in reducing inequality. The idea is that the more progressive a tax system is, the more equal the after-tax distribution of income and wealth becomes. Progressive income taxes will require those on higher incomes to pay a larger percentage of their total income in taxes compared to those on

 **Internal link**

There is more on taxation in section 2.5.

DP ready ATL **Research skills**

Comparing tax rates

Find personal income tax rates, corporate tax rates and indirect tax rates that apply in your country. Compare with another country in your region of the world.

low incomes. Also, progressive property and inheritance taxes will make the burden of the tax fall most heavily on the upper-income groups. In both cases, income and wealth can be redistributed more equitably; that is, inequality can decrease. However, in practice this may not be as effective with the low- and middle-income groups ending up paying a proportionally larger share of their incomes in taxes than the high-income groups. This is because the poor are often taxed at the source of their incomes or expenditures (by withholding taxes from wages, or through indirect taxes imposed on the purchase of goods such as cigarettes). By contrast, the rich derive the largest part of their incomes from the return on physical and financial assets, which can go unreported. Also, they may be able to exploit legal tax loopholes and end up paying fewer taxes. In some countries, where there is no fear of government reprisal, they may completely evade taxes.

Other policies to reduce poverty and inequality

Besides taxation a government may also resort to the use of other policies. These include the following.

- **Transfer payments:** these usually include pensions, unemployment and disability benefits and child allowances. These payments are made to the most vulnerable groups of the population using tax revenues, so they decrease income inequality. It is important to note that there is risk that the people receiving these payments may become too dependent on them.

- Targeted spending on goods and services: the government can subsidize or directly provide services such as education and health care services and infrastructure in order to make them available to the most deprived groups. Examples include: public health projects in rural villages and urban fringe areas; school lunches and preschool nutritional supplementation programmes; and the provision of clean water and electrification to remote rural areas.

- Investment in human capital: this can be achieved by improving the quality and access to education and health services for the lower-income groups. A healthier population with better education, training and skills will increase labour productivity and lead to higher incomes and wealth.

- The minimum wage: the government can set or increase the minimum wage in order to support the incomes of low-skilled workers. However, this may lead to an increase in unemployment.

- Universal basic income (UBI): this is a model for providing all citizens of a country or a geographic area with a given amount of money, regardless of their income, wealth or employment status. Typically, identical periodic payments are made to all, which are funded through the taxes paid by those with higher incomes. This sum should be enough to take care of basic needs but not enough to provide a lot more. However, the opportunity cost of funding UBI can be high. In June 2016 Switzerland's voters rejected such a plan.

Watch this

Search YouTube using these terms: UBI explained. Watch a video on how the UBI model could work.

TOK

Inequality may also arise because of differences in qualifications. These are reflections of a number of things such as natural ability, attitudes towards study, the quality of tuition and income of parents. Is there a role for the state in these cases? To what extent should the state intervene to compensate for such differences?

DP ready | ATL **Thinking, communication and research skills**

1. In class, discuss possible problems that the policies in the bullet list above could cause.

2. Search online using these terms: Bolsa Familia and Oportunidades. Collect information about these programmes. To what extent were they successful? Share this information with the rest of your class and discuss these programme's advantages and disadvantages.

 Creativity, activity, service

Get in touch with organizations assisting people in need in your local community and find out in what ways you could support these organizations. Arrange a "give away" event at your school—ask people to bring in things they might no longer need including clothing, books, cookware and kitchenware, linens or even small domestic appliances. Donate the collected items to the organizations you got in touch with so that they can distribute them to the needy. You can ask to participate in the distribution.

Alternatively, you could organize a fundraising event.

Focus point

Economic inequality refers to the unequal distribution of income and of wealth while poverty refers to the inability to cover minimal consumption needs. A number of reasons can give rise to both inequality and poverty. Inequality of opportunity, discrimination or different levels of human capital are among these reasons. Economic inequality can have a negative impact on economic growth and social stability. Progressive taxation, transfer payments and investment in human capital are some of the measures a government can use to reduce inequality.

Key terms—test yourself

Define these terms: absolute poverty, relative poverty, direct taxes, indirect taxes, progressive taxation, proportional taxation, regressive taxation.

In this section you will learn about:

→ monetary policy and the role of the central bank

→ fiscal policy

→ supply-side policies

→ how policies may promote economic growth and keep unemployment low and prices stable.

The issue

In order to achieve policy objectives, policy-makers use monetary, fiscal and supply-side policies. This section explains these policies, examines their strengths and limitations then evaluates how they may promote growth, low unemployment and price stability.

Policies—key points

Demand-side policies aim to affect aggregate demand (AD). They include monetary policy and fiscal policy. Monetary policy is conducted by the central bank of the country and involves changes in the money supply and interest rates. **Fiscal policy** is conducted by the government and involves changes in the level of government expenditures and/or taxes.

Supply-side policies aim to increase aggregate supply (AS). They focus on the production side of the economy. They are often categorized as market-based supply-side policies or interventionist policies.

Note that fiscal and monetary policy may try to increase AD, but may sometimes decrease AD, while supply-side policies aim only to increase AS.

Internal link

This section refers to AD, AS and the LRAS curve. There is more in-depth information in section 3.2.

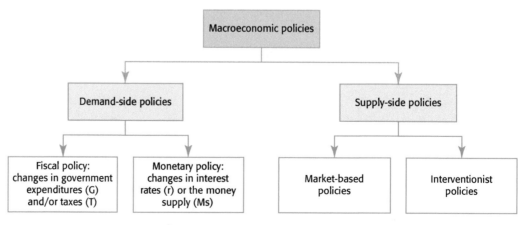

▲ Figure 3.6.1 Macroeconomic policies

Monetary policy

The role of a central bank

The **central bank** can be described as the bank of the government and the bank of commercial banks. **Commercial banks** are profit-oriented firms. They attract deposits by paying interest and grant loans for which they are paid interest. The central bank regulates the behaviour of commercial banks, making sure they do not engage in risky lending to increase their profits. The central bank is also the "lender of last resort" which is another way of saying that it does whatever it takes to make sure that banking crises are avoided. It also collects all government revenues from taxation and other sources and makes all government payments. Most importantly, it carries out monetary policy by affecting the money supply and thus interest rates. Interest rates are the cost of borrowing money and the reward for saving money over a period of time, expressed as a percentage. By increasing the money supply, the central bank can decrease interest rates and vice versa.

Goals of monetary policy

The single most important goal of monetary policy is to achieve and maintain price stability. For the UK, the US, the eurozone, Canada, Sweden and other central banks this means inflation rate below but close to 2%. For the Reserve Bank of India, it means maintaining inflation at around 4%.

If the economy is in recession or at risk of entering recession, monetary policy can be used to increase AD. Unemployment will decrease. In contrast, if growth is too fast and there is a risk of rising inflation, monetary policy can be used to decrease AD to cool off the economy and decrease inflationary pressures. So, by regulating AD monetary policy can, in principle, decrease the short-term fluctuations of real GDP, making the business cycle smoother. If monetary policy is successful and manages to achieve and maintain long-term price stability, then long-term economic growth may accelerate. Businesses are more likely to invest and expand if there is price stability and they face less uncertainty. Lastly, as will be explained later, monetary policy can influence the exchange rate, which helps to correct trade-related issues.

Tools to conduct monetary policy

The central bank uses three tools to affect the money supply and thus interest rates.

- The central bank can change the **reserve requirement ratio**. This is the percentage of a commercial bank's deposits that it cannot lend out and must hold as reserves. When a commercial bank provides you with a loan, it automatically creates money as it opens an account that you use to make payments. So, if the central bank wants to decrease the money supply it can limit the amount of loans a bank can make by increasing the RRR. If the central bank wants to increase the money supply it will decrease the RRR.

DP ready ATL **Research skills**

Inflation targets

Find inflation targets around the world by searching the web using these terms: central bank news inflation target. Record the lowest and the highest targets as well as the countries for each extreme.

Internal link

There is more on inflation in section 3.5.

- Commercial banks can borrow from their central bank. If the central bank would like commercial banks to make more loans, the rate it charges for this is kept low. This interest rate is referred to with many different names, such as the **discount rate** or the refinancing rate.

- The most important tool of monetary policy is **open market operations**. If the central bank were to buy $100 million worth of a food product, $100 million new dollars would enter the economy. The money supply would have increased. The opposite would happen if the central bank sold $100 million worth of that product. Of course, the central bank does not buy and sell food products. Instead, it increases the money supply by buying short-term government bonds from commercial banks and it can decrease the money supply by selling short-term government bonds.

Quantitative easing (QE)

QE is a relatively new policy. It has been used recently to help economies grow and reduce unemployment while avoiding deflation. It is very similar to open market operations. The main difference is that the central bank does not buy only short-term government bonds from commercial banks but many other financial assets commercial banks own, in order to pump more cash into commercial banks to encourage them to lend more aggressively. QE was used by Japan in 2001 and by the US Federal Reserve in 2008 in response to the financial crisis. The Bank of England followed in 2009 while it was adopted by the European Central Bank in 2015.

How does monetary policy work?

Monetary policy can be used to decrease AD so that inflation or the risk of inflation decreases. This is referred to as **contractionary (tight) monetary policy**. The central bank decreases the money supply, using the tools explained above; interest rates increase. This means that borrowing costs for both households and firms increase. Households borrow less and so they spend less on durables such as cars and appliances and, of course, on houses.

Households have a greater incentive to save and not to spend. Firms borrow less and so they spend less on capital goods. If C and I decrease, then AD will decrease, and an inflationary gap can close.

Monetary policy can also be used to close a deflationary gap, increasing AD and also real GDP and lowering unemployment. In this case, **expansionary (loose) monetary policy** will be used. Interest rates decrease, the cost of borrowing decreases, the incentive to save decreases and so more is spent, increasing AD. This sounds easy, but as will be explored below, it does not always work.

Positive features of monetary policy

Monetary policy is:

- flexible—the monetary policy committee meets frequently to set interest rates

Search the web

Search YouTube using these terms: ECB price stability important. Watch a short video from the European Central Bank on inflation and monetary policy.

- incremental—interest rates can be increased or decreased by 0.25% at a time
- reversible—if it becomes clear that say, interest rates were decreased more than necessary, risking inflation, it is very easy to reverse direction and increase interest rates in the next meeting.

In addition, monetary policy is independent of the government and politicians, even though this independence has recently been tested in the US and elsewhere. Politicians care more about their short-term re-election chances and less about the benefits of long-term price stability to the economy.

Search the web

Search using these terms: conversation fed independence matters. Read a very short article on the independence of the US Federal Reserve Bank.

DP ready | ATL **Thinking skills**

Politicians' involvement in monetary policy

1. To what extent do you think politicians should limit their involvement in central bank decisions?

2. What are the risks of prime ministers or presidents interfering with monetary policy decisions?

Internal link

Recall what you learned in section 3.4 about Truman's one-handed economist.

In the case of monetary policy, the issue is that lower interest rates alone may not convince households and businesses to borrow more and spend more. If there is low confidence, then more borrowing and spending will not easily take place. So, if an economy is in a deep recession, monetary policy may be ineffective. Also, interest rates have a lower limit of 0%. They cannot turn negative—a bank will not pay a household to borrow money and buy a house.

Fiscal policy

The government conducts fiscal policy. Fiscal policy refers to changes in government expenditures (G) and/or taxes (T) to affect AD.

Types of government expenditure

- Capital expenditures: these include spending on infrastructure such as roads, bridges, ports, airports, research and development facilities, schools and hospitals.
- Current expenditures: these include the salaries of public sector employees, spending on school and hospital supplies, also paying subsidies.
- Transfer payments, such as pensions, unemployment and other cash transfers: these payments are not included in GDP as they do not represent a contribution to current production.

Types of government revenue

- Government revenues are mostly received from direct and indirect taxes.
- Government revenues can also include any receipts from the sale of state-owned assets (such as firms, ports or airports) to the private sector (privatizations).

What are the goals of fiscal policy?

The goals of fiscal policy are not very different from the goals of monetary policy as both are demand-management policies. Perhaps the most important goal of fiscal policy is to lift an economy out of recession. If the government expenditures are capital expenditures that increase or improve the available infrastructure, not only will AD, and so real GDP, increase but long-term growth will also accelerate. Faster long-term growth may also result if fiscal policy is "prudent" which means that large deficits are avoided and the national debt does not increase to unsustainable levels. Businesses will feel less uncertain about the future and will be more willing to invest.

Fiscal policy can also be used to decrease inflation, particularly if inflation was the result of profligate government spending. As shown later in this section, it can also be used to decrease trade imbalances. All of these goals are also goals of monetary policy—but there is one goal that fiscal policy can address more directly, which is to decrease income inequality.

How does fiscal policy work?

Let's explain how fiscal policy can be used to increase AD so that a deflationary gap decreases. The government will increase government expenditures (G) and/or decrease taxes (T). This is referred to as **expansionary fiscal policy**.

If government expenditures (G) increase, then AD will directly increase as G is a component of AD. Interestingly, the resulting increase in real GDP will be greater than the increase in G. This is due to the multiplier effect (an HL topic) which shows that an increase in government expenditure will lead to a greater increase in national income.

If taxes (T) decrease then disposable incomes (Yd) increase and with higher disposable incomes, people will tend to spend more, increasing consumption expenditures (C) and so AD. If corporate taxes decrease then the resulting higher profitability that firms will enjoy may lead to an increase in investment spending (I), which also increases AD. Note, though, that typically fiscal policy does not refer to changes in the rates of indirect taxation.

If the goal is to decrease AD to close an inflationary gap and lower inflation then the government will adopt contractionary fiscal policy, decreasing government spending (G) and/or increasing taxes (T). This is simply the opposite logic to the one described above.

The above describes what is referred to as discretionary fiscal policy. The government "does" something. However, fiscal policy can be also fixed more firmly through what are called automatic stabilizers. Automatic stabilizers (HL topic) refer to changes in tax revenues collected and unemployment benefits paid by the government that result only from changes in national income and thus tend to stabilize the business cycle automatically. When an economy enters recession, government spending automatically

Internal link

See section 3.5 on inequality.

Search the web

A recent example of expansionary fiscal policy is the US government's response to the recession of 2008. It increased government spending, initially by $787 billion. Search the web using these terms: Obama stimulus package 2009. Read about this policy from several sources.

TOK

You will have read that most but not all economists agree that Obama's stimulus package was successful. You will notice that in many cases, ideology about the role of the state and the role of markets, drives opinions. What does this suggest about the discipline of economics?

increases as unemployment benefits "kick-in" making the recession milder. If an economy is overheating, income taxes rise, slowing down household spending and thus 'cooling-off' the economy

Positive features of fiscal policy

It should be clear that expansionary fiscal policy in the form of increased government expenditures (G) is most effective in lifting an economy out of a deep recession. This is because it is direct. Government spending is a component of AD and it directly increases incomes and output, increasing consumer and business confidence. The multiplier effect renders it also very powerful. In addition, spending can be targeted towards specific sectors of the economy, such as specific needs in infrastructure, research and development or green technologies.

A problem with fiscal policy

The biggest issue with fiscal policy is that the politicians who are in charge often use fiscal tools to their own personal or party benefit. Fiscal policy is a short-term stabilization policy. In principle, it should move against the business cycle, it should be "counter-cyclical". If the economy is booming too fast, contractionary fiscal policy should be adopted, whereas if the economy is rapidly declining, expansionary fiscal policy is expected. Politicians of course prefer to increase government expenditures and to decrease taxes because cutting government spending and raising taxes may cost them the next election. What is known as an "expansionary bias" is involved. This bias is dangerous because it means increased **budget deficits**, possibly unsustainable levels of national debt and risk of future inflation.

Time lags in policy-making

What are time lags in policy-making? It takes time to detect an economic problem, such as entering a recession. Policy-makers take time to gather data, process it and identify a recession. This is the detection lag. Then policy-makers will have to debate before a specific policy choice is made. This is the administrative lag. Policies also, once implemented, take some time to impact the economy. This is the execution or impact lag. Therefore, from the point in time when an economy starts to have problems until the point when a policy choice starts working, a certain amount of time elapses. Both fiscal and monetary policies suffer from time lags. This may present a problem as the policy may end up destabilizing instead of stabilizing the economy. For example, let's say the government decides to increase government spending in order to deal with a recession and close a deflationary gap. If exports unexpectedly rise before the full impact of the fiscal stimulus, an inflationary gap may result.

▲ Green technology in Warsaw, Poland

Monetary policy has the advantage

In terms of time lags, monetary policy is the clear winner. The time lags associated are significantly shorter. Both fiscal and monetary policies suffer exactly the same detection lag. However, the members of the monetary policy committee are not politicians, so it is easier to arrive at a policy response, such as a decrease in interest rates if there as a deflationary gap. For a government to decide which government expenditures to increase and by how much, and then for parliament to approve these changes, a much longer time is needed. For example, for a government project that increases spending on the construction of a new highway, rolling out the funds will take much longer.

Supply-side policies

These policies aim at increasing long-run AS and so potential output. Supply-side policies can be divided into market-based policies and interventionist policies. Market-based supply-side policies aim to increase the power of markets and decrease the role of the state. Interventionist supply-side policies rely on the state to improve the production side of the economy.

What are the goals of supply-side policies?

Supply-side policies are long-term policies. Their goals are to:

- expand the productive capacity of the economy and therefore accelerate long-term growth
- increase competition and efficiency in product markets as greater competition leads to more output, lower prices and faster rates of innovation
- decrease labour costs for firms as lower production costs provide the incentive to firms to increase their output
- improve incentives for firms to invest and for people to work
- decrease the risk of inflation and so increase the competitiveness of domestic firms, both abroad and domestically.

Market-based supply-side policies

These are policies that try to decrease the role of the government and focus on product markets, labour markets and incentives.

Supply-side policies related to product markets include the following.

- **Deregulation:** this refers to attempts by the government to decrease the regulations and bureaucracy that businesses face. The aims are to: decrease production costs, leading to higher levels of output; decrease burdensome red tape so that more entrepreneurs are encouraged to start businesses.
- **Privatization:** this refers to the transfer or sale of state-owned assets to the private sector These assets are typically firms but could also be, for example, airports and harbours. The idea is that the profit incentive that private firms have will force them to cut costs and decrease any inefficiencies, while improving the quality of the goods or services offered.

- ***Trade liberalization:*** eliminating policies that protect domestic firms from foreign competition (such as tariffs on imports) is arguably the fastest way to unleash the power of markets and competition. Domestic firms will be forced to cut costs and improve the quality of the products and services they offer.

- *Introducing and enforcing anti-monopoly legislation:* ensuring that collusion of oligopolistic firms and **abuse of monopoly power** are not tolerated allows society to enjoy the benefits of competition.

Supply-side policies related to the labour market include the following.

- *Decreasing or eliminating the minimum wage:* a lower or even no minimum wage decreases production costs of firms and allows them to hire more workers. Higher profitability may increase investment and so increase growth.

- *Reducing the power of labour unions:* labour unions keep wages higher for their members. The result is higher production costs for firms, so they hire fewer workers.

- *Decreasing job security:* high job security for a workforce implies significant costs for firms if they wish to dismiss workers. Decreasing job security would, in theory, enable firms to hire more workers.

- *Decreasing unemployment benefits:* if unemployment benefits are high, they may create the incentive for unemployed individuals to reject job offers and remain unemployed for as long as they are allowed to collect these benefits. Decreasing these benefits will force these individuals to accept a job offer, leading to lower unemployment.

The above measures are referred to as policies that increase labour market flexibility or policies that decrease **labour market rigidities**. You may recall that labour market rigidities are responsible for structural unemployment.

 Internal link

Unemployment is covered in depth in section 3.4.

Incentive-related supply-side policies include the following.

- *Reducing corporate taxes:* this will increase profitability and may lead to more investment and faster growth.

- *Reducing the marginal income tax rate:* in principle this will prompt individuals to work more or persuade more individuals to join the labour market.

- *Reducing capital gains tax:* the capital gains tax is a tax on profits made from selling financial assets, such as stocks, at a price higher than the price at which they were acquired. Reducing this tax may increase financial investments that could indirectly increase growth.

Interventionist supply-side policies

These include increased government spending on:

- better education and training that all can access
- better health care services that all can access
- research and development
- more and better infrastructure.

Why do these interventionist policies increase the LRAS?

Better education and health care services increase the stock of human capital of the economy. Labour productivity (output per worker) increases. The potential output of the economy rises as the LRAS curve shifts to the right.

Investment in research and development leads to better technologies. Improvements in technology are the most significant determinant of long-term growth. With the same resources, long-term growth permits the economy to attain greater levels of output.

Infrastructure is physical capital such as roads, telecommunication and transportation networks, electrical grids, sanitation and sewerage systems. Such capital generates benefits for the whole population. It also decreases the cost of all economic activity. A consequence of more and better infrastructure is an increase in potential output as the LRAS curve shifts to the right.

Industrial policies

Industrial policies are another category of supply-side policies. These are highly interventionist and many consider them counter-productive. Pro-market economists and politicians often overstate what markets alone can achieve and are critical of public action. However, industrial policies have been adopted by most economies at various points in time. There are many economies still employing them although they would not easily admit it. The idea is that the government 'picks winners'; that is, it selects industries that it considers crucial for long-term growth and sets industrial policies what will make doing business in these industries easier, to encourage investment and faster growth. The polices include subsidizing these industries directly or indirectly or providing tax cuts and tax relief. Examples of the industries involved include cement and steel, artificial intelligence and telecommunications (such as 5G technology). Some industrial policies are successful, but some have also been wasteful.

Spillover effects

The distinction between demand-side policies and supply-side policies is not completely fixed; there are spillover effects. There are supply-side effects of certain demand-side policies as well as demand-side effects that certain supply-side policies create. Some examples are given below.

- An increase in government expenditures (G) will lead to an increase in AD as G is a component. If these expenditures are on education, health care, research and development and infrastructure, the supply-side of the economy will be positively affected. So, in the short term, AD will increase but, in the long-term, potential output and the LRAS will increase.

- A decrease in direct taxes (personal or corporate) will increase AD as disposable income and thus consumption will increase, as will investment spending. However, tax cuts may improve incentives so that the supply-side of the economy may also be positively affected.

- Fiscal policy affects AD but if it is prudent (that is, with low budget deficits and sustainable levels of debt) it will also positively affect the supply-side of the economy.

- Monetary policy affects AD but if it achieves and maintains price stability, the supply side of the economy will also be positively affected as firms will tend to invest more.

- All interventionist supply-side policies, such as more spending to increase and improve access to education and health care, or to increase and improve infrastructure, will also increase the short-term AD as (G), a component of AD, will increase.

- An attempt to improve incentives by lowering direct taxes will also increase AD as both C and I may rise due to higher disposable incomes and after-tax profits.

Issues with pro-market supply-side policies

Market-based supply-side policies are very long-term policies. There are several reasons for this.

- These policies are difficult to implement because of vested interests. This refers, for example, to many large businesses that will fight to keep their monopoly power, as more competition will erode their economic profits. Often, large businesses have close ties with members of the government, so some product market supply-side reforms are never implemented.

- Even if a government manages to implement such supply-side policies, they take a very long time to have any effect on the economy. It is interesting to note that supply-side policies are also referred to as structural policies as they principally aim to change structural features of the economy.

- Supply-side policies related to the labour market increase income inequality. Remember that their goals include, for example, decreasing labour costs for businesses by decreasing the minimum wage, weakening the power of labour unions and reducing job security. To the extent that monopoly power in product markets persists, these policies may lead to wages decreasing as a proportion of national income while profits increase. Also, trade liberalization may displace workers in industries that shrink because of foreign competition.

 Search the web

Search for a podcast using these terms: Ostry growth inclusion podcast. What does the Deputy Director of Research at the International Monetary Fund (IMF) say about pro-market supply-side policies and their effect on growth?

Reducing environmental regulations will decrease the production costs of firms but will also adversely impact the environment. For example, reducing regulations on emissions and pollution, on drilling and extraction or on toxic substances and safety may increase several environmental risks.

Issues with interventionist supply-side policies

- Interventionist supply-side policies are also characterized by long time lags as it takes time to obtain the funds for, say, the construction of a new airport and for the positive effects to materialize.

- The necessary increase of government expenditures will add to the national debt. This is why many consider it sensible to start infrastructure projects when there is a deflationary gap, as the risk of inflation is low and low interest rates imply low borrowing costs for the government.

Advantages of supply-side policies

Market-based supply-side policies are considered necessary in economies where the extent of government intervention is very high and is counter-productive. The following issues may affect some economies:

- Labour unions and labour protection policies may lead to high labour costs that damage the competitiveness of domestic products both in the country and abroad.

- Monopoly power in product markets may lead to abuses that hurt competition and society.

- Taxes, both personal and corporate, may prove barriers to work, investment and innovation.

- Market-based supply-side policies may lead to improved resource allocation and encourage greater labour force participation, higher rates of investment and faster growth.

Interventionist supply-side policies are considered most necessary, especially for developing countries, as follows:

- The bigger and better stock of human capital can accelerate growth, decrease poverty and decrease income inequality.

- Interventionist supply-side policies can target specific needs in specific areas of the economy.

Which policy should policy-makers choose?

The choice of policy will depend on the issue that policy-makers are focusing on. Examples are explored below.

Long-term growth

Few would disagree that competitive markets and the profit motive are in the best position to promote long-term growth. Market-based supply-side policies are uniquely suited to unleash the power of markets. Decreasing excessive regulations and administrative costs on businesses can lead to greater levels of output and growth.

Search the web

Search using these terms: deregulation trump environment national geographic. Or search using: climate deregulation trump Reuters. Read about how deregulation may negatively affect the environment.

Decreasing labour costs can have the same effect. Lowering prohibitively high corporate tax rates can lead to more investments and lowering personal tax rates may also lead individuals to choose work over leisure. However, there are risks involved. Deregulation should not benefit the present generation at the cost of future generations and, as Jonathan Ostry writes concerning market-based supply-side policies, "some assessment of their impact not only on the size of the pie, but on the distributional consequences, should be taken into consideration".

Markets cannot reach their full potential if the human capital of the population is low, or if the necessary infrastructure is not present. Interventionist supply-side policies are in this respect a necessary condition for markets to deliver long-term growth. Better education and health care that everyone can access will raise labour productivity and allow firms and the economy to grow. Without a necessary and up-to-date telecommunications, railroad and highway network, firms cannot grow.

It should be understood that markets and the state have complementary roles in the process of long-term growth. In addition, all policies should ensure that the resulting growth is inclusive so that income inequality does not widen to the point where growth is not resilient.

Search the web

Search using these terms: IMF Ostry growth inclusion. You will find a short article on the subject in the IMF F&D magazine.

Inflation

To tackle inflation, tighter monetary policy is required. Remember that the most important goal of the central bank is to achieve and maintain price stability. If it becomes clear that inflationary pressures are rising, the central bank will increase interest rates to calm the economy. In addition, monetary policy has three very important advantages. It is flexible, incremental and reversible. Fiscal policy has none of these advantages. In addition, increasing taxes is politically unpopular and so is decreasing government expenditures. Lastly, monetary policy has shorter time lags compared to fiscal policy. Of course, if inflation was the result of profligate government spending, tighter monetary policy must be accompanied by spending cuts to be more effective.

One may claim that the above is fine if inflation is demand-pull. What if inflation is cost-push? Wouldn't it be logical for the government to use SSPs to try to increase aggregate supply? The answer is no. Why? Because supply side policies take forever to have any effect on the economy and, in the meantime, inflationary expectations will have gone through the roof creating higher and higher inflation. Interventionist SSPs are, of course, not even to be considered as AD would rise, fueling inflation. A tax cut would have the same effect. So, again, it is tighter monetary policy that does the job.

Unemployment

If unemployment is cyclical, then policy-makers will choose expansionary demand-side policies. Typically, they will choose monetary policy because of the advantages discussed earlier. Monetary policy is the 'first responder' to economic distress. Increasing government expenditures will be necessary though if the recession is deep. Lower interest rates may prove inadequate to encourage more borrowing and spending because of low consumer and business confidence. For the same reasons, decreasing taxes may not convince households and firms to spend more. In addition, it is not a good idea to change taxes often because certainty is a necessary characteristic of a good tax system.

If unemployment is structural, then supply-side policies are needed. Displaced workers have to acquire the skills that firms demand and the labour market will require increased flexibility. Improving skills requires education and training while flexibility requires the labour market reforms explained earlier (for example, a lower minimum wage and decreased labour union power).

DP ready | ATL **Thinking, social and communication skills**

One country's economic profile

Work in a small group.

1. Choose a country. Research its present economic condition and the economic challenges it faces, focusing on inflation, unemployment, growth rates and the level of debt as well as the extent of income inequality. Use websites such as countryeconomy.com, tradingeconomics.com, the IMF, the World Bank, and any other site your teacher suggests.

2. Assume that each of you is the chief economic advisor in the country you have chosen. Based on your research, each member of the group recommends short-term and long-term policies. Constructively criticize any differences in recommendations. Reach a consensus.

3. Create posters that communicate your research and your findings to the rest of the class.

Focus point

The toolkit that policymakers have at their disposal includes demand-side policies (fiscal and monetary) and supply-side policies (pro-market and interventionist). Each has advantages and disadvantages. The decision as to which policies or policy mix to use always depends on the particulars each economy faces. A careful consideration of expected short-term and long-term benefits and costs is thus necessary. Policies are crucial for the performance of an economy but also for the livelihoods of ordinary people.

Key terms—test yourself

Define these terms: demand-side policies, fiscal policy, supply-side policies, central bank, commercial banks, Reserve Requirement Ratio (RRR), discount rate, open market operations, quantitative easing, contractionary (tight) monetary policy, expansionary (loose) monetary policy, expansionary fiscal policy, deregulation, privatization, trade liberalization, infrastructure, industrial policies.

The global economy

This unit focuses on issues related to international trade and development. The extensive benefits of free trade are explained, along with acknowledgment that not everyone wins from free trade. The methods and the arguments in favour of and against protection will follow, as well as descriptions of the routes available to countries to liberalize trade. You will also learn the factors that affect the exchange rate of a currency and the basics for understanding the balance of payments of a country. The meaning of economic development is examined, together with the ways in which it can be measured and its relationship to economic growth. Factors that act as barriers to economic growth and development are explored, as well as strategies that developing countries can adopt to promote growth and development.

In this unit you will learn about:

→ benefits gained from free trade

→ why protection exists

→ trade liberalization through two routes: multilateral and regional

→ foreign exchange markets and exchange rates the balance of payments (BOP) and what it means to import too much

→ the distinction between developed and developing countries

→ strategies that developing countries can use to overcome barriers, and promote growth and development.

4.1   WHY TRADE?

In this section you will learn about:

→ the benefits of free trade

→ Adam Smith's theory of absolute advantage and David Ricardo's theory of comparative advantage

→ the limitations of complete specialization.

The issues

Countries import and export goods and services. In this section you will learn about the possible benefits countries may enjoy from engaging in trade and why free trade is considered an engine of growth. You will also learn, through a very simplified model, which goods a country should specialize in and export and, through an example, the gains from specialization. Lastly, this section explores general limitations of this model, and of specialization in particular.

Imagine a country inside an impenetrable dome. There are no imports and no exports. The population can only consume what they produce. This is called **autarky**. This section shows that this is not a desirable situation; there are huge benefits from selling and buying goods and services in world markets.

The benefits of free trade

When there is free trade, firms face increased competition. If monopoly power of domestic firms decreases and competition increases, all the benefits of competition will follow: prices decrease and the quality of the products offered improves. Firms are forced to innovate and to cut costs, becoming more efficient, to withstand competition from imports or to penetrate foreign markets and export more. Consumers will enjoy a greater variety of goods to choose from. Their choice will not be limited to what domestic firms offer.

Domestic producers will be able to find capital goods (machinery, equipment, tools and intermediate products) that more closely meet their exact specification, often at a lower cost, increasing quality and profitability. They will also be able to import any necessary raw materials not available in their country, such as oil, natural gas, timber, ores and minerals. Domestic firms will have access to larger markets, which will allow them to grow in size and possibly benefit from economies of scale. Lower average costs may lead to lower prices, domestically and abroad. This benefit is mostly relevant to firms exporting from small countries with small markets. For example, think of Danish firms being able to export to all of Europe or the world instead of being limited to their domestic markets.

Free trade permits faster transfer of technology. This is because technology is embodied in the capital goods a country imports. The biggest benefit of all is that free trade permits specialization of resources. Specialization leads to greater output and higher levels of consumption.

Specialization, the benefits of more competition, the faster diffusion of technology, the possibility of economies of scale and the increased exports of the country, all permit an economy, especially a developing economy, to experience faster growth. For this reason, trade is referred to as an engine of growth.

Absolute advantage: Adam Smith (HL)

You should be convinced that free trade carries benefits, but a crucial question needs answering. Which goods should a country specialize in and export, and which goods should it import?

Search the web

Search in YouTube using this phrase: role trade growth world bank. Watch the World Bank video on the role of trade in supporting growth and reducing poverty in developing countries.

To answer this question, we will simplify the situation by considering a model with two countries producing two goods. The first explanation relied on Adam Smith's theory of absolute advantage published in 1776. A country has an **absolute advantage** in the production of a good if compared to its trading partner, it can produce more units with the same resources or, equivalently, it can produce a unit of the good using fewer resources. A country should thus specialize in and export that good in which it has an absolute advantage. Table 4.1.1 and Figure 4.1.1 show the production possibilities of two countries, country Red and country Green, each producing two goods: apples and bananas. It is assumed that both countries have the same amount of labour and of capital or, to simplify matters, each country has just one unit of labour. The numbers are the maximum amount of each good that each country can produce if it uses all of its resources in that good's production.

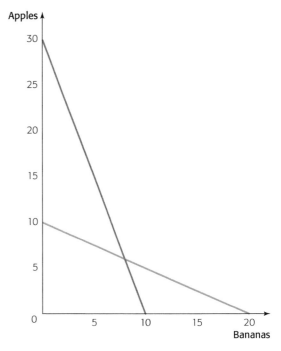

▲ **Figure 4.1.1** Production possibilities for countries Red and Green—illustrating comparative advantage

	Country Red	Country Green
Apple production: maximum	30	10
Banana production: maximum	10	20

▲ **Table 4.1.1** Countries Red and Green apple and banana production—maximum production of each good when using all available resources in that good's production

It should be clear that Red has the absolute advantage in apples, as with the same resources (say, one unit of labour) it can produce 30 apples whereas Green can produce only 10 apples. Green has the absolute advantage in bananas as it can produce 20 bananas while Red can only produce 10 bananas. Red should specialize in and export apples while Green should specialize in and export bananas.

What if one of the countries has the absolute advantage in the production of both goods? What if the production possibilities were as in Table 4.1.2 and Figure 4.1.2.

	Country Red	Country Green
Apple production: maximum	40	60
Banana production: maximum	20	90

▲ **Table 4.1.2** Example production possibilities for Red and Green

In this case, Green (with the same resources) can produce both more apples than Red (60 versus 40) and more bananas (90 versus 20). Green has the absolute advantage in the production of both goods. According to Adam Smith, there is no room for mutually beneficial specialization and exchange.

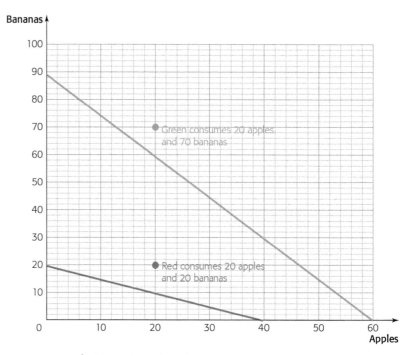

▲ **Figure 4.1.2** Introducing comparative advantage

Comparative advantage: David Ricardo (HL)

In 1817, Ricardo showed that even in the case above there is still room for mutually beneficial specialization and exchange. He showed that what matters is comparative and not absolute advantage. Relative, and not absolute cost of production is important. That means that we should look at the opportunity cost of producing each good for each country. A country has a **comparative advantage** in the production of a good that it can produce at a lower opportunity cost than its trading partner. Table 4.1.3 focuses on which country sacrifices fewer bananas to produce an apple and which country sacrifices fewer apples to produce a banana.

Focusing on country Red	Focusing on country Green	Analysis
It can produce either 40 apples or 20 bananas. If it produces 20 bananas it will sacrifice 40 apples: opportunity cost of 20 bananas = 40 apples. Dividing by 20: **opportunity cost of 1 banana = 2 apples**	It can produce either 60 apples or 90 bananas. If it produces 90 bananas it will sacrifice 60 apples: opportunity cost of 90 bananas = 60 apples. Dividing by 90: **opportunity cost of 1 banana = $^2/_3$ of an apple**	Green can produce a banana at a lower opportunity cost: it needs to sacrifice $^2/_3$ of an apple whereas Red must sacrifice 2 apples. Green has a comparative advantage in banana production: it should specialize in and export bananas.
It can produce either 40 apples or 20 bananas. If it produces 40 apples it will sacrifice 20 bananas: opportunity cost of 40 apples = 20 bananas. Dividing by 40: **opportunity cost of 1 apple = $^1/_2$ of a banana**	It can produce either 60 apples or 90 bananas. If it produces 60 apples it will sacrifice 90 bananas: opportunity cost of 60 apples = 90 bananas Dividing by 60: **opportunity cost of 1 apple = 1.5 bananas**	Red can produce an apple at a lower opportunity cost: it needs to sacrifice $^1/_2$ of a banana whereas Green must sacrifice 1.5 bananas. Red has a comparative advantage in apple production: it should specialize in and export apples.

▲ **Table 4.1.2** Analysis of comparative advantages for Red and Green

We have established which country should produce apples and which should produce bananas. Now, how can they trade and increase their consumption?

Green, which will specialize in bananas, sacrifices two-thirds of an apple to produce one banana, so it will be willing to sell (export) one banana if it earns more than the opportunity cost to produce it (that is, more than two-thirds of an apple). Red will be willing to buy (import) one banana if it can pay less than two apples, which is the opportunity cost Red experiences by producing the banana itself.

A mutually beneficial exchange can occur if the countries trade one banana for one apple.

Green will sell (export) one banana to buy (import) one apple.

Looking at it the other way around leads to the same conclusion: Red will be willing to sell (export) one apple if it earns more than half of a banana, which is the opportunity cost of producing it. So earning one banana for one apple is acceptable. Green will be willing to buy (import) an apple if it pays less than the opportunity cost to produce one, which is one and a half bananas.

Red will sell (export) one apple to buy one banana.

If these two countries trade they will be able to consume combinations of the two goods that are outside their production possibilities. For example, Red can sell (export) 20 apples for 20 bananas. Therefore it could consume 20 apples *and* 20 bananas.

Green can sell (export) 20 bananas for 20 apples. It could therefore consume 70 bananas *and* 20 apples. Both countries can consume outside their production possibilities curves.

Sources of comparative advantage (HL)

Ultimately, comparative advantage depends on:

- the productivity of the country's factors of production
- the level of available technology.

More educated and skilled workers, and labour working with more advanced capital equipment, can produce more output. If technology advances faster in one sector than another, then more can be produced in that sector with the same inputs.

Limitations of the model (HL)

Despite this model being helpful in determining which goods a country should export and which goods it should import, the model does not fully explain actual trade flows. The limitations arise from the underlying assumptions of the model.

- It is assumed that goods are homogeneous. This may be the case for agricultural goods but it is definitely not the case for services or for manufactured goods. For example, both Italy and Germany produce, export and import cars because cars are highly differentiated products. Also, a country may export a good but many of its components may have been imported from a number of countries.

Search the web

Search using this phrase: where is the iphone made?. How many countries are providing and exporting iPhone components to Foxconn, an iPhone assembler, before it is exported from China? Do you think the US or China profit the most from the sale of an iPhone? Search for the answer using these terms: country profits the most iphone.

TOK

What are the advantages and
limitations of models in economics?

- It is assumed that opportunity costs are constant but they are not, as there are often economies of scale.

- It is assumed that factors of production are perfectly mobile, easily switching from producing one good to producing another. This depends on whether labour is geographically and occupationally mobile—but a worker may not have the relevant skills or may not be able to move location.

- It is assumed that there are no transportation costs. Although these costs are often low because of container shipping, this may not always be the case.

- It is assumed that there are no trade barriers but, as we will see, there are plenty of barriers that restrict trade in the world.

Limitations of complete specialization (HL)

A country must diversify, specializing and exporting a wide range of products in order to decrease risks. If a country relies only on tourism then, if something happens that decreases the number of tourists arriving, its export revenues and aggregate demand (AD) will collapse, leading to a recession. If the country relies only on exports of primary products, as some developing countries still do, then a world recession will have devastating effect on exports and real output. In addition, there is greater value added in manufactured products.

> **DP ready** **Research and communication skills**
>
> **Adam Smith and David Ricardo**
>
> 1. In a small group, find out basic information about Adam Smith and David Ricardo. Divide tasks between the people in your group (that is, specialize) to prepare a short presentation.
>
> 2. Present your findings to the rest of the class.

Focus point

One of the few ideas that most, if not all, economists agree on is that free trade is an engine of growth. The theory of comparative advantage is also a most powerful theory explaining why specialization and trade is beneficial, permitting all countries to engage in trade. However, the model cannot explain all actual trade flows because of its assumptions, and complete specialization, as our simple model may suggest, is very risky.

Key terms—test yourself

Define these terms: autarky, absolute advantage, comparative advantage.

4.2 WHY IS THERE PROTECTION?

In this section you will learn about:

→ why protection exists

→ types of protection

→ arguments for and against protection.

The issue

Despite the many benefits of free trade, there is still protection. **Protection** refers to policies that aim to restrict imports into a country. This section analyses several different types of protection and evaluates their impact. It also assesses arguments in favour of and against protection.

Reasons for protection

If the benefits of free trade are so many and so extensive, why do countries often restrict trade using various trade barriers? The simple answer is that in unrestricted trade there are losers as well as winners. The losers are often powerful and willing to fight. Figure 4.2.1 illustrates this point, using the example of the wheat market in a country called Kay.

P_A represents the autarky price (with no trade) and Q_A the autarky quantity. Assume that the price of wheat in the world market is at P_W and that it is below the domestic price P_A. We assume that Kay is a very small country, so the world price P_W is not affected whatever amount Kay produces or consumes. Kay thus faces a perfectly elastic (horizontal) supply curve at P_W.

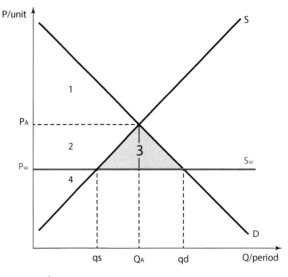

▲ **Figure 4.2.1** The wheat market in Kay

Consumers in Kay are better off with free trade. They consume more ($qd > Q_A$) and pay a lower price ($P_W < P_A$). Producers of wheat in Kay are the losers. They sell less wheat ($qs < Q_A$) at a lower price (P_W).

It is time to apply knowledge of consumer surplus, producer surplus and welfare analysis. You should be able to realize that the consumer surplus increases by areas(2,3) while the producer surplus decreases by area(2). Free trade therefore increases social welfare by area(3)—but domestic producers are worse off. Since they are fewer in number than consumers, they each lose quite a lot of money, so they will be willing to lobby and pressure the government for protection.

Search the web

Search for a podcast using the terms: imf podcast three chief economists. The chief economists of the IMF, the World Bank and the OECD discuss the role of trade liberalization and of advances in digital technology in increasing income inequality within countries, as well as the consequences. Pay attention to what the World Bank chief economist says about winners and losers from free trade.

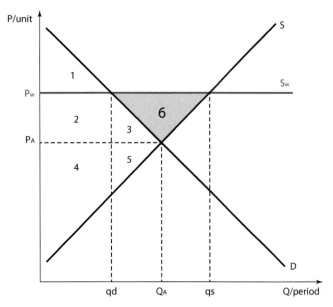

▲ **Figure 4.2.2** The price in the world wheat market is higher than the domestic price

Now assume that the price of wheat in the world market (P_W) is higher than the domestic price P_A. This is shown in Figure 4.2.2.

Now, domestic producers are better off with free trade as they sell more (qs > Q_A) at a higher price (P_W > P_A). Domestic consumers are now the losers. They enjoy less (qd < Q_A) and pay a higher price (P_W > P_A).

In this case, the producer surplus increases by area(2,3,6) while the consumer surplus decreases by area(2,3). Free trade thus increases social welfare by area(6). Domestic consumers are worse off, though. Usually the number of consumers is large (unless the good is a capital good, bought by relatively few firms) and so each suffers a small loss. This means that it is not worth it to them to organize and demand protection.

DP ready **ATL Thinking skills**

Issues relating to free trade

When free trade hurts producers, many are forced to downsize or even close down. Workers lose their jobs. Each of these displaced workers may not have the resources to lobby the government against free trade and in favour of protection, but each one has a vote. When the negatively affected domestic industry, and the resulting unemployment, are concentrated in one or a few areas, these votes may count a lot for representatives of the area and for national elections.

Outline the risks involved.

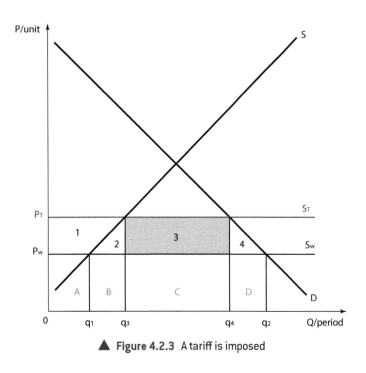

▲ **Figure 4.2.3** A tariff is imposed

Types of protection

Tariffs

The most common form of protection is to impose a **tariff**, which is a tax on imports.

Figure 4.2.3 returns to the market for wheat in Kay and shows the effect of a tariff on imported wheat.

Let's assume that initially there was free trade and that the world price was at P_W. Since Kay is a tiny country, it faces a perfectly elastic (horizontal) supply for wheat at S_W. At that price, Kay's producers will be willing to offer q_1 units of wheat while Kay's consumers will be buying q_2 units of wheat per period. So, the difference $q_2 - q_1$ (that is, distance q_1q_2) will represent imported wheat.

Watch this

Search YouTube using this phrase: "Let's Talk Tariffs". Watch the WTO video you will find.

Assume now that a tariff (P_WP_T) is imposed on imported wheat. As a result, the price of wheat in Kay rises to P_T. The tariff may be imposed on imported wheat but it also allows domestic producers of wheat to sell at the higher price. They now have the incentive to sell more wheat $(q_3 > q_1)$ and so earn more revenues. Consumers are not happy. They pay a higher price (P_T) for wheat and consume less (q_4 units). Imports of wheat, the difference between domestic consumption (q_4) and domestic production (q_3), decrease to (q_3q_4) units. The government collects tariff revenues equal to the tariff (P_WP_T) per unit times the number of units (q_3q_4) imported. This is equal to area(3).

You should realize that the consumer surplus decreased by area(1,2,3,4) while the producer surplus increased by area(1). The tariff led to a welfare loss equal only to area(2,4) because area(3) represents the tariff revenues collected by the government which could be spent on schools, for example, and so cannot be considered a welfare loss for Kay. Area(2) represents the resulting production inefficiency and area(4) the consumption inefficiency.

Spending on imports (the import bill) before the tariff was area(B + C + D) while after the tariff it shrunk to area(C). Remember that the tariff is paid by Kay's consumers and that area(3) is not paid to the foreign exporters but is collected by the domestic government.

DP ready ATL **Thinking skills**

Impact of the wheat tariff in Kay

Refer to Figure 4.2.3.

1. Determine the increase in the revenues Kay's producers collect because of the tariff.

2. Using PED, explain why we cannot be sure whether Kay's consumers spend more or less on wheat as a result of the tariff.

 TOK

Figure 4.2.3 suggests that it is straightforward to measure not only who gains and who loses from tariffs but also by how much. To what extent do you agree with this?

DP ready ATL **Thinking and research skills**

Tariffs on various products

1. Listen to the Planet Money podcast "Tariffied". Search using these terms: Planet money episode 835 tariffied. You will hear about an American pig farmer whose pigs lost 10% of their value as a result of the Chinese tariffs imposed, as pork prices dropped in the US. Why did US pork prices drop when China imposed a tariff on US pork products? Hint: think of demand and supply and the size of China.

2. Since protectionist policies increase output of domestic firms, it means that more jobs are created. Is the employment effect on the country necessarily positive, though? Think of tariffs on imported steel. Who buys steel and for what reason?

3. Research online using these terms: US tariffs Canadian paper. You will find several articles. Using one or more of these, outline the impact of this tariff on the newspaper industry and other industries that use paper as an input.

DP ready ATL **Thinking and communication skills**

Analysis of articles on tariffs

Find and read the following articles:

"Import Tariffs Squeeze Small Businesses Here and Elsewhere" by J Podsada

"The Limits of 'Made in America' Economics" by A Lowrey

"New China Tariffs Increase Costs to U.S. Households" by M Amiti et al.

1. Working in small groups, write a summary of the main points made by each article.

2. Groups present their findings to the rest of the class and participate in a class discussion.

Quotas

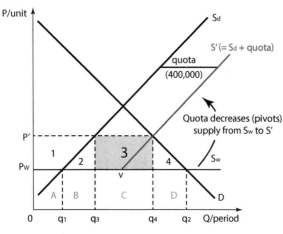

▲ **Figure 4.2.4** A quota is imposed

Another form of protection is to impose a **quota**—a quantitative restriction of imports. For example, the EU rule in place in 2019 permitted only 228,389 tons of sheep meat and goat meat to be imported from New Zealand annually and 6600 tons of duck meat from China.

Figure 4.2.4 illustrates the effect of a quota on the market for wheat in country Kay. This will help to analyse the impact of a quota compared with that of a tariff.

Once again, initially assume free trade and that the world price was at P_W. Kay is a very small country so it faces a perfectly elastic (horizontal) supply for wheat at S_W. At P_W Kay producers offer q_1 units and Kay consumers buy q_2 units of wheat per period. The distance q_1q_2 represents the quantity of imported wheat.

To make matters simple, assume that a quota is set equal to half of distance q_1q_2. So, if distance q_1q_2 was 800,000 tons of wheat per year, the quota was set at 400,000 tons of wheat per year. This means that Kay allows only 400,000 tons of wheat to be imported from abroad. Kay no longer faces an infinitely (horizontal) elastic supply as it cannot import as much as its consumers perhaps would like. At each price the amount supplied in the domestic market will be equal to whatever its domestic firms are willing to offer plus the quota (for example, plus 400,000 tons). Figure 4.2.4 is a simple supply and demand diagram that shows this. The effective supply of wheat is now S' and it is drawn parallel to the domestic supply of wheat S_d and to its right by the amount of the quota (here, by 400,000 tons). To draw this, find the midpoint of q_1q_2 and lightly trace a vertical line to S_W to point v. From point v on S_W, now draw a parallel to S_d. The new, effective supply of wheat for Kay is S' (or more precisely, P_WvS').

Note that supply with free trade was at S_W. Now, it has pivoted to S', as the quantity that can be imported was restricted; S_d was just the domestic supply. As a result of the decrease in supply, the price of wheat in Kay will increase to P'. More will be produced domestically ($q_3 > q_1$) and less will be consumed ($q_4 < q_2$). Up to now, the analysis is the same as the one for tariffs.

The difference is that with a quota the government collects no revenue. Area(3) is known as "quota rents" and is typically collected by foreign exporting firms who can sell now in Kay at a higher price only because of the quantitative restriction of imports.

Concerning welfare: the consumer surplus decreases by area(1,2,3,4) and the producer surplus increases by area(1), illustrating that consumers are worse off and producers of wheat better off. Since area(3) is not collected by the government and is typically collected by foreign firms, it is also part of the welfare loss. The welfare loss of a quota is therefore equal to area(2,3,4) and is bigger than the welfare loss resulting from a tariff. Area(2) reflects the production inefficiency, area(4) the consumption inefficiency and area(3) the quota rents that foreigners capture.

DP ready ATL **Thinking and communication skills**

Tariff versus quota

1. If you were one of the foreign exporting firms, would you prefer Kay to impose a tariff or a quota on your product, and why?

2. A protectionist measure invites retaliation. Your country is thinking of imposing a trade barrier to protect a domestic industry but you want to minimize the probability of retaliation by your trading partner. Explain whether you would advise for a tariff or a quota.

3. "The effects on imports of a tariff on the quantity of imports are less certain than that of a quota."

   a. To what extent do you agree with this statement?

   b. Outline the connection here with price elasticities.

4. Prepare a poster that illustrates with one diagram the effects of a tariff and the effects of an equivalent quota (one that leads to the same quantity of imports). Clearly indicate who wins and who loses in each case. Make sure you also incorporate foreign exporting firms in your analysis.

Subsidies

Subsidies lower production costs and increase supply. In an open economy with trade and imports, the increased domestic supply decreases import penetration. Figure 4.2.5 is a simple demand and supply diagram that illustrates the expected effects of a subsidy in this context.

Focusing once again on the wheat market in the small country Kay, we assume that the world price is at P_W and Kay has a perfectly elastic supply of wheat at S_W. Kay's farmers offer q_1 units at P_W while q_2 units are consumed. The difference, q_1q_2, reflects the quantity of wheat that Kay imports. The subsidy (ab) that the government of Kay pays to its wheat farmers, decreases their production costs and increases their supply to S_s. They are now willing to offer more wheat at P_W. Quantity supplied by Kay farmers increases to q_3. Since the price in Kay remains at P_W, consumption of wheat is not affected but the quantity imported decreases to q_3q_2. Farmers in Kay are better off. They sell more wheat ($q_3 > q_1$) and they earn more per unit: they earn the world price P_W plus the subsidy by the government. Since the subsidy is the vertical distance between the two supply curves, they now earn P_p. Their total revenues increase from area(A) to area(A,B,1,2). Consumer expenditures on wheat

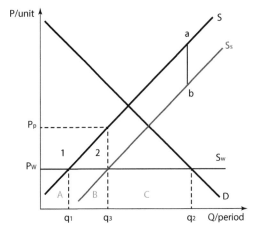
▲ **Figure 4.2.5** The effect of a subsidy

are the same as the price they pay (P_w) and they still consume q_2 units, so spending remains at area(A,B,C). The cost of the subsidy to the government is the quantity subsidized ($0q_3$) times the per unit subsidy ($P_w P_p$) or area(1,2).

Concerning welfare: the consumer surplus is unchanged, so consumers are not adversely affected if a subsidy is used to protect domestic producers from import competition. The producer surplus increases by area(1). Since the cost of the subsidy is area(1,2) there is a welfare loss equal to area(2). This represents the production inefficiency that results from the subsidy. There is no consumption inefficiency.

DP ready   ATL **Thinking skills**

Subsidy versus tariff or quota

Using your knowledge and appropriate diagrams explain why:

1. paying a subsidy to domestic firms as a method of protection may be preferable to a tariff or a quota

2. a quota may minimize the probability of retaliation

3. tariffs may be preferable for a developing country that needs to construct more schools.

Administrative barriers

An important principle in international trade states that any product exported must meet the requirements of the importing country. **Administrative barriers** are the bureaucracy (known as "red tape"), or the health, safety or environmental requirements, aimed to restrict the flow of imports.

Documents have to be prepared, shipments are subject to inspections, and imports have to clear customs. All of this administration is costly and decreases the volume of trade. Some of the health and safety regulations claim to protect consumers, but are actually meant to slow down the flow of imports. A famous example of excessive red tape used for this purpose happened in 1982. It is known as the Poitiers effect.

 Search the web

1. Search the web to find out why there is a trade issue between the UK and the US concerning chlorinated chicken.

2. Search for: car safety trade 533 npr. Listen to podcast #533 by Planet Money on why car safety is a trade barrier.

3. Search using these terms: latest Poitiers Lewis nyt.
   Read a *New York Times* article (14 January 1983) about how France tried to limit the imports of video cassette players from Japan.

Arguments for protection

There are several arguments in favour of protection. Let's look at the most common. Remember that protection creates winners, which are invariably found in the protected industries.

■ Protection creates jobs. Politicians love this argument as it is seemingly always true, and it attracts positive headlines. Protecting an industry will increase output and employment will probably increase. However, if the protected product is an input (such as steel) that other domestic industries use (such as the construction industry), then their production costs will increase, decreasing their supply. Jobs may be lost in these domestic industries. The jobs that are lost are not as visible as the jobs gained, so politicians usually escape criticism.

■ Protection is required to create a "level playing field" when competition from abroad is considered unfair. It is often claimed that foreign cheap labour is responsible when domestic firms cannot compete. The validity of this is questionable because if the higher domestic wages are not a result of higher labour productivity, then the domestic industry has a comparative disadvantage and should be importing the product. In different circumstances, foreign governments sometimes assist their country's businesses with subsidies—sometimes illegal ones— to increase export penetration, in this way hurting the domestic industry. In these cases, protection may be justified.

■ If there is indeed unfair competition from abroad, and imports flood the market, then the domestic government can claim that dumping is taking place. Dumping is when a firm sells abroad at a price below average cost or below the price it charges in its home country. In these cases, anti-dumping tariffs that equate the foreign price to the domestic price are imposed and the World Trade Organization (WTO) settles the dispute.

TOK

An argument used by President Trump in 2018 for imposing tariffs on steel imports was that these imports posed a "national security threat" to the US.

Watch this

Watch the following two videos. Search YouTube using the terms:

Trump tariffs are about national security PBS newshour.

Or search using: Steel tariffs national security issue fox news.

There are two sides to every argument. In a small group, debate the merits of each side using reason and evidence to support your position.

DP ready | ATL **Research and thinking skills**

Turkey's steel quotas

Find out why Turkey imposed quotas on steel imports in October 2018.

1. Do you support Turkey's decision?

2. Are there risks in declaring that emergency "safeguard" measures are required?

■ In developing countries with high rates of poverty and ineffective tax collection, the revenue that governments earn from tariffs may be important.

■ Protection may also be used to correct a growing trade deficit. If import expenditures are much higher than export revenues, protection can be employed to decrease imports. This is risky because any correction comes at the expense of trading partners, who may retaliate.

- Administrative barriers are necessary for valid safety, health and environmental considerations. The problem is how to reach a decision on the validity of the claim.

- Trade barriers may be erected to help establish a new industry that has not grown sufficiently large to benefit from economies of scale or to have acquired the necessary know-how needed to compete in open world markets. This is the "infant industry" argument and it has been used by all countries. It makes economic sense to support the growth of infant industries, but often the problem is that, as the industry grows, so does its political power. Some governments have proven to be unable or unwilling to withdraw support for fear of losing votes or because of powerful vested interests. This can result in inefficient "perpetual infant" businesses.

Arguments against protection

- Protection increases prices for domestic buyers of the good. Buyers can be households; they will suffer a decrease in their purchasing power. Buyers can also be other firms; they will face increased production costs. Higher production costs lead to lower levels of output and employment. If the protected product is an input, such as steel, the higher production costs for firms in other industries will force them to raise their prices, making them less competitive in export markets.

- Protection of an industry may breed inefficiency as it faces less competition.

- Consumer choice is reduced if an imported product is more expensive.

- Protection causes an increase in output that is inefficient.

- Protection results in misallocation of domestic and world resources.

Focus point

Should there be free trade or protection? Predictably, the answer is, it depends. In general, trade liberalization since the Second World War has produced immense benefits for the world. Free trade has indeed been an engine of growth.

However, in free trade there are also losers. Businesses that cannot withstand import competition may shut down. Workers will be displaced. Freeing up trade may have to be a gradual process in order for governments to ensure that resources can be reallocated in other areas. Most importantly, there should be sufficient care that the displaced workers acquire new skills. Protection, if needed, should be temporary and not a result of pressure from vested interests.

Search the web

Search using these terms: why open markets matter OECD.

Read the article, which gives supporting data on the benefits of trade.

TOK

Does freeing up trade involve moral issues? Should policy-makers be guided by moral judgments in their policy prescriptions?

Key terms—test yourself

Define these terms: protection, tariff, quota, administrative barriers.

4.3 BIG GROUPS, LITTLE GROUPS

In this section you will learn about:

→ preferential trade agreements
→ the role of the World Trade Organization (WTO)
→ regional trading blocs (or agreements)
→ trade creation and trade diversion.

The issue

Free trade may have both winners and losers but the net effect on countries is positive and trade also accelerates growth. Historically, free trade has not been the norm; as mentioned in section 4.2, serious efforts started after the Second World War to achieve **economic integration** (when countries progressively decrease or eliminate trade and other barriers to the free movement of goods, services, capital and labour) and trade liberalization. **Trade liberalization** (the process of moving from protection to free trade) has two routes: the multilateral route through the World Trade Organization (WTO) and the regional route through the formation of regional trading blocs. This section explains these routes and their effects.

Preferential trade agreements

A **preferential trade agreement** is any agreement between countries that lowers trade barriers. If the trade agreement is:

- between two countries it is a **bilateral agreement**
- between several, usually neighbouring, countries it is referred to as a regional agreement
- between several countries that may not be in the same region it is referred to as a plurilateral agreement
- between many countries through the WTO, it is a **multilateral agreement**.

Big groups

The World Trade Organization (WTO)

The **WTO** was established in 1995. It is the successor of the GATT (General Agreement on Tariffs and Trade), a 1947 agreement between 23 countries to promote free trade by phasing out or eliminating tariffs and other trade barriers. The WTO currently has 164 members representing roughly 98% of world trade. GATT and the WTO agreements are known as multilateral agreements and are anchored on the **Most-Favoured Nation (MFN) principle** that requires every member country to treat all other member countries as it treats it most-favoured trading partner, effectively not allowing discrimination.

What does the WTO do?

- The WHO provides a forum for trade negotiations that cover goods, services and intellectual property.

- It ensures that agreements are implemented and adhered to by requiring that national trade policies are transparent and by carrying out periodic reviews.

- It provides additional assistance to developing countries to build their technical expertise and their trade capacity.

- It is the arbitrator of trade-related disputes. This means that disagreements or grievances are settled within the WTO. The seven-member **Appellate Body** makes the final decision, which all parties in any dispute must accept.

Evaluating the WTO

The GATT, and its successor the WTO, have been quite successful in decreasing trade barriers over the past 70 years or so. This has resulted in world trade growing dramatically. According to OECD and World Bank data, world trade (sum of exports and imports) as a percentage of world output (gross world product) has increased from roughly 25% in 1960 to almost 60% in 2017.

However, the greatest benefit resulting from the WTO is that, as an institution, it has established rules and order in the trading world and so has managed to decrease uncertainty. Rules are enforced because members have agreed that the WTO has the authority to impose sanctions on the parties that lose in a dispute.

The Appellate Body, the "supreme court" of the WTO, consists of 7 judges whose four-year appointment has to be accepted by all 164 members, each with the right to veto a nomination. The US has recently been blocking the appointment of new judges, and by the end of 2019, there were only two judges left. There is the risk that the dispute settlement system of the WTO will be paralyzed, ending 23 years of resolution enforcement that prevented countries from resorting to trade protection.

The WTO proved instrumental in preventing national governments from resorting to escalating trade protection in response to the 2008–09 recession following the global financial crisis. Members, bound by the rules of the WTO, did not resort to raising tariffs and quotas to appease domestic political pressure.

Of course, the WTO has been subjected to plenty of criticism. With 164 members it is very difficult and time consuming to reach an agreement. The WTO has been accused that it lacks transparency in its decision-making and that it has mostly catered to the needs of advanced economies, neglecting those of the developing world. It has also been accused of paying insufficient attention to the displacement of labour that trade liberalization unavoidably brings about, as well as to rising income inequality issues. According to critics, it also does not sufficiently consider the possible adverse effects of trade liberalization on the environment and it has not been sufficiently concerned about the issue of child labour.

Search the web

Search using these terms: transcript showdown at the WTO npr. Listen to the transcript to understand, in simple terms, the WTO arbitration process, as well as the risks faced.

TOK

The WTO has been accused of not paying sufficient attention to child labour issues and to production processes in so-called "sweatshops" (to learn more, search for this term online). A question of ethics is involved. Should child labour be banned? Could that deprive the poor of a source of much-needed income, hurting the very people it aims to help? Should a "fair" wage be set across developing countries? Could establishing a "fair" wage in a developing country lead to a decrease in its exports and so to slower growth? Is any job better than no job?

Few would disagree that the WHO's net effect on world welfare has been positive. It would be truly frightening if there were no international body regulating the rules of world trade.

Little groups

Regional trading blocs (or agreements)

Bilateral or plurilateral (involving several but not all WTO countries) agreements exist between groups of usually neighbouring countries that wish to decrease protection and integrate further within the group. By definition this implies departing from the Most-Favoured Nation (MFN) WTO principle. These agreements are known as **regional trading blocs (or agreements)**. Under the WTO they are allowed as long as trade within the bloc is essentially free and that barriers against non-members are not increased.

According to the WTO, in 2019 there were 294 regional trade agreements (RTAs) in force. There has been a proliferation of RTAs because such agreements are faster to achieve and because of growing demand for deeper integration between countries.

Watch this

Search for: let's talk WTO on wto.org. Watch the short video on why the WTO is important.

Types of trading bloc

- **Free trade agreement or area (FTA):** when a group of countries agrees to phase out or eliminate trade barriers between them, while each maintains its own tariff (or trade barriers) toward non-members. An FTA requires "rules of origin" to prevent non-members shipping goods into the area through the country with the lowest external tariff. For example, it may be required that at least 80% of the components of a laptop are manufactured within the group to qualify for 0% tariff.

- **Customs union:** an FTA may evolve into a customs union if, in addition, members agree to a common external tariff or, more generally, to a common trade policy toward non-members.

- **Common market:** a customs union may evolve into a common market if, in addition to the free flow of goods and services within member countries, there is also free flow of inputs—that is, of capital (cross-border investments) and free flow of labour (citizens of a member country can work in any other member country).

The highest form of integration is for the bloc to evolve into an economic and possibly to a monetary union. Members of an **economic union** share common regulatory policies (on, for example, competition issues), as well as other policies such as on climate, the environment, health, security, justice and migration. Members of a **monetary union** in addition adopt a common currency and share a common central bank.

Examples of regional trading blocs or agreements (RTBs)

- Free trade area (FTA): the prime example is the USMCA (United States, Mexico and Canada) agreement which is expected to come into force by the end of 2019. It is referred to as the new

NAFTA (the 1994 North American Free Trade Agreement). Another example is the ASEAN Free Trade Area. This has been recently established by the original ASEAN 6 (Brunei Darussalam, Indonesia, Malaysia, the Philippines, Singapore and Thailand) and the newer members (Cambodia, Laos, Myanmar and Viet Nam).

- Customs union: the Southern African Customs Union (SACU), which includes Botswana, Lesotho, Namibia, South Africa and Eswatini, was established in 1910 and is the world's oldest customs union. The European Union was initially a customs union when, in July 1968, the six member countries of the European Economic Community (EEC) (Belgium, Germany, France, Italy, Luxembourg and the Netherlands) eliminated all customs duties between them and adopted a common external tariff.

- Common market: the European customs union transformed into a common market in 1993 when adopting the four freedoms of movement of goods, services, people and money.

There are other RTBs that you should perhaps be aware of, such as MERCOSUR, COMESA and CPTPP.

Evaluating RTBs

Advantages of RTBs

- It is much easier for a country to reach an agreement when negotiating with just a few other countries rather than with 163 other countries within the WTO.

- As the number of member countries is smaller than the WTO members, RTBs can go further than they would have within a multilateral agreement. RTBs have started to cover areas such as investment and labour movement, competition issues, intellectual **property rights**, e-commerce and anti-corruption efforts that a country alone cannot deal with.

- For smaller countries, membership in an RTB permits its firms to access a larger market, giving them the opportunity to grow, achieve economies of scale and become more competitive.

- If there is free movement of labour within an RTB then employment opportunities increase, resulting in less unemployment.

- Countries enjoy greater bargaining power in negotiations. This is especially true for smaller countries but even a large country such as France has more bargaining power in negotiations with, for example, the US, if it is negotiating through the EU.

- If the RTB leads to increased prosperity then greater political stability may follow.

Disadvantages of RTBs

- A country will sacrifice to various degrees its sovereignty, as some decisions will either be a compromise or will be made outside the country.

Search the web

Go to https://rtais.wto.org and click on the right-hand side: "search RTAs".

In "coverage of agreement" select goods; in "signatories" select any country, then add to your search as in the following example. If you select India, in "region" select "West Asia", and then "extra regional". The results will be quite a few trade agreements.

DP ready ATL **Research skills**

Your country's trade agreements

Using the procedure described in "Search the web" above, explore https://rtais.wto.org to see agreements your country has signed.

■ RTBs may prove discriminatory against smaller, often developing, countries. For example, in bilateral trade negotiations, when large economies such as the EU, the US or China negotiate with smaller countries, the latter are in a weaker position to defend their trade interests.

■ A major criticism of RTBs and their proliferation is that they undermine multilateral trade liberalization through the WTO. The latest WTO Doha round of trade negotiations was launched in 2001 but as of late 2019 had yet to reach an agreement.

Trade creation and trade diversion (HL)

Whether a RTB improves or decreases welfare depends on whether such an agreement leads to more trade creation than trade diversion.

Since tariffs and other trade barriers between members are lowered, each of these economies can more fully exploit any comparative advantage they have. Production switches from higher to lower cost members, allowing more imports from these lower cost members. This is referred to as **trade creation**.

However, the agreement may lead to imports being switched away from a more efficient non-member to a less efficient member. Why? The member becomes artificially cheaper because tariffs are eliminated within the group but maintained with outsiders. This is referred to as **trade diversion**.

Focus point

Trade liberalization may proceed either through the World Trade Organization or through Regional Trading Blocks. The WTO has been instrumental in advancing freer trade and, therefore, in promoting growth. But it has also been criticized on many grounds, for example, that its deliberations are not transparent, that it caters more to the interests of the advanced economies or that it neglects labour or environmental issues.

Regional agreements have proliferated and are also successful in advancing the interests of many countries as it is easier within a smaller group to reach consensus on more issues. But they may prove a stumbling block to the efforts of the WTO for achieving multilateral agreements.

Key terms—test yourself

Define these terms: economic integration, trade liberalization, preferential trade agreements, bilateral agreement, multilateral agreement, the World Trade Organization (WTO), Most-Favoured Nation (MFN) principle, Appellate Body (of the WTO), regional trading bloc or agreement (RTB), free trade agreement (FTA), customs union, common market, economic union, monetary union, trade creation, trade diversion.

In this section you will learn about:

→ foreign exchange markets

→ exchange rate systems—floating (or flexible), fixed and managed systems

→ factors affecting exchange rates

→ managed exchange rates and disequilibrium exchange rates

→ the consequences of changes in the exchange rate on inflation, economic growth, unemployment, the current account balance and living standards.

The issue

The exchange rate of a currency is perhaps the most important price in an economy. When it changes, it affects almost everything and everyone. Being a price, it is determined in a free market by demand and supply. This section helps you to understand the factors that affect the demand and the supply of a currency in the foreign exchange market (also known as the forex market). There is also an explanation of the consequences of changes in the exchange rate on the economy.

Foreign exchange markets

The exchange rate is determined in the foreign exchange (forex) market, which operates on a 24-hour basis, 365 days a year. The **exchange rate** of a currency is its price expressed in terms of another currency. For example, on 12 July 2019 €1.00 = $1.1288, so you needed $1.1288 to buy one euro. If we divide both sides by 1.1288 we get the price of a dollar expressed in terms of the euro, or $1.00 = €0.8859. You should realize that the one is the inverse of the other—if the euro value goes up with respect to the dollar, then this means that the dollar value of the euro went down. You should also realize that whoever is buying euros in the foreign exchange market is at the same time also selling dollars and vice versa.

DP ready | ATL **Research and thinking skills**

Exchange rates

1. Find the exchange rate of the currency of your country today against a number of major world currencies. Find the same exchange rates a month earlier.

    a. Has your currency increased or decreased in value during this period?

    b. Calculate the percentage change.

For question 2, use the currency calculator at x-rates.com. It provides more decimal places for greater accuracy in your conversions.

2. Start with US$1000 and visit the following countries sequentially. Spend nothing but exchange your money every time you visit a new country. Go from the US to the UK then France, Egypt, Turkey, South Korea, Indonesia, Australia and finally New Zealand.

    a. Explain whether the number of units of one currency needed to buy another reflects anything about the "strength" of a currency. Do prices of goods and services in each country matter?

    b. Compare the value of a currency today with its value a year earlier. Explain whether the terms "strengthening" or "weakening" make more sense in this case.

Exchange rate systems

There are three different exchange rate systems within which exchange rates are determined: floating (or flexible), fixed and managed exchange rate systems.

- A currency is traded in a **floating (or flexible) exchange rate system** if there is no government or central bank intervention in the market.

- In a **fixed exchange rate system** the price of the currency is set by the government and maintained at that level through appropriate central bank intervention.

- In a **managed exchange rate system**, the exchange rate is allowed to float but there is periodic intervention by the authorities whenever the direction or speed of change is considered undesirable. The frequency of such interventions of course varies. Most currencies are traded using this system (also called a "managed float" system).

Factors affecting exchange rates

Imagine the forex market where only UK pounds and US dollars are bought and sold by the participants of this market. Who would demand and buy pounds in this market and what for? Who will supply and sell pounds in this market and what for?

Pounds are demanded by people for many reasons.

- People in countries with other currencies want to buy UK goods and services (that is, UK exports). If Americans are buying UK

Search the web

Exchange rates of major currencies may change by the minute or even every second. Search the web using: live foreign exchange rates. Add any two major world currencies to your search string to find a site that shows charts with live changes. For example, for sites that give you rates by the minute, search using: live forex rupees to dollar. Or search using: live forex yen to dollar.

goods and services, then US dollars will have to be sold so that UK pounds can be bought. An American attending the London School of Economics will have to exchange her US dollars to UK pounds to pay for tuition. The UK is exporting education services to her.

■ Some people want to make investments into the UK (for example, they want to buy UK bonds or stocks, to make deposits in pounds, to buy a UK firm or to establish a new firm in the UK). If an American wants to make deposits in UK pounds, he will have to buy UK pounds with his US dollars. The same applies if he wants to buy UK bonds, shares or a UK company, or if he wants to set up a factory in the UK.

■ Some people want to buy UK pounds now, hoping to sell these later at a higher price and make a profit. These people are referred to as speculators and they can make or lose a lot of money.

Pounds are supplied by people for many reasons.

■ People need pounds in order to import US goods and services. A UK firm buying (importing) shirts from the US company Abercrombie & Fitch will have to sell UK pounds to buy the necessary US dollars for the purchase.

■ Some people want to make investments into the US (for example, they want to buy US bonds or shares, to buy a US firm or to establish a new firm in the US). A British investor wishing to take advantage of higher US interest rates on dollar deposits will have to sell UK pounds to buy the necessary US dollars to make the deposit.

Trade flows and cross-border investment flows give rise to most of the demand and supply of a currency. There are also other reasons for trading currency in the foreign exchange market. Consider, for example, a Mexican migrant worker in the US who sends money to his family in Mexico every month. Money that migrants send to their country of origin is referred to as **remittances**. This worker needs to sell US dollars to buy Mexican pesos. Now consider a US corporation earning profits in India. If it repatriates its profits, it will need to sell Indian rupees to buy US dollars.

 Internal link

Section 4.5 on a country's balance of payments (BOP) has more information.

Focusing now on the US dollar–UK pound market, Figure 4.4.1 shows the equilibrium exchange rate for the UK pound expressed in terms of US dollars.

Since Figure 4.4.1 focuses on the exchange rate of the UK pound with respect to the US dollar, the vertical (y-axis) is the price of the pound and the horizontal (x-axis) is the quantity of pounds traded per period. On the y-axis the price of the pound is expressed in US dollars so it gives US dollars per one UK pound or $/£.

Demand for pounds (for UK exports and financial and other investment flows into the UK) is equal to the supply of pounds (reflecting UK imports and investment flows out of the UK) at the exchange rate e_1; say, \$1.26 per pound.

Now let's ignore investment flows between the two countries. Instead, imagine that only export and import flows affect demand and supply for the pound and thus its exchange rate.

Looking at Figure 4.4.2, assume that the exchange rate is at e'. At e' the value of UK exports is equal to (e'a). This is because at e' foreigners demand (e'a) pounds to buy UK goods and services, the value of which is (e'a). The value of UK imports is equal to (e'b). This is because at e', (e'b) pounds are offered to buy imports valued at (e'b). Since the value of imports exceeds the value of exports, we say that the UK has a trade deficit equal to distance (ab). A trade deficit exists if expenditures on imports of goods and services (M) exceed revenues from the export of goods and services(X)—or if M > X.

This distance also reflects the excess supply for UK pounds in the foreign exchange market. If there is excess supply in a market then the price, in this case the exchange rate, will tend to fall. The term used to describe a decrease in the exchange rate in a floating exchange rate system is depreciation.

This depreciation of the pound makes UK goods and services cheaper in the US. UK exports become more competitive abroad and will tend to increase. At the same time, US products become more expensive in the UK when their dollar price is expressed in pounds. UK imports become less attractive and will tend to decrease. So, as the pound depreciates, more pounds will be demanded and fewer will be supplied; the trade deficit shrinks until the exchange rate reaches e_1.

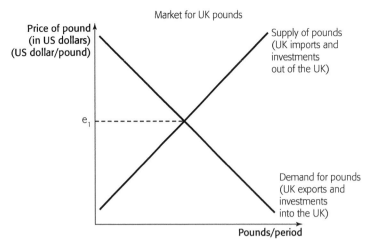

▲ **Figure 4.4.1** Equilibrium exchange rate for the UK pound against the US dollar

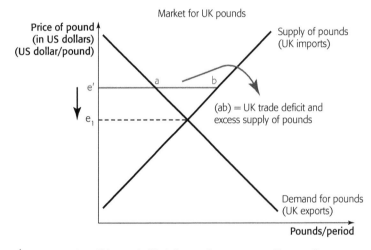

▲ **Figure 4.4.2** UK pound–US dollar market: export and import flows

DP ready ATL Thinking skills

Analysis of an exchange rate

Analyse what would happen if the exchange rate was below e_1. Explain why the price of the pound would increase or, using the correct term, appreciate, and reach e_1.

Changes in demand and supply for a currency

As explained above, the demand for and the supply of a currency reflect trade flows. If exports of, for example, Egypt increase, the demand for the Egyptian pound will increase and shift to the right, leading to an increase in its price. The Egyptian pound will appreciate. If Egypt's exports for some reason decrease, then the opposite will occur.

If Egypt starts importing more goods, more Egyptian pounds will be offered to buy these goods as Egyptian importers buy more foreign currency. The supply of Egyptian pounds will increase and shift to the right, decreasing the value of the Egyptian pound. The Egyptian pound will depreciate. The opposite will happen if Egypt starts to import less.

The demand for, and the supply of a currency also reflect cross-border investment flows. These include portfolio investments and foreign direct investments (FDI). **Portfolio investments** include the buying and selling of stocks and bonds as well as deposits across borders. They are short-term financial capital investments. FDI refers to buying a controlling interest in an existing foreign firm or establishing a new presence abroad, so it is a long-term investment. When foreigners buy South Korean bonds or shares, the demand for the Korean won increases and shifts to the right. The won will appreciate. If investors become worried about the outlook of the Malaysian economy, many may sell their Malaysian assets (such as shares and bonds), increasing the supply of ringgit and shifting the supply of ringgit to the right. The ringgit will depreciate.

Currency speculation and remittances

Currency speculators buy and sell currencies to make a profit by fluctuations in the value of currencies. Currency speculation is mostly responsible for the continuous ups and downs seen in any currency chart. If currency speculators expect the Turkish lira to appreciate, they may buy Turkish liras hoping to sell them later at a profit. The demand for Turkish liras will rise and the lira will indeed appreciate. This is an example of "self-fulfilling expectations".

Remittances flowing into a country will tend to appreciate the currency. An increase in remittances flowing into Bangladesh will increase the demand for the Bangladeshi taka as migrant workers living and working in the eurozone will sell euros to buy taka to send to their families.

 TOK

Currency speculation may lead to sharp movements in the exchange rate of a country. As outlined later in this section, movements in the exchange rate may disrupt an economy and adversely affect living standards. Is there an ethical basis to limit currency speculation?

 Search the web

Visit the Migration Data Portal at migrationdataportal.org. Click on the Data drop-down menu and then on the Development tab on the left-hand side of the page. Read information about remittances that your country receives and/or pays as well as other migration-related information.

Illustrating changes in currency demand and supply

Figures 4.4.3a and 4.4.3b show, as an example, the effect on the Swiss franc of an outflow of financial capital from the eurozone. If investors who own euro deposits and bonds lose confidence in the euro, they will start selling euros and buying safer Swiss francs and Swiss assets. Figure 4.4.2a focuses on the euro and shows the sale of euros and its effect on the price of the euro. Figure 4.4.2b focuses on the Swiss franc and shows the purchase of Swiss francs and its effect on the price of the Swiss franc. Notice that the euro depreciated from e_1 to e_2 which implies that the Swiss franc appreciated from $(1/e_1)$ to $(1/e_2)$.

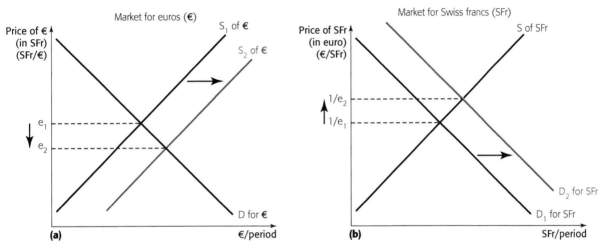

▲ **Figure 4.4.3 a and b** The effect on the Swiss franc of an outflow of euros

Factors influencing trade and cross-border investment flows

You have learned that changes in trade flows and in cross-border investment flows affect the exchange rate. The factors that influence trade flows and cross-border investment flows are explained below. If these factors change, the exchange rate will change.

To recap: the exchange rate depends on the demand for and the supply of the currency. The demand and the supply of a currency mostly reflect trade flows and cross-border investment flows.

Therefore, factors affecting trade and cross-border investment flows will in turn affect the exchange rate. These factors include changes in:

- inflation rates
- interest rates
- growth rates.

Changes in inflation rates

Assume that inflation accelerates in Brazil. How will the Brazilian real (BRL) be affected?

Rising prices in Brazil mean that Brazil's exports become less competitive abroad and will tend to decrease. Demand for BRL will decrease. However, foreign products (imports) will be relatively more attractive so Brazil will import more. To do so Brazil will have to sell and supply more BRL to buy more foreign currency. If demand for BRL decreases and shifts left, and supply of BRL rises and shifts right, then the BRL will tend to depreciate. Higher inflation leads to depreciation of the currency.

Changes in interest rates

Remember that the interest rate is the return someone earns from saving money (and bonds pay interest to the holder of the bond). Now think of financial investors such as commercial banks, insurance companies, or companies managing pensions or hedge funds. If US interest rates rise this means that (a) dollar deposits and (b) US bonds become more attractive. They offer a higher return, so holders of US dollar deposits and US bonds earn more money. To take advantage of this development, financial investors will sell other currencies to buy more US dollars. Demand for dollars will increase and shift to the right, leading to a rise in the price of the dollar. Higher interest rates in the US lead to an **appreciation** of the dollar.

DP ready | ATL Thinking skills

Effect of US interest rates

1. Explain the effect of higher interest rates in the US on other currencies such as the BRL, the Mexican peso or the Indian rupee. (Remember, investors will sell other currencies to buy dollars.)

2. Explain what would happen to the other currencies if the US Federal Reserve decreased US interest rates. Use appropriate diagrams to illustrate your answer.

Changes in growth rates

Remember that growth refers to an increase in real income. If an economy is growing and incomes are rising, more imports will be consumed. This leads to an interesting effect: a growing economy, such as Vietnam, may see its currency depreciating. When Vietnam wants to buy more imports, it will have to sell more Vietnamese dongs to buy the necessary dollars. Supply of the dong will increase and shift to the right, pushing down its value.

However, there is a contrasting issue. If the Vietnamese economy is also expected to continue to grow, then this will attract foreign direct investment (FDI). Multinational firms will take advantage of the prospect of higher profits in Vietnam by acquiring controlling share of existing Vietnamese companies or by building factories there. The multinationals will need to buy dongs to make these investments. Demand for dongs will rise, pushing up its value. The positive forecasts for the Vietnamese economy will also attract financial investors who want to buy stocks of Vietnamese companies to take advantage of the expected rise in share prices. In such cases, expectations of strong growth may lead to a currency appreciation.

Fixed exchange rate systems

What if the exchange rate is set by the government or the central bank of a country? The UAE dirham (AED) has been fixed for a long time against the US dollar at AED3.67 per one US dollar. The Danish currency, the kroner (Kr), has been fixed against the euro at a "central" rate of 7.46 kroner per 1 euro. "Central" means that the kroner can fluctuate within a +/– 2.25% band around that rate, so between Kr7.62 and Kr7.29 per euro.

Maintaining a fixed exchange rate

How does a central bank maintain the price of a currency fixed at some level or within a band? Firms and individuals still buy and sell the currency so the demand for it and the supply of it continuously shift. To maintain the fixed exchange rate, a central bank must intervene in the foreign exchange market and start buying or selling its currency and/or adjust interest rates to induce investors to buy or sell the currency.

The idea is simple. If the currency tends to fall then the central bank must increase demand for the currency. It can do this either by buying the currency itself or by inducing foreign investors to start buying it. How can it induce investors? By increasing interest rates and thus making deposits denominated in its own currency and domestic bonds more attractive.

In a fixed exchange rate system, if the government abandons the fixed level of the currency and sets it at a lower level, it is referred to as **devaluation**. If the government abandons the fixed level of the currency and sets it at a higher level, it is referred to as **revaluation**. The terms "devaluation" and "revaluation" are used in a fixed exchange rate system whereas "depreciation" and "appreciation" are used in a floating system.

Let's illustrate the above using Figure 4.4.4. This features a fictitious country Laylaland with the Layla (L) as its currency. Let us further assume that the Layla is fixed against the dollar at a parity of \$1.50/L. Originally, demand (D_1) and supply (S_1) conditions are such that the exchange rate is at \$1.50.

Search the web

Search using these terms: Denmark's fixed exchange rate policy.

Find out more about why and how Denmark has been successfully keeping the kroner fixed against the euro.

DP ready ATL **Thinking skills**

Central bank intervention

Explain what a central bank will have to do if the currency tends to rise above the bank's fixed level.

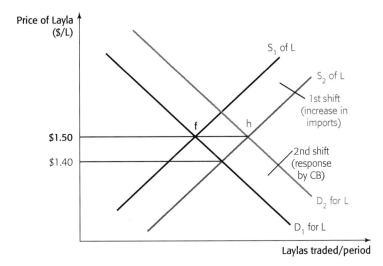

▲ **Figure 4.4.4** US dollar–Layla

Assume that incomes in Laylaland are increasing. Imports will increase so the supply of Laylas will increase to S_2 as more Laylas will have to be sold to buy the necessary dollars. At the foreign exchange market there is now an excess supply of Laylas equal to distance (fh) at the original $1.50/L exchange rate. This will tend to push the Layla down to a lower exchange rate ($1.40/L). To maintain the parity at $1.50/L, Laylaland's central bank must intervene in order to increase demand for Laylas to D_2. It can do this either by starting to buy (fh) Laylas in the foreign exchange market, or it can increase interest rates to induce investors to buy (fh) Laylas, since deposits in Laylas and Laylaland's bonds will become more attractive. Laylaland's central bank probably cannot continue either of these interventions over a long period. First, it has limited dollar reserves in its vaults to continue buying Laylas in the foreign exchange market. Also, higher interest rates in Laylaland will reduce domestic consumption and business investment spending (purchases of capital goods), decreasing AD and risking recession.

Managed exchange rates

Between floating and fixed exchange rates we have the most common exchange rate system: managed exchange rates. Within a managed exchange rate system, the authorities try to decrease exchange rate movements and, at the same time, maintain some flexibility. The exchange rate floats but there is periodic intervention by the central bank whenever the currency starts to move in a direction or at a speed considered undesirable. In some managed float systems the currency floats but within a desired but undisclosed band. A country may allow the currency to trade at an undisclosed band below or above the equilibrium level. The central bank intervenes to steer the exchange rate back to the desired level.

The three systems—a final note

This section has distinguished between floating (or flexible), fixed and managed exchange rate systems in order to explain how these work in principle. In the real world, the classification is much more complicated because central banks deal with the exchange rate in whichever way they consider most appropriate for their policy objectives. Fully fixed and free floating systems are rare and, in between them, there are very many different types of managed arrangements. They differ regarding the degree and the frequency of central bank intervention in foreign exchange markets.

Disequilibrium exchange rates

An economy may try to keep its exchange rate undervalued; that is, below its equilibrium value. The reason is that if the exchange rate is lower than its equilibrium rate, then exports will be cheaper and more competitive abroad. This could be a policy aimed at penetrating export markets for an economy that relies on export-driven growth. China has repeatedly been accused of this.

Search the web

Search using these terms: managed float MAS 2019 (channelnewsasia.com). Find out about the managed float system that operates in Singapore.

How could the authorities of a country maintain the exchange rate below its free market equilibrium level? How could China, for example, keep the yuan undervalued? Its central bank will have to purchase US dollars by selling yuan or it must keep interest rates low. There are several risks involved. First, the US will get upset and may retaliate. The US will object to Chinese exports being artificially cheaper in US markets and outcompeting US firms. In addition, US products in China will be more expensive and will not sell well. Another issue for China is that continuously selling yuan to keep its price low raises the risk of inflation in China.

The opposite may also occur. An economy may try to keep its exchange rate overvalued; that is, above its free market equilibrium level. The reasons for this are more complicated. Countries that pursue import substitution as a strategy to promote economic growth would keep their currency overvalued. These countries would try to substitute domestic production for imports in order to create their own manufacturing industries and diversify out of the primary sector, which lacks opportunities for growth and development. By keeping their currency overvalued they artificially keep import prices low. This sounds absurd but it is not. They block out imports of the good they are trying to produce domestically, using very high tariffs and other trade barriers but the overvalued exchange rate keep prices of necessary imported inputs low, such as machines and parts.

How could the authorities of a country maintain the exchange rate above its free market equilibrium level? The central bank would have to buy its currency in the foreign exchange market or keep interest rates high. The risks were that imports may have been cheaper domestically but as exports become more expensive and less competitive abroad the traditional export sector was thus penalized.

▲ People's Bank of China headquarters in Beijing

Economic consequences of changes in the exchange rate

Movements in the exchange rate affect a range of issues including inflation, unemployment, output, growth and living standards. The key to understanding the impact of changes in the exchange rate is to remember the two bullet points below.

- A depreciation makes exports cheaper abroad and therefore more competitive. It makes imports more expensive in the domestic market and therefore less attractive.

  Example: think of a miniature BMW toy car produced in Germany and priced €1.00. Let the dollar–euro exchange rate be €1.00 = $1.20. An American would need $1.20 to buy the toy. If the euro depreciates to €1.00 = $1.10 then the toy priced at €1.00 in Germany will be sold at $1.10 in the US market. It is cheaper and therefore more competitive.

  Now, think of a shirt made by US company Abercrombie & Fitch and priced $120.00 in the US. With the initial exchange rate, an Italian customer would need €100.00 to buy it. After the depreciation of the euro, €100.00 can be exchanged for only $110.00 so more euros are needed now to buy the shirt—the Italian customer will now need €109.09 euros to buy it. The shirt imported from the US is now more expensive in the eurozone and so is less attractive.

- An appreciation works the other way round. It makes exports more expensive abroad and thus less competitive, while imports become cheaper and thus more attractive.

Effect on inflation

What if the currency depreciates? How is inflation affected? Since exports become cheaper and more competitive abroad, while imports become pricier and less attractive domestically, exports will tend to increase and imports to decrease. Net exports (X – M) are a component of AD so net exports will tend to increase and AD will shift to the right. Depending on how close to potential output the economy is operating, demand-pull inflation may result.

In addition, the depreciation brings about rising import prices. To the extent that domestic firms buy imported raw materials and intermediate goods, the higher cost of their inputs may lead to a decrease in AS and so to cost-push inflation.

Effect on economic growth

If the currency depreciates, exports become more competitive as prices decrease, and imports become less attractive as they become more expensive. AD will tend to increase and shift to the right because net exports (NX), a component of AD, will increase. If AD shifts to the right, real output will increase and the economy will grow, but there may be a higher risk of inflation.

DP ready | ATL **Thinking skills**

Illustrating AD/AS

You have learned that if AD shifts to the right, real output will increase and the economy will grow, but there may be a higher risk of inflation. Explain what this risk depends on. Use a Keynesian AD/AS diagram to illustrate your answer.

Effect on unemployment

A depreciating currency, as explained above, may increase AD and therefore economic activity. Cyclical unemployment will tend to decrease. An appreciation will tend to increase cyclical unemployment as net exports and AD will decrease.

Effect on the current account balance

The basic idea of the current account is simple.

If import expenditures exceed export revenues (M > X), the country has a trade deficit. A depreciation will decrease its size because exports become more competitive and increase while imports become less attractive and decrease. If the country had a trade surplus (X > M), a depreciation will tend to increase its size.

If the currency instead appreciates, exports become less competitive and tend to shrink while imports become more attractive and tend to rise. A trade deficit (M > X) will tend to widen while a trade surplus (X > M) will tend to shrink.

> **Internal link**
>
> The current account is discussed in detail in section 4.5.

Effect on living standards

The typical basket of goods and services that consumers purchase includes imports. If the currency depreciates, then the prices of imported goods in the country increases—automatically the cost of living increases. The purchasing power of households shrinks. This decreased access to goods and services mostly affects poorer families—if fuel, pharmaceuticals and food are imported, the depreciation will disproportionately hurt lower income households.

A depreciation, as already noted, will also increase exports. The growth of the export sector will increase employment and income-earning opportunities for many with the appropriate skills. Since imports will also become less attractive, domestic firms competing with imports may grow and also generate jobs. Of course, these effects on employment and living standards require a significant depreciation to take place.

DP ready ▏ATL **Thinking and communication skills**

Effect of appreciation on living standards

In a small group, analyse the possible effects on living standards of a sizeable appreciation of the currency. Present your ideas in the form of a poster to discuss with the rest of the class.

Focus point

The exchange rate is arguably the most important price for an economy. It is determined by market forces but often governments, through their central banks, intervene in its determination. If the exchange rate depreciates then exports become cheaper abroad and thus more competitive; while imports become more expensive domestically and thus less attractive. Changes in the exchange rate affect all macroeconomic variables such as inflation, unemployment and growth and of course the living standards of the population. Consequently, the exchange rate is central stage for all policy-making decisions.

Key terms—test yourself

Define these terms: exchange rate, floating (or flexible) exchange rate system, fixed exchange rate system, managed exchange rate system, remittances, portfolio investment, devaluation, revaluation.

In this section you will learn about:

→ the balance of payments (BOP)—the current account, capital account and financial account

→ the implications of a persistent current account deficit

→ ways to correct a persistent current account deficit—expenditure-reducing policies, expenditure-switching polices and supply-side policies.

The issue

This section examines an important account for a country—the balance of payments (BOP). It is a record of exports and imports, and a little more. The section explains what the BOP includes, what it means to import too much and what can be done about it if it proves to be a problem.

The balance of payments (BOP)

The **balance of payments (BOP)** is a record of all transactions of a country with the rest of the world over a period of time, usually a year. Any item that leads to an inflow of currency is recorded with a plus sign and is referred to as a **credit item**. If an item leads to an outflow of currency it is recorded with a negative sign and is referred to as a **debit item**. Table 4.5.1 gives some examples of transactions considered from the point of view of Mexico's BOP.

Item	For Mexico's BOP, currency inflow or outflow?	Credit or debit?	Plus or minus?
Raquel, who lives in Mexico City, buys a $250 Italian jacket.	outflow from Mexico	debit item	minus sign
Jorje, a wealthy Mexican entrepreneur, buys $200,000 worth of US stocks from the New York Stock Exchange.	outflow from Mexico	debit item	minus sign
Bob, an American college student, visits Mazatlan and spends $1,200 on his stay.	inflow into Mexico	credit item	plus sign
Raquel's mother receives $18,000 in dividends and interest payments from US shares and bonds she owns.	inflow into Mexico	credit item	plus sign
Arturo's Steel Company, Mexico's largest, acquires a Turkish steel manufacturing firm for $1.2 billion.	outflow from Mexico	debit item	minus sign
Arturo's Steel Company earns $120 million in profits from operations abroad.	inflow into Mexico	credit item	plus sign

▲ **Table 4.5.1** Examples of BOP items (measured in US dollars)

Breaking the BOP into pieces

The components

The BOP is broken down into three separate sub-accounts: the current account, the capital account and the financial account.

The important ones for us are the current and financial accounts. The capital account is small. The **current account** records trade flows, income flows and transfers across borders. The **financial account** records cross-border investments. Cross-border investments include portfolio investments (buying and selling of bonds and shares, deposits and loans) and foreign direct investment (FDI). Table 4.5.2 presents these sub-accounts in greater detail.

Balance of payments (BOP)		
A. Current account (CA)		
Net exports of goods and services Exports of goods and services − imports of goods and services (X–M) = **Balance of trade** in goods and services	If (X − M) > 0 then trade surplus If (X − M) < 0 then trade deficit	
Net income from abroad = Income from abroad − Income paid abroad	If income earned abroad exceeds income sent abroad then (+) If income sent abroad exceeds income earned abroad then (−)	
Net current transfers = Current transfers from abroad − current transfers sent abroad (Current transfers include foreign aid and workers' remittances)	If current transfers from abroad exceed current transfers sent abroad then (+) If current transfers sent abroad exceed current transfers earned abroad then (−)	
Current account balance = Sum of net exports of goods and services plus net income plus net current transfers	If sum > 0 then current account surplus If sum < 0 then current account deficit	
B. Capital account (KA)		
Net capital transfers Capital transfers received − capital transfers sent (Capital transfers include debt forgiveness, and buying and selling of non-produced, non-financial assets such as patents and trademarks)		
Balance on capital account (KA) If > 0 then capital account surplus If < 0 then capital account deficit		
C. Financial account (FA)		
Portfolio investment Inflows and outflows	Net portfolio investment = sales of bonds and shares − purchases of bonds and shares	If sales of domestic bonds and shares exceed purchases of foreign bonds & shares, then (+) If purchases of foreign bonds and shares exceed sales of domestic bonds and shares, then (−)
Foreign direct investment (FDI) inflows and outflows	Net FDI = FDI inflows minus FDI outflows	If FDI accepted from abroad > FDI made abroad, then (+) If FDI made abroad > FDI accepted from abroad, then (−)
Changes in reserve assets or official borrowing/lending (Reserve assets include assets readily available to the central bank for meeting balance of payments financing needs; usually this refers to US dollars but also gold etc.)	If (+) the reserve assets decreased If (−) then reserve assets increased	
CA + KA + FA = 0		
(Errors and omissions): balancing item (if above ≠ 0)		

▲ **Table 4.5.2** The three accounts of the BOP

Current account balances for five countries

Determine the latest current account balance for five countries, noting the value of exports and imports of goods and services. Find the information on the tradingeconomics.com website or any other appropriate site.

A **current account deficit** results if the sum of net exports of goods and services plus net income plus net current transfers is negative. A **current account surplus** results if this sum is positive.

Interdependence between the accounts

Let's ignore the capital account (as it is small and insignificant) and also simplify things a little by considering that the current account only includes export revenues and import expenditures. The goal is to understand why the sum of the current and financial accounts (remember, we are ignoring the capital account) must equal zero, or why $CA + FA = 0$ so that $CA = -FA$.

Assume that during the month of June (choose any month or any year) the country Laylaland collected revenues from the export goods and services equal to $1,000 (credits) but it spent $1,200 (debits) on imports of goods and services. Since $X = \$1000.00$ and $M = \$1200.00$ there is a current account deficit equal to $200, or $CA = \$ -200.00$. The question is, in June, how did Laylaland residents manage to spend $200 more on imports than they collected from exports? Where was the $200 found?

The answer is simple: investment inflows (credits) into Laylaland by foreigners were more than investment outflows (debits). But what if inflows of foreign direct and portfolio investment into Laylaland were only $160? Laylaland would still be missing $40. Remember, Laylaland did pay for its imports. The answer is again simple: Laylaland's central bank must have used $40 of its foreign (dollar) exchange reserves. This $40 decrease in the foreign exchange reserves of Laylaland's central bank together with the investment inflows of $160 ensured that Laylaland's current account deficit was financed and its BOP did balance. So, if foreign investment inflows are insufficient, then it is the official reserves that solve the issue and, if necessary, there will be official borrowing by Laylaland's government from abroad.

In this way, the sum of all accounts is necessarily zero. If there is a deficit in the current account, there must be an equal surplus in the financial account. If there is a surplus in the current account, there must be a deficit in the financial account. Remember the role of the changes in the foreign exchange reserves held by the central bank and/or the possibility to borrow or lend officially.

If the sum is not zero, it must be because of unavoidable errors and omissions. That is why we have at the very bottom of the BOP accounts the "balancing item", an artificial entry that solves the issue.

Unfortunately, the foreign exchange reserves of any country are limited (the US is a special case as it can issue dollars) and a country can borrow for only so long before lenders get very nervous. The country must make adjustments to avoid a crisis. The currency may have to significantly depreciate or devalue but most importantly, it must correct the root cause of a persistent current account deficit. This is explained below.

Implications of a persistent current account deficit

A current account deficit is not necessarily a problem, especially if it is small as a proportion of GDP. It implies that the country is consuming more than it is producing. It may be a sign of a growing economy as higher incomes lead to greater import absorption.

To the extent that foreigners "trust" the country's long-term growth prospects—and so they are willing to buy its stocks and bonds, or to set up long-term business interests there, such as factories— the current account deficit is financed from the currency inflows in the combined capital and financial accounts. There is no pressure on the currency to depreciate.

It becomes a problem when the exchange rate starts to depreciate. This may prove helpful as it makes exports cheaper and imports more expensive, so export revenues increase and import expenditures decrease—the current account deficit will shrink. However, as you have learned, the increase in import prices may lead to higher inflation. The situation may worsen if policy-makers do not successfully deal with inflationary pressures.

It may also become a problem if policy-makers are forced to increase interest rates to induce financial investors to buy domestic bonds. Remember that higher interest rates will decrease AD because households and firms will borrow less to spend less on durables and capital goods. Growth will slow down and there is even risk of a recession.

If financing forces the state to sell off assets (such as utility companies, airports or harbours) to foreigners in order to finance the current account deficit, this may also deprive the state of future revenues and threaten the loss of economic sovereignty. If the country is forced to borrow heavily from abroad then its foreign debt increases and it runs the risk that international credit rating agencies, such as Moody's, may downgrade the economy's credit rating. This would put more pressure on the country, as even higher interest rates would be required to attract investors to compensate for the increased risk they face.

Persistent current account deficits cannot continue for long. They are a sign of an "ailing" economy. Chronic inflation, uncompetitive product markets and rigid labour markets can all contribute to uncompetitive exports and rising imports. Policy-makers will have to make adjustments to correct the imbalance. They can adopt **expenditure-reducing policies, expenditure-switching policies** and/or supply-side policies to narrow the deficit.

Correcting a current account deficit

Expenditure-reducing policies

These include contractionary fiscal and monetary policies. If AD decreases, then the decrease in national income leads to fewer imports being absorbed. Since a decrease in AD will also decrease inflation, the country's export competitiveness will increase. The resulting decrease in imports and increase in exports will reduce the current account deficit.

However, such an adjustment policy has its disadvantages. Growth slows down, incomes decrease, firms fail to grow or shut down and unemployment will increase.

Expenditure-switching policies

These are policies that aim at switching expenditures away from imports and towards domestic goods and services. They have to make imports less attractive, which means making them more expensive.

A sharp depreciation or a devaluation of the currency will achieve this result. Not only will imports become more expensive and so less attractive, but also exports will become cheaper abroad and more competitive.

The risk of such a policy is that the higher import prices together with the increase in exports may lead to higher inflation. If inflationary pressures are not effectively dealt with then any benefits from the lower exchange rate will quickly be lost.

Imports also become more expensive if trade barriers, such as tariffs, are imposed. This route carries risks. Trade frictions with trading partners will increase, as any benefit comes at their expense. WTO trade rules will be violated, risking sanctions if the WTO appellate considers the tariffs illegal. Protection also leads to inefficiency and misallocation of resources.

Supply-side policies

Typically, persistent current account deficits also require the use of supply-side policies. A persistent deficit is a sign of an uncompetitive economy. There may be too much monopoly power in product markets, businesses may be burdened by excessive regulation, the state may be too heavily involved in the workings of markets. Also, labour costs may be high owing to rigid labour market rules and regulations or to the presence of powerful labour unions. The key to addressing persistent current account deficits may be to use supply-side policies that:

- decrease monopoly power and render product markets more competitive
- decrease labour costs and render labour markets more flexible
- improve incentives.

The drawbacks are that supply-side policies are difficult to implement as often powerful domestic interests block them; and if they are implemented, they take long to have an effect. For many economies, though, they are absolutely necessary.

Focus point

The balance of payments keeps track of all inflows and outflows of currency from a country. It is broken down into the current account, the capital account and the financial account. The current account is most important as it primarily records export revenues and import expenditures. The financial account records cross-border investments. Since a country has to pay for its imports it must earn enough foreign exchange from its exports and investment inflows. If it doesn't and the imbalance persists then it will have to introduce policies to correct it such as expenditure reducing, expenditure switching or even supply-side policies.

Key terms—test yourself

Define these terms: balance of payments, credit item, debit item, current account, financial account, current account deficit, current account surplus, expenditure-reducing policies, expenditure-switching policies.

In this section you will learn about:

→ the meaning of sustainable development and the UN's Sustainable Development Goals (SDGs)

→ measuring development—commonly used indicators

→ the relationship between economic growth and economic development

→ barriers to growth and development—economic, social and political barriers.

The issue

You are probably aware of the distinction between developed and developing countries. Even if you are not, if you take a look at life around the world, you will realize that people in different countries start their days under very different conditions. Some live in comfortable homes, have more than enough to eat, and are well clothed and healthy. Others, however, have inadequate food and shelter, poor health and they do not know how to read or write. This section examines the concept of development and its relationship to economic growth. A number of factors that act as barriers to growth and development, and are therefore responsible for the world's great divide, are also explored.

The meaning of sustainable development

Sustainable development is a central concept for our age. A wide range of definitions of sustainable development exists. The most common is that of the Brundtland Commission of the United Nations, which defined **sustainable development** as "development that meets the needs of the present without compromising the ability of future generations to meet their own needs" (Brundtland 1987).

Sustainable development has three dimensions: economic development, social progress and environmental protection and requires a balance between them. This means that the promotion of human well-being, which involves both economic and social dimensions, does not result in the destruction of the environment. Sustainable development therefore necessitates that the needs and well-being of future generations are taken into account, given that human actions today might jeopardize the ability of future generations to meet their needs. For example, failure to maintain an adequate natural resource base could make it impossible for future generations to have sufficient food supplies. Therefore, resources must not be depleted so that they are available from one generation to the next.

The Sustainable Development Goals

The Sustainable Development Goals (SDGs) are 17 global goals set by the United Nations General Assembly in 2015 to be met by the year 2030. The SDGs build on the previous Millennium Development Goals (MDGs) but they go further and aim to promote prosperity while protecting the planet.

The goals are shown below.

Watch this

Search YouTube using these terms: michael green global goals progress. Watch a 2018 TED talk on the progress made towards achieving the SDGs.

SUSTAINABLE DEVELOPMENT GOALS

DP ready ATL **Research and communication skills**

One SDG investigated

Work in small groups to investigate an SDG. Each group chooses one of the SDGs. Make sure that there is only one group investigating a particular SDG. Each group searches online using this phrase: sustainable development site:.un.org.

Look at the United Nations web page on the SDGs.

For your group's SDG, investigate the progress that has been made so far towards achieving that goal and the main challenges involved. Present your findings to the other groups.

Measuring development

Economic development is an aspect of sustainable development— but what exactly is it and how can we measure it? **Economic development** is a multidimensional concept as it refers to an improvement in living standards, which involves increased per capita income levels, reductions in poverty, increased access to health care and education, increased employment opportunities and reduced inequalities of income and wealth. Economic development can be measured either with the use of single indicators that record the progress made towards a particular dimension of development, or with the use of composite indicators that are summary measures of several dimensions of development.

Single indicators: per capita GDP or per capita GNI

Per capita GDP or per capita GNI can to some extent provide information on the level of development of a country, as there is a positive correlation between per capita income and well-being. The UN and the World Bank keep systematic records of per capita GDP and GNI and classify countries on this basis. For example, the World Bank uses per capita GNI to place countries into three main categories: high income, middle income and low income. A country is low income if GNI per capita is below $975 per year. GNI per capita for a middle income country is between $976 and $11,905 per year and for a high income country it is above $11,906. The middle income group, which is quite big, is split between the upper middle income and the lower middle income, with the dividing line at $3,855.

To have a basis of comparison, however, we need to convert each country's per capita income figure to a common currency, which is typically the US dollar. Yet, prices of goods and services can vary significantly across countries. A haircut in Lagos is much cheaper than a haircut in New York. Cost of living differences must be considered in the conversion of per capita income to US dollars. Therefore, instead of the market exchange rate we use "PPP dollars". PPP stands for "purchasing power parity" dollars. These are dollars of equal purchasing power; that is, they buy the same basket of goods and services that the national currency buys. Therefore, we can classify economic development based on GDP or GNI per capita expressed in PPP dollars. The problems with this system are that:

- the cost of living varies a lot even within a country so using PPP is still quite imprecise

- increases in per capita income do not necessarily imply improved living standards, so classifications based on per capita income can be problematic.

Other single indicators

According to the definition of economic development, health care and education are important parts of a country's development process. Keeping track of health-related and education-related indicators helps to monitor progress in these areas.

- Health-related indicators include: health expenditure per capita, life expectancy at birth (years), infant mortality (per 1,000 live births), maternal mortality ratio (per 100,000 live births), prevalence of HIV (% of population aged between 15 and 49 years), physicians (per 10,000 people) or hospital beds (per 10,000 people).

DP ready | ATL **Research and thinking skills**

Income levels in different countries

1. Search online using these terms: World Bank map income country. Select the first (WDI) web page. Explore the map with the World Bank's classification of countries by income level.

   a. In which income group does the majority of the world's population belong to?

   b. In which regions are the low-income countries mostly concentrated?

2. The United Nations has identified a subgroup within the low-income countries called the Least Developed Countries. Use the web to find out which countries belong to this sub-group. What are the issues these countries face that have put them in the least developed countries group?

Internal link

There is more on per capita income in section 3.1.

■ Education-related indicators include: literacy rate (% who know how to read and write), mean years of schooling (of people aged 25 years and older), pupil–teacher ratio, school enrollment—primary, secondary and tertiary enrollment—(% of school age children enrolled in each level).

DP ready | **Thinking, research and communication skills**

Indicators—data from three countries

Choose three countries from each of the World Bank income groups. Use the World Bank, the UN, the World Health Organization (WHO) or perhaps the indexmundi websites for the following research.

1. Find the GNI per capita in PPP dollars for each country and enter the data into a table.

2. Choose two health-related and two education-related indicators and collect data on each of your chosen countries. Add this data to your table. Compare and contrast the different indicators across the different countries.

   a. Identify whether there is any country with low GNI per capita that scores well in health-related or education-related indicators.

   b. To what extent is it safe to infer the level of development of each country from this data?

   c. Share your data and observations with the rest of the class.

There are many other single indicators that can be used to measure the different aspects of economic development, such as energy consumption per capita, newspaper circulation per 1,000 of population or percentage of GDP derived from each sector of the economy and from the urban population. No single indicator is powerful enough to illustrate the complex issue of development adequately. It is therefore preferable to rely on composite indices.

Search the web

Search using these terms: World Bank development indicators. Explore the different indicators that are available.

Composite indicators

The most widely used composite indicator is the **Human Development Index (HDI)**. The HDI measures average achievements of a population in terms of health, education and access to goods and services. These three dimensions are measured by the indicators of:

■ life expectancy at birth

■ mean years of schooling and expected years of schooling

■ GNI per capita (in US$ PPP).

Each dimension takes a value between 0 and 1, with 0 being the lowest possible value and 1 being the highest. The composite index is the average of the three dimensions, so each country receives an HDI value from 0 to 1 and is then ranked accordingly. The HDI was successful in displacing per capita income as a summary measure of development. However, it remains an average, as it does not consider income distribution or gender inequalities.

HDI ranking

1. Search online using these terms: HDI ranking. Go to the United Nations web page where you will find a list of all countries ranked according to their HDI value.

   a. Record some rankings that surprise you.

   b. Were you expecting these countries to have scored higher or lower?

2. GNI per capita is included in the HDI measurement. There are countries with a higher HDI than GNI per capita rank and others that have a lower HDI than GNI rank. Explain what this implies.

Other composite indicators

To overcome some of the shortcomings of the HDI, the United Nations Development Programme developed two further indicators: the Inequality-adjusted HDI (IHDI) and the Gender Inequality Index (GII).

The IHDI measures development in the same three dimensions as the HDI, but adjusted for inequality in each dimension. The IHDI attempts to capture losses in development that arise from inequality. If there were no inequality the IHDI and the HDI would be equal.

The Gender Inequality Index (GII) measures inequalities between the genders in three dimensions. Often women and girls are discriminated against in health, education and in the labour market. The GII captures the loss in development of women due to inequalities in these areas.

Another composite indicator that could be used to track development is the Happy Planet Index (HPI) that measures how well nations are doing at achieving long, happy and sustainable lives for their people.

Internal link

Section 3.1 has more information about the Happy Planet Index (HPI).

Watch this

Search YouTube using these terms: Marks happy planet index. Watch a TEDx talk by Nic Marks, the creator of the HPI, on the importance of measuring success differently.

TOK

What knowledge questions might be encountered in constructing a composite indicator to measure development?

Economic growth and development

Economic growth refers to increases in the real GDP of an economy through time. Growth does not necessarily involve development. A country may grow without any development objective being met. The UN Development Programme has described four types of growth that impede the development process. They are:

- jobless growth, where employment opportunities for the poor do not expand

- ruthless growth, where income inequality widens

- futureless growth, where the environment is degraded and natural resources depleted

- voiceless growth, where individual empowerment falls behind.

As such, economic growth does not guarantee that economic development will occur. However, development usually requires growth. Some economic development may be possible in the absence of growth in the short term, if the policies followed provide access to basic social services for the poor. In the long-term, though, the development process necessitates that developing countries are growing.

Barriers to growth and development

There are a number of factors that prevent some countries from growing and developing.

A poverty cycle

Poverty locks individuals into a **poverty cycle** or poverty trap, shown in Figure 4.6.1. Poor people live on a very low income, which is spent entirely on necessities. This means that they cannot save money. The absence of savings does not allow for the necessary investments to be made, which implies that human, natural and physical capital remain low. As a result, there is low productivity that leads to low income and so they are trapped in a situation where their poverty leads to more poverty.

The poverty cycle is transmitted across generations as children are caught in the trap along with their parents, which limits both generations' possibilities for higher earnings. The poverty cycle therefore poses a significant barrier to growth and development both in the short and the longer term.

▲ **Figure 4.6.1** The poverty cycle

Economic barriers

Rising economic inequality

Rising inequality implies that a large part of the population does not have access to education and health services. The economy is deprived of their skills and talents.

The poor have limited or no access to credit. They cannot borrow to invest in their children's education or to start or expand a business. Rising inequality also reduces the overall savings in the economy. This results in reduced funds and resources available for domestic investments and lower demand for domestically produced goods and services.

High inequality also increases corruption. It may lead to social unrest and political instability, discouraging domestic and foreign direct investment (FDI). These factors lead to lower growth rates and lower incomes for the poor, thereby restricting economic development.

Internal link

Foreign direct investment (FDI) is covered in section 4.7.

Lack of access to infrastructure and appropriate technology

Infrastructure refers to the economy's physical capital such as transportation systems (roads, railways, ports and airports), telecommunications, energy systems (electricity and gas), water supplies, sanitation and sewerage systems. Infrastructure is a major facilitator of economic activity. Lack of infrastructure limits growth and development prospects. For example, a poor road network increases transportation costs and limits access to local markets, schools and health facilities.

Infrastructure is funded by government but, in developing countries, governments may not have the required resources. In many parts of Africa the most basic infrastructure does not exist or is not maintained. Closely related to the lack of infrastructure is the lack of access to **appropriate technology**; that is, technology suited to a country's factors of production. In general, technologies can be distinguished into capital-intensive (relying mostly on machines) and labour-intensive (relying on workers). Since, in most developing countries, labour is the relatively abundant factor of production, appropriate technologies are usually labour-intensive. Lack of appropriate technologies means that there is less employment, less income, more poverty and therefore less growth and development.

Low levels of human capital

In developing countries, levels of human capital are low, which limits economic growth and development. In many developing nations, the necessary resources to maintain adequate health and education facilities are not available; or poverty prevents people's access to health and education. This results in decreased labour productivity, individuals facing fewer employment opportunities, higher risk of spreading diseases, fewer technological improvements (because of the lack of skilled individuals) and more poverty. Human capital formation is absolutely necessary to achieve higher labour productivity, long-term growth and improved living standards. Remember that achieving better health and education are themselves development goals.

Dependence on the primary sector

In developing countries, the majority of people live in rural areas and are employed in the primary sector. As a result, developing nations have overspecialized in the production and export of primary commodities, or even rely on a single commodity. This can be a major obstacle to growth and development. Demand for most primary exports is income inelastic, and does not grow fast enough in high-income countries to boost growth and development in developing countries.

Lack of access to international markets

Developed economies, such as the US, the EU and Japan, provide large agricultural support to their farmers, mainly in the form of subsidies. This results in lower world prices. Developing countries cannot compete; they cannot expand their exports to international markets. This is a barrier because it leads to lower incomes, lower agricultural investment, lower employment opportunities for farm workers and increased poverty. Apart from the agricultural support that developed economies offer farmers, they also impose trade barriers—mainly tariffs—to protect their economies from foreign competition. This further limits the ability of developing countries to access international markets and obstructs growth and development.

Informal economy

The **informal economy** lies outside the formal one and is where unregistered, unregulated and untaxed economic activities take place. Unregistered activities include the jobs of street vendors and unlicensed taxi drivers and often become a way for people to survive. However, there is no protection for workers, who may become subject to exploitation and be exposed to health dangers, while limited possibilities exist for education and training. As a result, living standards for these workers are low. As long as the informal economy remains unregulated the development prospects are limited.

Indebtedness

High levels of indebtedness characterize many developing countries as their governments had a past history of high-level spending and borrowing. High debt levels require large debt repayments and can mean that the government has reduced funds available to invest in health, education and infrastructure, which are all necessary for economic growth and development.

Geography

The geographic location of many developing countries may act as a barrier to their growth and development. For example, many of the poorest developing countries around the world are landlocked. Examples in Asia are Afghanistan, Nepal, Bhutan and Laos. In Africa, roughly one third of countries are landlocked. Economic growth and development depend heavily on international trade, which is significantly more difficult and costly for landlocked countries. If not landlocked, countries may be in mountainous regions, for example Bolivia. This makes it particularly difficult for them to engage in farming and low-cost manufacturing. Also, some developing countries are in geographic locations that are exposed to natural disasters such as cyclones, storms, floods and droughts. This applies to a number of small island economies such as the Philippines and Haiti.

Tropical climates and endemic diseases

Almost all developing countries have tropical climates. Climate has a huge effect on crop productivity, water scarcity or availability and even labour productivity. These factors tend to be problematic in tropical climates. Climate also plays an important role for endemic diseases. Places that are warm all year, such as tropical Africa, generally have very high year-round malaria transmission. Since development depends on a healthy population, regions with a heavy disease burden struggle.

Watch this

Search YouTube using these terms: Sachs Sustainable Development Lecture 4 Chapter 2. Listen to a discussion of geography and climate as barriers to development.

Political and social barriers

Weak institutional framework

There are many economic, legal and social institutions that influence economic growth and development. However, in developing countries, the institutional framework is rather weak and does not allow for this. Specific reasons are given below.

Ineffective taxation structures

Tax revenues are needed by governments to make investments in health, education, infrastructure and other areas important for economic growth and development. Tax revenues in developing countries are low because incomes are low. Also, the tax system is ineffective in collecting tax revenues due to complicated procedures, tax exemptions for the wealthy with political influence and corrupt tax authorities.

Banking system

Banking services and access to credit are very important to economic growth and development, as they allow for investments in human, physical and natural capital. Yet the commercial banking system in many developing countries does not function properly, as it does not accommodate poor and small-scale producers, farmers and traders. The result is a major restraint on growth and development.

Property rights

Property rights involve laws that ensure legal rights to ownership and transfer of ownership from one owner to another. In developing countries, property rights are usually not well defined and enforced. This leads to lower investment, as there is risk of loss of the investment, which can in turn limit growth.

Gender inequality

In many developing countries there is gender inequality. Gender inequalities result in women and girls having limited access to social and economic opportunities compared with men and boys, with significant consequences for growth and development.

Poor governance and corruption

High corruption levels hold back growth and development because the country is suffering from poor governance. As ideas, the economic policies look good. In practice, they may be damaged by corruption, inefficiency, incompetence or all of these. Poor governance and corruption, if carried to extremes, can stop economic growth and development.

The barriers described above do not apply equally to every country.

Focus point

Economic development is a multidimensional concept that refers to an improvement in living standards involving increases in per capita income levels, reductions in poverty, increased access to health-care and education, increased employment opportunities, as well as reduced inequalities of income and wealth. Economic growth does not guarantee that economic development will occur, though economic development requires economic growth. There are many factors that act as barriers preventing countries from both growing and developing, such as rising economic inequality, lack of access to health care, education, infrastructure and appropriate technology as well as geography and climate.

Search the web

Search using these terms: De Soto property rights Reuters. Read a short article on the importance of property rights in the developing world.

TOK

To what extent can one confidently claim that an advanced economy is a developed economy?

| DP ready | ATL | Thinking, research and communication skills |

Barriers in a developing country

Work in a small group. Choose a developing country. Carry out an investigation exploring which barriers have been more significant in holding back this country in its growth and development process.

Present and discuss your findings in class.

Key terms—test yourself

Define these terms: sustainable development, economic development, Human Development Index (HDI).

4.7 IS THERE A WAY OUT?

In this section you will learn about:

→ foreign direct investment (FDI)

→ foreign aid

→ international trade strategies

→ diversification

→ market-oriented supply-side policies (SSPs)

→ social enterprise

→ microfinance

→ provision of merit goods

→ women's empowerment

→ redistribution policies

→ debt relief

→ the World Bank and the International Monetary Fund (IMF)

→ government intervention versus market-oriented approaches.

The issue

This section explores the strategies that can help developing countries overcome the barriers that are holding them back, which they can use to promote their growth and development. The appropriateness of some of the approaches and policies that can be pursued is highly debatable. Also, some strategies come with significant costs, as their application does not always bring the benefits that were expected when the strategies were designed. Therefore, the way out is not an easy path.

Foreign direct investment (FDI)

You are probably familiar with **multinational corporations** (MNCs), companies that operate in several countries. Some examples are AT&T, Kia Motors, HSBC, Siemens and Unilever. MNCs are able to establish their presence in more than one country through **foreign direct investment (FDI)**. FDI refers to long-term investment by firms from one country in productive facilities in another country. FDI includes investing in new facilities and acquiring a controlling percentage of the shares of existing local companies.

Encouraging FDI would mean more MNCs are attracted to developing countries. MNCs have good reasons to be willing to expand their operations in developing nations.

- They gain access to more markets and so they can expand their sales.

- They can lower costs of production, as labour costs are usually lower in developing countries.

- If involved in extractive activities, MNCs can benefit from the rich natural resources of oil, bauxite, copper or other metals and minerals found in developing nations.

▲ An International Technology Park in Bengaluru, India

In order to attract FDI, certain conditions must exist or be created within the developing country. These include:

- economic and political stability

- large and growing markets

- public policy with favourable tax treatment and ease of profit repatriation

- low labour costs

- high levels of human capital and labour productivity

- infrastructure such as roads and ports or telecommunications

- membership in free trade areas or trading blocs to avoid tariffs

- clearly defined property rights and a functioning legal system.

How does FDI help growth and development?

FDI can increase employment opportunities in developing countries as MNCs hire local workers in their production facilities. The local workforce may receive training, which leads to skill creation and improves human capital. In addition, FDI can bring organizational and managerial know-how, as well as new production technologies, which can all be learned and adopted by the local workforce and local businesses. This contributes to further improvements in human capital and also to technological improvements. FDI inflows are a source of foreign exchange, which may be used to finance much needed imports and a trade deficit. If the government of the developing country taxes MNCs, then tax revenues will increase and provide the government with funds to spend in other areas that will assist growth and the development process. Lastly, the inflows of FDI funds into the developing country can increase savings, which will increase the amount of investment.

All these improvements present the positive results of FDI, but there are contrasting aspects.

- The skills of the local workforce may not improve if workers are used to fill only the low-skill positions and no training is provided.

- The technology brought may be capital intensive and thereby inappropriate, not creating employment positions.

- MNCs may hurt local firms by eliminating competition and by importing intermediate products instead of buying them from domestic suppliers.

- The tax contribution of MNCs may be considerably less than it should be, as a result of favouring tax conditions.

- MNCs may use their economic power to influence government policies in directions unfavourable to the development process, such as through weakening labour protection laws or environmental protection laws.

■ In many cases the operation of MNCs has caused environmental damage in the developing country, which is against both development and sustainability.

These facts suggest that although growth may come about through FDI the development prospects of the country may not necessarily improve.

Foreign aid

Foreign aid refers to the transfer of funds to developing countries in the form of loans or grants, or to the transfer of goods and services in the form of gifts. Aid is non-commercial, as the transfers do not involve buying and selling. Note that in order for loans to be considered part of foreign aid, they must be offered in concessionary terms—that is, at lower than market interest rates and with longer repayment periods.

When aid comes from the governments of donor countries it is referred to as **Official Development Assistance (ODA)** and can be bilateral or multilateral.

■ Bilateral aid involves one donor country; aid flows from one advanced economy to the developing country.

■ Multilateral aid involves an international organization such as the United Nations, the World Bank or the IMF; aid flows through that organization to the developing nation.

Aid may also come from non-governmental organizations (NGOs). NGOs are organizations pursuing objectives for the public interest and aim to provide services to the public, directly or indirectly. Oxfam, Friends of the Earth and WWF are well-known NGOs but there are many other smaller organizations that serve similar purposes.

Aid is usually in the form of humanitarian aid or development aid that is offered through ODA and also by NGOs. Humanitarian aid aims to save lives and ensure access to basic necessities such as food, water, shelter and health care. For example, humanitarian aid may be provided in emergency situations resulting from violent conflicts or natural disasters such as floods, earthquakes and tsunamis. Development aid aims to help developing countries achieve their growth and development objectives and can take the form of:

■ **project aid**, where the funds must be used to finance the construction of a particular project such as a dam, a road or a hospital

■ programme aid, where the funds are used to support sectors of the economy, such as health care or education

■ **tied aid**, where the funds must be used to buy imports from the donor country.

Search the web

Use the web to find information about Shell's operation in Nigeria. There are opposing views. To what extent was Shell's presence in the country beneficial? What might be the negative aspects of its operation?

Foreign aid is a highly debated topic. Table 4.7.1 shows some of the views that exist on foreign aid.

Positive views	Negative views
Aid is linked with higher growth rates.	Aid can lead to dependency, as it creates the need for more and more aid.
Aid can help developing countries escape the poverty trap.	Aid may be abruptly terminated if a donor's budget changes.
Aid is effective when it is narrowly targeted to specific pro-development projects and objectives, such as the prevention and elimination of certain diseases.	Aid can be ineffective when it is given to countries with corrupt governments.
Aid is effective when it is reinforced by appropriate domestic policies and institutions in a non-corrupt government environment.	Aid can be ineffective when it induces countries to postpone improvements of macroeconomic conditions.
Aid is effective when it is not tied to buying products from donor countries.	Aid can be ineffective when the technologies transferred and the advice given are inappropriate.

▲ **Table 4.7.1** Positive and negative views of foreign aid

Search the web

Search using the terms: Nobel prize Duflo interview.

Read or listen to the interview with Esther Duflo, Economics Nobel prize winner in 2019, together with Abhijit Banerjee and Michael Kremer. They applied the randomized control trial approach in order to learn about the effectiveness of small-scale policy interventions in helping improve the lives of some of the world's poorest households.

This will give you an additional insight as to whether aid is effective or not.

DP ready ⫶ **Thinking, research and communication skills**

Foreign aid

Watch this

Search YouTube as follows to watch three videos.

■ Search using these terms: Sachs Official Development Assistance.
   Watch Jeffrey Sachs talking about the importance of foreign aid.

■ Search using: Easterly on foreign aid.
   Watch an interview with William Easterly arguing that aid does more harm than good.

■ Search using: Moyo Aid Tedx Brussels.
   Watch Dambisa Moyo's argument that aid has harmed the African Continent.

1. Make a list of the arguments you heard on the three videos that you consider to be important.

2. As a class, discuss whether aid helps developing nations or not.

3. The Global Fund to Fight AIDS, TB and Malaria (GFATM) is a form of ODA. Investigate how this aid programme works.

   a. Explain the programme's objectives.

   b. Analyse whether it has been successful in meeting its objectives.

 TOK

To what extent are developed nations morally obliged to assist developing nations through foreign aid?

International trade strategies

Developing countries can base their growth and development on the trade strategies explained below.

Import substitution

Import substitution (also known as import substitution industrialization) is a strategy where a country begins to manufacture simple consumer goods, such as textiles or shoes, aiming to substitute imports with these domestically produced goods, and therefore promote its domestic industry. Import substitution requires trade barriers such as tariffs and quotas to prevent the entry of imports and to protect the newly established industries. At the same time, the exchange rate is kept overvalued so that prices of necessary imported manufacturing inputs are low.

Import substitution has been practised by a number of developing countries in Latin America, Asia and Africa in an attempt to create a manufacturing sector and thereby reduce reliance on the primary sector. Nevertheless, such a strategy is associated with inefficiency as protection reduces competition. Also, the overvalued exchange rate can harm primary exports, which may increase poverty for some parts of the population. Lastly, the newly established industries may use capital-intensive production methods limiting employment opportunities and leading to jobless growth that is usually not followed by development.

Export promotion

Export promotion is a trade strategy where a country attempts to achieve economic growth by expanding its exports. Japan was the first country to have adopted this strategy and was followed by Korea, Taiwan, Hong Kong and Singapore (known as the East Asian Tigers) and other countries including, of course, China. The government's role is very important for export promotion to be a successful growth and development strategy. It can help exporting firms with state subsidies, investment grants and tax exemptions while making large investments in key areas. For example, it can invest in education to improve the skills of the workforce, research and development that can lead to innovation, as well as in transport and communications infrastructure that can assist production.

Export promotion has been successful for many countries, but this may not always be the case. Strong dependence on exports makes the economy vulnerable. For instance, if trading partners go into a recession, the exporting economies are strongly affected. Trade barriers imposed by developed economies may hurt exports and export revenue. The income distribution may worsen as the rural sector may be left behind while those involved in the exporting sector will enjoy a larger share of national income.

Trade liberalization

Trade liberalization refers to the reduction, or complete removal, of protectionist measures that prevent free trade, such as tariffs, quotas and subsidies to domestic producers.

Internal link

See section 4.1 on free trade.

This will allow developing countries to expand their exports in international markets and enjoy greater export revenue.

Together with all the other benefits of free trade, trade liberalization can allow for greater economic growth. Yet, trade liberalization on its own may not be enough. Developing countries lack skills, technology and are focused on the primary sector. This means that, even with greater access to global markets, they will still export a narrow range of products and will therefore have low export shares in world trade.

Economic integration

Regional integration among developing countries may prove beneficial as a trading bloc increases the size of the potential market for each exporting firm and helps to avoid the obstacles of the protectionist barriers of developed countries. It can also decrease the level of dependence on developed countries' markets while providing member countries with greater political and bargaining power in negotiations with developed economies. Examples of economic integration among developing countries include the Latin America Free Trade Association (LAFTA), MERCOSUR, a customs union among Argentina, Brazil, Uruguay, and Paraguay and the Asia-Pacific Economic Cooperation (APEC), a group of 21 nations that border the Pacific Ocean. Still, many attempts of forming trading blocs among developing countries have encountered significant organizational and administrative problems, while the transport costs are especially high since infrastructure is poor.

Diversification

One of the major problems that many developing countries face is their over-dependence on a narrow range of agricultural products. **Diversification** involves broadening the range of goods and services that developing countries are able to produce. This would allow such economies to benefit from worldwide economic growth as manufactured products and services have higher income elasticity of demand. Also, they will no longer be subject to price volatility, which will stabilize incomes and export earnings. Diversification may create new jobs and can lead to the improvement of skills and technologies in order to support the broader range of production.

However, diversification may not guarantee that developing countries' exports will no longer be subject to trade protectionism, while the benefits of specialization in the form of efficiency will be lost.

DP ready ATL **Thinking and communication skills**

Trade strategies

Discuss the following question in class. Which trade strategy do you find most effective in terms of encouraging growth and development?

Market-oriented supply-side policies (SSPs)

The idea behind market-oriented supply side policies (SSPs) is that markets are the most effective mechanism for growth and in turn for development.

Market-oriented policies, such as privatization and deregulation, increase efficiency and contribute to economic growth. More specifically, the profit motive forces privatized firms to cut costs and decrease inefficiencies, while deregulation decreases production costs and leads to higher levels of output. In both cases there is faster economic growth.

Labour market reforms are also part of market-oriented SSPs and aim to increase labour market flexibility. As a result, labour costs decrease, firms' profitability increases and employment increases. Higher profits may increase investment and accelerate growth.

However, market-oriented SSPs can only be effective in the long term; they are not capable of dealing with short-term problems. Also, privatization often has led, at least in the short term, to increased unemployment and it can lead to monopoly pricing. Is this something developing countries can afford?

Lastly, note that market-oriented SSPs related to the labour market increase income inequality. This is particularly damaging for developing countries where income inequality is often already high.

Social enterprise

Social enterprise refers to for-profit businesses engaged in socially beneficial activities. Social enterprise is a ground-breaking response to the funding problems that many non-profit organizations are facing. Developing countries can greatly benefit from social enterprise, as it can provide aspects of aid that are not addressed through conventional routes. This can be achieved through innovation. For example, in Myanmar the Phandeeyar tech hub connects those seeking to develop products in line with the country's economic growth with technology professionals. The Buffalo Bicycle Company built their bicycles specifically for the Southern African terrain in order to assist local people with the geographical challenges they were facing. The progress made by these types of enterprise has increased recognition that social entrepreneurship can benefit the developing world.

DP ready ATL **Thinking skills**

Social enterprises

Identify any social enterprises operating in your local community or in your country.

Microfinance

Microfinance focuses on making available very small loans to the very poor, helping them to start a small business, expand an existing one, or meet an emergency arising from disease or bad weather. The scheme was initiated by Muhammad Yunus who created the Grameen Bank several decades ago.

Microfinance can help developing nations as it has positive impact on poverty reduction and it can allow for improvements in health, nutrition and primary school attendance. Many microfinance loans have been offered to women, which has helped them in their empowerment; their participation in such programmes gives them greater bargaining power and enables them to take part in family decision-making.

However, microfinance has recently come under attack. According to some studies and analysts, most borrowers do not appear to be climbing out of poverty while some are getting trapped in a spiral of debt.

Watch this

Search YouTube for the following videos.

- Search using these terms: Wagner rethinking microfinance.
  Watch a video on what has gone wrong with microfinance.
- Search using these terms: duflo anti poverty fight.
  Watch an interview with Esther Duflo, a leading MIT economist, on the aid debate and on microfinance.

DP ready | ATL **Thinking skills**

The spread of microfinance

Although initially intended for developing countries, in the recent past microfinance has expanded to advanced economies as a source of credit. Explain why you think this has happened.

Provision of merit goods

Health and education

Health and education are vital drivers of growth and development. Better health and education increase labour productivity and since productivity is the key to growth, this can also lead to development. Improved health and education allow individuals to have more, better and higher paid employment opportunities.

Something that adds further to the importance of health and education is that they are interdependent. Improved health improves education because health is a critical factor in school attendance. At the same time, greater education improves health, because basic skills such as personal hygiene and sanitation are often learned at school. Provision of health and education programmes can therefore be of substantial importance in growth and development.

Infrastructure

Infrastructure increases productivity and lowers costs of production. Some examples follow. Transportation systems allow more output to be transported and production costs to be lowered. Irrigation contributes to higher levels of agricultural output. Reliable energy systems allow for increased productivity from workers through the introduction of simple electrically powered machines and equipment. Access to clean water and sanitation have major effects on the health of a population by preventing illnesses and premature deaths. Therefore, the provision of infrastructure is also crucial for growth and development.

However, it should be noted that health and education as well as infrastructure are largely dependent on the government, which can be an issue when the government is short of funds that would allow for provision. For example, many governments in developing countries have their investment plans at the ready. They plan for improvements in health and education, building of roads, ports and power grids, access by the poor to safe water and sanitation— but they lack the financial resources to carry out those plans. Also, poor governance and corruption may impede investments in human capital and infrastructure.

Women's empowerment

Reducing gender inequality can significantly improve a country's development. Not only do deprived girls and women benefit but also the growth and development process accelerates.

The most important way to empower women is through educating girls. An educated mother will enjoy higher earning ability outside the home for each extra year of schooling. She will have fewer children, increasing the income available per child, which can result in even higher long-term productivity and output gains. Her children will be healthier and she will probably make sure that they are also educated, creating a virtuous circle. Educating women decreases mortality in children, decreasing the costs of health-care intervention. Lastly, better and more educated women can lead to higher female participation in the labour force as well as in politics, allowing them to influence policy.

Education for girls is considered by many as the most influential investment for accelerating the development process.

Search the web

Search using these terms: Rwanda success women empowerment. Read an article on how women empowerment in Rwanda helped the country become one of the fastest growing and developing nations in the African continent.

Redistribution policies

High and rising inequality is one major factor that prevents growth and development. Therefore, implementing policies to redistribute income can be of particular importance. To do so, governments can use progressive income taxes and transfer payments. Taxing households with higher incomes more heavily than those with lower incomes and spending more on transfer payments, means that national income may be redistributed, which reduces inequality and allows for more growth and development. Yet, many developing countries have ineffective taxation systems and governments usually run on very low budgets.

Perhaps a more useful route to a more equitable distribution of income and wealth is to improve the quality and access to education and health care. Schools, health-care centres, better sanitation and clean water supplies will all contribute to an increase in human capital, which will increase labour productivity and lead to higher incomes, growth and development. Nevertheless, the government's lack of resources may still be an issue.

Another policy focuses on defining and enforcing property rights. This can significantly help towards reducing inequality. People without property rights cannot use their resources to create wealth, so their assets become "dead capital". If property titles are provided, the capital will no longer be "dead" and will be used to generate income, reducing inequality while allowing for growth and development.

Debt relief

High levels of indebtedness is another setback for developing nations. Remember that high debt levels require large debt repayments that do not allow enough funds for spending in other areas. Debt relief involves cancelling a portion of debts: the amount that must be repaid is reduced. This releases some funds that can finance growth and development strategies.

The World Bank and the International Monetary Fund (IMF)

- The World Bank is a development assistance organization that extends long-term loans to developing countries for the purpose of promoting economic development and structural change.

- The IMF is a multilateral financial institution that oversees the global financial system, stabilizes exchange rates and helps countries in financial crises by extending loans. In recent years, IMF lending has been almost exclusively focused on the developing world.

Both the World Bank and the IMF help developing countries by giving them loans. The loans offered are conditional and require that recipients agree to adopt particular policies (structural adjustment policies). For example, these policies may involve deficit reduction, privatization, deregulation, improved tax collection and labour market reforms. However, such loans deprive the borrowing country of control over its domestic affairs and may have negative effects on economic development. For instance, in some cases, IMF and World Bank officials have asked impoverished nations to cut budgets, and even to privatize health services as part of the conditions for lending. Such measures may prevent human or physical capital improvements and therefore act against development objectives.

Government intervention versus market-oriented approaches

Here is one of the biggest debates in development economics. Should countries adopt a more interventionist rather than market-oriented approach? Or should they do the opposite?

Adopting a market-oriented approach is based on the idea that market powers always lead to the best possible outcome. Indeed, free markets lead to allocative efficiency as the market mechanism directs resources in their best possible use.

The market also provides the necessary incentives, such as higher incomes and profit, that encourage economic activity and generate growth. Even so, the role of government in economic development is crucial. The government is vital for building the infrastructure and is also essential for human capital formation, which are both necessary for any economy to develop. Remember that health care and education are merit goods so, if they are left to the market, they are underprovided. Public financing is essential to ensure that the poor have access to merit goods.

 Internal link

See section 2.2 for more on allocative efficiency.

However, if the government is not functioning properly—which can be the case in developing countries—then public schools and health conditions are poor. Yet, when it comes to reducing poverty a market approach is highly problematic as markets are basically designed to "ignore" the poor, as their incomes are low and they cannot, therefore, "vote with their dollars". So, the government is needed to ensure economic opportunity for all.

The government is also needed to regulate key sectors of the economy. The banking sector is one of them. Unregulated banking systems tend to experience crises. Nevertheless, corrupt governments may encourage or allow illegality, which neither helps in regulating markets nor in creating equal opportunities. Overall, national governments have played an important role in the successful development experiences of the countries in East Asia.

However, in other parts of the world, including some countries in Africa, Latin America and the Caribbean, the government often appears to have been more of an obstacle.

A market-oriented approach is preferable when there is government failure, whereas good governance is needed when there is market failure. That is to say, that the roles of the market and the government are complementary.

Focus point

There are several strategies that can be used to promote economic growth and development. In some cases these strategies have worked but in others they haven't. This suggests that care must be taken when designing and implementing policy so that each strategy matches the needs of the particular country pursuing them. There is no uniform approach.

Index